America and its Critics

Virtues and Vices of the Democratic Hyperpower

Sergio Fabbrini

polity

First published in Italian as *L'America e i suoi critici* © Società editrice il Mulino, Bologna, 2005

This English edition © Polity Press, 2008

Polity Press
65 Bridge Street
Cambridge CB2 1UR, UK

Polity Press
350 Main Street
Malden, MA 02148, USA

ISBN-13: 978-0-7456-4250-5
ISBN-13: 978-0-7456-4251-2 (pb)

A catalogue record for this book is available from the British Library.

Typeset in 10.5 on 12 pt Palatino
by SNP Best-set Typesetter Ltd., Hong Kong
Printed and bound in the United States by the Maple-Vail Book Manufacturing Group

The publisher has used its best endeavours to ensure that the URLs for external websites referred to in this book are correct and active at the time of going to press. However, the publisher has no responsibility for the websites and can make no guarantee that a site will remain live or that the content is or will remain appropriate.

Every effort has been made to trace all copyright holders, but if any have been inadvertently overlooked the publishers will be pleased to include any necessary credits in any subsequent reprint or edition.

For further information on Polity, visit our website: www.polity.co.uk

To the memory of Nelson W. Polsby,
teacher of separation of powers

Contents

Preface   ix

1   Anti-Americanism in Europe   **1**
1.1   Introduction   1
1.2   Anti-Americanism in the European Context   2
1.3   America and the European Left   5
1.4   America and the European Right   9
1.5   America and the European Catholic Center   12
1.6   Misunderstanding America   16
1.7   Conclusion   19

2   A Plebiscitary Democracy?   **20**
2.1   Introduction   20
2.2   The Origins of Separated Government   23
2.3   Congressional Government   31
2.4   The Crisis of Congressional Government   33
2.5   Presidential Government   37
2.6   The Difficulties of Presidential Government   45
2.7   Conclusion   57

3   A Democracy without the People?   **59**
3.1   Introduction   59
3.2   The Characteristics of the Electoral System   62
3.3   The Development of the Electoral Process   71
3.4   Why Americans Don't Vote: The Debate   82
3.5   Political Parties from Decline to Transformation?   91
3.6   Conclusion   95

4   A Democracy for the Rich?   **98**
4.1   Introduction   98
4.2   The American Commercial Republic   101
4.3   The Neoconservative Revolution   114
4.4   The Weakness of the Democrats: The Two Clinton
      Presidencies   121
4.5   The Anti-politics of the Elites: Term Limits and Recall   125
4.6   The Social Implications of American Liberalism   131
4.7   Conclusion   134

5   An Imperial Democracy?   **135**
5.1   Introduction   135
5.2   Foreign and Domestic Policy in America   137
5.3   Hegemonic America and the Cold War   142
5.4   The End of the Cold War and the First Gulf War   148
5.5   The 1990s and the Schizophrenic Power   152
5.6   George W. Bush's America and the Second Gulf War   159
5.7   Conclusion   166

6   America as Method   **170**
6.1   Introduction   170
6.2   American Exceptionalism   170
6.3   The Societal and Institutional Antinomies   174
6.4   Political Change and American Antinomies   178
6.5   America: A Model or a Method?   180
6.6   Conclusion   184

Notes   187
Index   212

Preface

No other country in the world evokes such contrasting sentiments as the United States of America (which I will refer to here as America, in keeping with a tradition initiated by one of the first observers and scholars of this country, namely the Frenchman Alexis de Tocqueville, who visited it between May 9, 1831 and February 20, 1832; I am of course aware that the term more appropriately refers to an entire continent). This is no new feat. Ever since its birth America has evoked admiration or rejection amongst Europeans, as if it represented their alter ego. But these reactions certainly also owe much to the fact that America has remained the world's only superpower after the end of the Cold War. Or rather, America has become a veritable hyperpower, to use the felicitous expression coined by the then French minister of foreign affairs Hubert Védrine during a conference held on June 12, 1995. America, that is, has become a superpower without apparent limits to the exercise of its might. Because the fate of the world in large part lies in the hands of its power, America should rightly be the focus of our attention. Yet, it would seem that these contrasting sentiments have not been informed by an adequate understanding of the country, i.e. by the willingness to understand America *sine ira et studio*.

In this book I analyze some of the criticism of America advanced by European observers. America's critics (and for this reason I owe them a debt of gratitude) have given me the opportunity to examine American democracy, both its institutional and electoral structures as well as its political choices in domestic and foreign policy. Although critical analyses of America abound in the literature, here

I refer to the most widely available contributions in order to discuss the main issues raised by them. I do so with the intent of contributing to a more informed political discussion rather than for the purpose of rebutting America's critics. I immediately add though that even if this book seeks to show that its vices are fewer and different than those that are commonly bemoaned, American democracy nevertheless cannot be read as an exemplary catalogue of virtues, as its apologists would have us believe. Resting on contradictions rather than coherence, American democracy cannot be seen as a model. Like all democracies, the American democracy is a combination of virtues and vices, although its history and its power tend to exacerbate both. This is why I wish to count myself neither amongst the critics nor the unconditional supporters of America.

This book is an updated and significantly revised version of the Italian edition published in 2006 which received the 2006 European Amalfi Prize for the Social Sciences. The first edition benefited from the comments of several scholars, among them Stefano Bartolini, Vincent Della Sala, Beppe Di Palma, Maurizio Ferrera and Gianfranco Poggi. Daniela Sicurelli and Barbara Krippl have provided competent research assistance. Ton Notermans assisted me in editing the English version. I would like to thank each one of them, as well as to absolve them from any responsibility for what I have written and how I have written it. This book builds on my long-standing research into the nature and transformations of American democracy, which I conduct shuttling back and forth between both shores of the Atlantic. The book is dedicated to the memory of my friend Nelson W. Polsby, who generously hosted me for years at the Institute of Governmental Studies at the University of California, Berkeley. Although we did not always share the same interpretation of American democracy, in our discussions he persuasively convinced me not to underestimate the strength of the system of separation of powers in keeping America within the democratic track. This book seeks to honor his wit, his teaching, his loyalty to friends.

School of International Studies
Trento University

1

Anti-Americanism in Europe

1.1 Introduction

Notwithstanding the rhetorical celebration of the common values shared by both America and Europe, mutual understanding of the transformations taking place in the two continents is still dramatically lacking. Anti-Americanism has resurfaced in Europe after September 11, and anti-Europeanism has become a sort of implicit public philosophy of the neoconservative elite which undisputedly has run the country with the two George W. Bush presidencies (2001–8).[1] In this chapter, I will deal mainly with the European attitude toward America, not only because it is much more militant and diffused than its counterpart in America, but also because it represents a significant hurdle to the Europeans' understanding of the transformations taking place on their own continent.

Certainly, the terrorist attacks of September 11, 2001 in New York and Washington, DC and the killing of thousands of people immediately triggered a mood of solidarity with Americans throughout Europe. However, the *nous sommes tous américains* of the aftermath of the attacks quite soon became the *nous sommes contre les américains* once America defined its strategy for dealing with global terrorism.[2] The attacks did not suffice to reverse a mood of suspicion among European elites and the public toward America. Indeed, as soon as the discussion on the right strategy against terrorism had started, the initial mood of identification with America significantly abated. And when America, without the backing of the United Nations' Security Council, moved toward an armed intervention in Iraq in the Spring of 2003, European anti-Americanism emerged vocifer-ously.[3] Thus, alongside the armed intervention, a social mobiliza-tion against the American war unfolded, apparently losing sight of the fact that a terrorist attack had occurred previously in America. What interests me here is why anti-Americanism regularly rears its head in large sections of European public opinion and amongst the elites. In Europe, anti-Americanism seems to be one of the few public philosophies able to unite large sections of the left, the right, and the Catholic Church.[4] This public philosophy tends to emerge especially in periods of war and during international crises in general.

I will argue that this public philosophy has historical roots in Europe, but that it is also fostered by more recent criticisms of American power in the post-Cold War international system. Although these criticisms have a different quality than those that have historically justified European anti-Americanism, nevertheless confusion continues to characterize many of them. The criticism of what America does intermingles with the criticism of what America is, as was the case historically. It is the aim of this chapter to trace the reasons of that intermingling. I will proceed as follows: first, I will locate anti-Americanism in the European context; second, I will discuss the rationales of the anti-Americanism of the European left, right, and center; third, and finally, I will delineate the implications of what I call the European misunderstanding of America.

1.2   Anti-Americanism in the European Context

Anti-Americanism is an ambiguous concept and a loaded term that needs a more precise empirical definition.[5] It has been used, by some, to label those positions attempting to criticize either Ameri-can decisions and choices or America as such.[6] Anti-American is akin in its ambiguity to un-American, the term used to disparage and delegitimize domestic critics throughout American history. As Ellwood has noted, in America, "external hostility is called anti-American and internal hostility is called un-American."[7] Anti-Americanism is thus a loose concept, one comprising both the criticism of the American system as such (what America is) and the criticism of specific American policies (what America does). But, of course, the two criticisms have different qualities and different implications. Although ambiguous, anti-Americanism is a recurrent sentiment throughout the world, Europe included. Tony Judt explains this widespread negative reaction, claiming that "anti-American sentiment . . . in the first place is driven by humiliation, the feeling of worthlessness and hopelessness shared by hundreds of millions in the Islamic world and elsewhere."[8] In itself, this would not be sufficient to feed a specific anti-American sentiment; in fact, Judt adds, "what ties this widespread sentiment of wounded pride to a certain image of America in particular is American arrogance," or, as Stanley Hoffmann calls it, American "bossism."[9]

Thus, anti-American sentiment is not only attributable to non-western public opinion[10] but also to many constituents of European public opinion,[11] long before the American invasion of Iraq in 2003.[12] One year after September 11, 2001, the German journalist, Petra Pinzler wrote:

> America first, the others follow – today's problems can hardly be resolved according to this old slogan any longer. Examples? Almost the whole world has approved the International Climate Protection Agreement, the ban on nuclear testing, the ban on land mines, and the punishment of war criminals by an International Criminal Court. But the United States stonewalls because it fears disadvantages and prefers the law of the jungle to international law. Death penalty, children behind bars: Europe protests, but the United States refuses to tolerate any criticism. "No" is its most frequent answer.[13]

In sum, in Europe, pre-9/11 America was perceived by many as the country that relied primarily on military strength to deal with international crises. The perception of America as an unscrupulous military power was thus magnified by the invasion of Iraq in 2003 but it was not created by that invasion. The Eurobarometer opinion poll of November 2003 indicated that 53 percent of Europeans considered America a threat to world peace. The same percentage was recorded for Iran and North Korea; only for one country, Israel, was the percentage higher, namely 59 percent.

Continental European countries have been at the core of the criticism of America. In the United Kingdom and Scandinavia, anti-Americanism has been subdued by a more vociferous anti-Europeanism, and has taken the form of uneasiness with America.[14] In particular, Britain's long-standing special relationship with America did nothing to help the post-Second World War British elites who grudgingly accepted an inferior status in that relationship. This inferior status was made evident by the Suez crisis of 1956, when America sided with the Egyptians against the colonial ambitions of Britain (and France). The Labour Party of the 1980s tried to transform this inferior status into a position of equidistance between the two superpowers. Of course, frustration with America is not the same as anger toward America. Nevertheless, "the postwar era has seen frequent and repeated outbursts of British anti-Americanism as the former superpower struggled to adjust to its subordinate position in the cold war Pax Americana."[15]

On the continent, anti-Americanism has appeared to be one of the few public philosophies able to unite the left, the right, and the Catholic center. France, in particular, has led the anti-American movement.[16] As Sophie Meunier has remarked, "one well-known peculiarity of French cultural identity is its anti-Americanism."[17] Indeed, Alain Joxe, the director of France's elite postgraduate School of Social Science, declared to *Le Monde*, during NATO's military intervention in Kosovo in April 1999, that "the strategic and economic views of America are not only dangerous but alien to our political ethic." He further added that, "an American victory in Kosovo would have created the condition not for reconstruction but for Mafia-style chaos." In the same newspaper, the well-known writer (and foreign policy advisor of President François Mitterrand in the first half of the 1990s) Régis Debray, fulminated against "the emptying of the European mind by the Americans," to the point of admonishing his readers, "America: you must be against it. This is the fundamental requirement."[18]

French anti-Americanism, however, has traditionally been of a different ilk than that of other European countries.[19] It springs not only from a national conviction that French civilization is of universal importance[20] but also from its difficulty in dealing with the new international status of America. As Bruno Racine, chief advisor of the French conservative Prime Minister, Alain Juppé, pointed out, "America's hyperpower irritates us because it forces us to acknowledge our historical downgrading."[21] In other European countries, anti-Americanism was not fueled by considerations of national pride, national civilization, or the desire to play an international role distinct from America; their respective histories could not justify such ambitions. In fact, one need only consider the self-restraint of German elites (or, for that matter, of Japanese elites) during the entire post-Second World War period, to be convinced of this, although this self-restraint was severely called into question in Germany during the Iraq war in the Spring of 2003.[22]

The end of the Cold War helped to unleash anti-Americanism, at least in Europe. In fact, the presence of the Soviet Union at the heart of Europe had constrained most political and cultural elites from criticizing America, thereby confining the debate to issues of management.[23] This mood, however, has been nourished by several different fears that continue to be perceived and shared by elite groups across Europe. An older anti-Americanism came to be interwoven with new anti-American critiques, of which two are politically significant.[24] The first fear has to do with the process of Americanization brought about by globalization. Anti-globalization activists, as well as journalists, academics, and politicians have interpreted the process of globalization as an opportunity for the US to Americanize the world. America has been considered the culprit of the transformation of European society and economy, the source of all undesired political changes across Europe. Although the available evidence does not seem to justify this fear (in fact, globalization seems to be controlled as much by European as by American economic interests), it has contributed significantly to creating the context for the growth of anti-Americanism. As Giddens has remarked, we

> have got too much of a conspiracy theory here . . . It's too easy to blame the ills of the world economy on US power . . . Obviously the USA is by far the dominant economic power in the world and most big corporations are US based. Yet, the global marketplace isn't just an extension of American power. The USA doesn't control financial markets any more than any other country or agency does.[25]

The second fear has to do with the hyperpower status of America in the international system.[26] Indeed, the American decision to invade Iraq was like holding a match to a haystack.[27] The unilateral assertion of American views, notwithstanding the shock of 9/11, ignited a militant anti-Americanism among the elites and the public of several European countries. The deeper roots of European anti-Americanism (based on a rejection of what America *is*) and the contemporary fears of American economic and military power (motivated by a critique of what America *does*) combined in pushing Europe further away from America.[28]

1.3 America and the European Left

America has never been to the liking of the European left: this is true not only of the Communist left, which became the largest political force after the Second World War in countries like Italy, France of the IV Republic (1946–58), and Greece, and which was very influential in the democratic transition of Spain and Portugal, but also of the Socialist left, which looked for an alternative between (American) capitalism and (Soviet) communism. Matters could not be otherwise. The Communist left, in fact, sought to destroy capitalism and to supersede democracy, and America combined the power of the former and the vitality of the latter. America was the capitalist system by definition, the kingdom of the market, the society of profit. Moreover, ever since the beginnings of the communist challenge, America stood out as the alternative to the Soviet route to social emancipation: Americanism as the democratic ideological alternative to communism, Woodrow Wilson as the alternative international leader to Vladimir Ilych Lenin. The long Cold War confrontation did nothing except to solidify revulsion of a country viewed as the spearhead of an anti-communist coalition, allegedly intent on subjugating the world to the dominance of the capitalist market and the hypocrisy of the democratic plutocracy.[29]

In the post-Second War World period this state of mind also influenced the reformist Socialist left, as well as pervading the radical left that arose from the student and worker movements of 1968–9. To be sure, especially on the Socialist left (but also on the libertarian radical left), there was no lack of individual politicians and intellectuals who put forward an alternative interpretation of the "American model." These were exceptions, however. Also the reformist Socialist left disdained America more than anything else because it was so capitalist that not even a Socialist party could develop in this context. Werner Sombart's question of 1906, "Why is there no socialism in America?" dwelt in the European socialist conscience, keeping alive a sense not only of distance from but also of rejection of the American political experience.[30]

This is why the European left as a whole, although more the Communist camp than the Socialist, was anti-American throughout the Cold War period. But things soon changed after the Cold War. Within the left a process of revision was set in motion which led to a distinction (if not a rupture) between a reformist and a radical component. The leftist view of America, or rather the interpretation of its political and economic regime, also underwent a revision. The reformist left had started to interpret America in more pragmatic terms, making a distinction between capitalism and democracy, thus reassessing the importance of the latter, no longer merely a veil for the former. American democracy has been reassessed for its capacity to promote an open and dynamic society. Yet, its institutional structure has continued to be eyed with suspicion because of the excessive powers it allegedly bestows upon the president. Thus, references to its potential "plebiscitary dynamics" (due also to declining electoral participation in the wake of the crisis of the political parties and to the growing political role of the media that makes the relationship between the president and the citizens more direct) have continued to characterize the writings and speeches of the representatives of this part of the left.

At the same time, American capitalism has come to be understood as a publicly regulated system in order to safeguard its competitive logic, and no longer as an economic arena devoid of any rules and principles where the weak are necessarily subject to the strong. Yet, the possible alliance between the political and military power of the president and the economic power controlled by a small number of powerful groups and individuals close to him continues to be perceived as a constant threat to domestic democracy and the international equilibrium. Moreover, this analysis of America's internal structure has pushed the reformist left to support the project of a European Union (EU) intended as a civilian power able not only to provide a counter-weight to America on the international scene but also to influence its domestic evolution. In short, there can be no doubt that the present-day reformist left has fully recognized the democratic nature of America. Nevertheless, the (ill-founded) worries concerning the (potential) plebiscitary tendencies of America and their international implications continue to create unease for this part of the left. It is no coincidence that the left has come to embrace the traditional arguments of the balance of power: America is no longer a hostile power but it is not yet a friendly one either.

The radical component of the European left, in contrast (which is influential in pacifist and anti-globalization movements), has proudly continued to parade its diffidence toward America.[31] This diffidence takes on the characteristics of a rejection of both its economic and political regime. America continues to be perceived as a veritable empire of money. Notwithstanding Giddens' insistence that American capitalism "is more open, more transparent and even more regulated than German corporate capitalism,"[32] American capitalism continues to be seen as unregulated both domestically and internationally. Only such an unregulated capitalism, in this view, would permit the emergence of a society so unjust as the American one. Simultaneously, after having abandoned the plutocratic interpretation, American democracy is seen as a political system with highly centralized decision-making power and thus as a potentially authoritarian system. Such an interpretation is maintained notwithstanding the role played by the Electoral College in the presidential elections of November 2000, and thus the role of the judicial guardian, the Supreme Court, in deciding what the electoral system failed to do on that occasion.

Afflicted by a curious squint, these components of the left see America as a Latin American or Asian country whose presumed presidentialism means that its president does whatever he wants. In other words, American democracy is considered a veiled form of presidential authoritarianism. In fact, especially the more militant sections of the radical left tend to view America as a military fortress headed by a supreme commander who is subjected to few, if any, domestic checks on the exercise of his power, or even as a Latin-American type of regime in which the president can do as he or she pleases. A military fortress, moreover, that is engaged in imposing its own power on the entire world. This is not in the least so, it is argued, because the presidents operate in a democracy "without the people," i.e. a democracy in which few citizens vote. As Giddens has caustically remarked,

> all the things the traditional left said about the USA are still there, and even accentuated – the accumulation of fortunes, the vulgarity of new monied elites and so forth . . . But I'm strongly against the knee-jerk anti-Americanism that so many of the European (and some of the American) left go in for.[33]

American democracy no doubt displays more social disparities than its European counterparts. Yet, with the passing of anti-trust legislation, i.e. the Sherman Antitrust Act, already in 1890 American capitalism was the first to be regulated in the history of the West, and it continues to be tightly controlled by the federal institutions (legislature, executive, and judiciary) in order to safeguard competition and to prevent the emergence of monopoly power. For this reason America has adapted to a system of global governance, such as the World Trade Organization (WTO), which is based on the principle of regulation, even if, both internally and externally, there have been repeated attempts by the large corporations to neutralize the constraints of market regulation. Above all, it is rather questionable to maintain that American democracy displays a centralized structure as the separation of powers constitutes a formidable obstacle to its governmental decision-making capabilities. Nor is it plausible to maintain that America is a democracy without the people, even if it is true that at least half of the citizens do not vote in federal (presidential and congressional) elections.

One might say that this part of the political left tends to interpret domestic American politics in the light of its foreign policy, seeing its hegemonic international ambitions as the inevitable consequence of its internal hierarchy of power. But above all, it tends to reduce each foreign policy decision of America to its imperial ambitions. Is this really so? Of course, America has its vices but they are of a different nature and degree than claimed by the radical left. Although the reformist and radical left differ significantly in their attitude toward America, their opinions are based on an insufficient knowledge of the country. Both are struck by the excessive powers of the president, even if one camp interprets this as potential plebiscitary drift whereas the other camp sees in it a demonstration of the authoritarian nature of the presidential regime. Both are struck by the low voter turnout in federal elections, even if one camp interprets this as the outcome of the weakness of the parties and the other as the consequence of a manipulated democracy. Both are struck by America's military might, although one camp sees this as a threat that needs to be re-equilibrated whereas the other sees it as the expression of an empire that needs to be opposed. In sum, the scant knowledge of American democracy continues to impinge negatively, although to different degrees, on the two camps of the left.

1.4   America and the European Right

America has never been to the liking of the European right, either.[34] Conservatives could not be sympathetic to a country born out of a revolution that was not only anti-colonial but also, and especially, liberal-progressive and which from the outset was marked by a pronounced egalitarianism.[35] For the European rightist parties, America's democratic origin and its egalitarian spirit coincided in the sense that the one nourished the other. Consequently, since the nineteenth century, the European right has instinctively embraced Edmund Burke's theory that the French Revolution was largely inspired by the revolution which had taken place on the other side of the Atlantic some 15 years before,[36] and if the former was to be rejected, then so too was the latter. After all, the liberal-conservative de Tocqueville, who arrived in America at the height of the Jacksonian revolution of the 1830s, and who was largely sympathetic to the new country, was shocked at how widespread the passion for equality was among the former English colonies.

Throughout Europe's history, the political right has constantly fostered an attitude of contempt toward America. For the right, America represented a challenge to traditional hierarchies, a refusal to defer to constituted authority, the kingdom of the individual, the society that showed no respect for the past (nor wished to). Indeed, de Tocqueville observed "(a)s in America the European ladder of power has been turned upside down; the wealthy find themselves in a position analogous to that of the poor in Europe: it is they who often mistrust the law."[37] Therefore, the European Conservative right regarded the Americans as crude, uncouth, ill-mannered, ingenuous, if not stupid,[38] or, in other words, lacking the sophistication and refinement that the representatives of the right believed they possessed (by birthright or as the result of long acculturation). For the European Conservative right, moreover, America represented the passion for political participation, the organization of party machines able to mobilize millions of voters, the ascent to power of ordinary people. Again, de Tocqueville noted that "American democracy constantly brings new men forward to direct affairs; consequently there is little consistency or order in government measures."[39]

In short, America represented mass democracy, unruly, anarchic, and (above all) based on the affirmation of particularistic interests. A vulgar democracy compared to its superior European counterpart with its orderliness based on a restricted electorate and a plethora of notables (in its Tory conservative version) or on an amorphous mass which founded its identity solely on its (subordinate) relation with the leader (in its Bonapartist and later Gaullist version). We need not dwell on the fact that the radical right too shared with the Conservative right this disdain for America. In the 1920s and in the 1930s (in Italy and Germany) and until the 1960s (in Spain, Portugal, and Greece) fascist and authoritarian regimes styled themselves as a response to Americanism and its (purported) crude materialism.[40] To an America without a state, without a "spirit," without an ethnic identity; to "mongrel" America, fascist and authoritarian regimes sought to oppose the Europe of the state, the Europe of the spirit, the Europe of "organic" ethnic and racial purity.

The disdain of the European right for America endured after the Second World War. Certainly, during the Cold War era it was kept under control. Because America was engaged in a mortal confrontation with the Soviet Union, it was not easy for the European Conservative right to be critical. Indeed, America was even presented by some leaders of the European Conservative right as the new conservative power of the West, the legitimate heir to the old European colonial powers of the pre-Second World War period. Also at the domestic level the European Conservative right found reasons to sympathize with America. For example, the growing apathy of the American electorate was employed to justify an elitist, or better still, hierarchical interpretation of American democracy. Of course, things were not that simple, because America continuously witnessed forceful social movements that questioned the decisions of the governmental elite, and which, for example, prompted Democratic President Johnson not to run for re-election in 1968 and Republican President Nixon to proffer his resignation in 1974. Yet, the European Conservative right continued to interpret American democracy in paternalistic and hierarchical terms, although America made no secret of its intolerance of elites, even if it had few of them.[41] Notwithstanding the changes to the propensity toward social cooperation wrought by a mass-communication society,[42] America's anti-paternalism, when translated into policies, continues to produce a mixture of individualism and self-organization that is the antithesis of the statist and dirigiste culture of the European Conservative right.[43]

With the end of the Cold War, a significant democratic evolution has also occurred amongst the European radical (or post-fascist) right (in Italy, Spain, and Greece especially). No longer fixated on its communist enemy, the European radical right was able to initiate an important process of theoretical and ideological revision that has steered it toward a traditional conservative perspective. This revision has also affected its interpretation of America. America, which was already valued for the international role of bulwark against communism it played during the Cold War, has now come to be reassessed on the level of its domestic democracy. In particular, American democracy has come to be appreciated as a political regime marked by a pronounced governmental decision-making capacity. Indeed, especially in continental Europe, both the radical and Conservative right has come to appreciate American presidentialism for its allegedly plebiscitary traits. Thus, for the European Conservative and radical right, America shows how a system with only one man at the helm can guarantee a superior efficiency and coherence of decision-making with respect to parliamentary systems. However, also in this case, the positive predisposition toward America is informed by a rather shaky knowledge of American democracy. The European right does not seem to be aware that America is not strong *because of its governmental system*, but *notwithstanding* it.

If the European left and right have historically joined hands in rejecting America, their respective reasons for doing so were diametrically opposed ones. Although both have rejected American democracy, the left did so because of its allegedly plutocratic character whereas the right bemoaned its allegedly mass-society character. Although both had rejected American capitalism, the left did so for the disparities it produced whereas the right condemned the egalitarian leveling it promoted. But above all, both the European left and the right were united by their rejection of so-called American individualism, although the left justified its rejection in the name of a social solidarity threatened by individualism while the right justified it in the name of an "organic state" or "natural society" that individualism undermined. Both European left and right had communitarian (the former) or organicistic (the latter) ideological roots. Despite their differences concerning international politics during the Cold War era (the left opposed America whereas the right supported its policy of containment of Soviet communism), both continued to share a common interpretation of America. The end of the Cold War has finally called into question that interpretation. It has permitted both the left and the right to embark on a revision of their interpretation of American democracy and society. However, the re-interpretation of America has not been informed by an adequate knowledge of the functioning of that country.

1.5   America and the European Catholic Center

Nor has America ever been to the liking of the European Catholic world, which comprises a large area of national political parties and groupings (such as Popular and/or Christian Democratic parties). Indeed, the higher echelon of the Vatican has never concealed its distance from, and rivalry with, America.[44] There are numerous underlying reasons for this attitude, but mainly that America is a Protestant country, in fact the largest in the world. America was born from the wars of religion that devastated Europe in the seventeenth century, and were followed by the Reformation and Counter-Reformation. America's religious origin is like no other country in the world. It was colonized by communities of protestant dissidents fleeing to the New World in order to construct (finally) "the city upon the hill"; dissidents, moreover, who were the dissidents of dissidents, the heretics of heresy, or in other words the radicals of the Reformation. As Walzer puts it, "American civil society has its origin in acts of resistance to and flight from religious persecution."[45]

Sectarian Protestantism even today is the hallmark of American identity and it manifests itself, for example, in the defense of the death penalty.[46] The difference between America and Europe, thus, is that the former has sects while the latter has churches. As Lipset noted:

> [t]he United States . . . is the only country where most churchgoers adhere to sects, mainly Methodists and Baptists [and nowadays Evangelicals], but also hundreds of others. Elsewhere in Christendom the Anglican, Catholic, Lutheran, and Orthodox churches dominate. The churches are hierarchical in structure and membership is secured by birthright. Sects, by contrast, are predominantly congregational; each local unit adheres voluntarily . . . Churches outside the United States historically have been linked to the state; their clergy are paid by public authorities, their hierarchy is formally appointed or confirmed by the government, and their schools are subsidized by taxes. [47]

Of course, with successive waves of immigrants the other great monotheistic religions reached the American side of the Atlantic.[48] Catholicism first arrived with the Irish in the mid nineteenth century and then with the Italians and the Poles at the end of the century. Islam arrived after the Second World War, while even more recently America has received a substantial influx due to the rediscovery by the African-American community of its ancestral (i.e. African) religious roots. And, of course, Judaism spread after the Diaspora of the 1930s, with the (modest) welcome of the Jews fleeing the Holocaust, and thereafter with the all-embracing welcome extended to its survivors.

However, once these religious groups were settled in America, as Walzer remarked, the American "expanding toleration regime tended to protestantize the groups that it included. American Catholics and Jews gradually came to look less and less like Catholics and Jews in other countries."[49] Thus American Catholicism is the least hierarchical of the national Catholic Churches.[50] American Islamism openly uses the language of religious tolerance. And it is known that American Judaism is the backbone of so-called Judaism of reform. In sum, the religious pluralism of America fostered a more tolerant religious climate than elsewhere, although it has not prevented the birth, at regular intervals, of fundamentalist and illiberal religious movements, as happened in the 1990s and 2000s. Why, then, should we be surprised that the Holy See is not at ease with America?[51] As Lipset remarked, "The European churches ... retain structures and values formed and institutionalized in medieval agrarian societies. . . . Thus, as with aristocracy and gentry, the European churches, particularly the Roman Catholic, have disliked the logic of bourgeois society,"[52] which found its ideal breeding ground in America.

But there is a second reason for the Catholic Church's suspicion of America, namely the liberalism that has influenced the public behavior of that country since its origins. Since the beginning of the new federal republic, the American political elite has consented to maintaining a rigorous separation between state and church (that is, between the federal state and the various religious congregations) either out of conviction or necessity. Whatever may be the case, the fact remains that, in America, secular power and religious power were assigned to two different spheres.[53] Of course, American history did not lack attempts to call into question that distinction. Especially on the level of the individual states (and in particular in the southern and western states of the so-called Bible Belt), pressures toward a biblical interpretation of American democracy have regularly emerged. Christian fundamentalist movements have mobilized in order to gain influence over legislation concerning the family and education, demanding, for example, that homosexual relations be outlawed or that Darwinian theories be removed from school textbooks. At the federal level, those movements have been especially active in supporting restrictive legislation on abortion, if not its outright abolition. However, these powerful pressures to "re-Christianize America" have encountered opposition in other states, in Congress and above all (at least up to now) in the judiciary. As the Supreme Court has recognized, the Constitution (and especially the first ten amendments, known as the Bill of Rights) cannot easily be made to serve the interests of specific religious majorities. However, the battle is far from over.[54]

American liberalism has never been fully accepted by the Catholic Church hierarchy.[55] In predominantly Catholic Europe, in fact, the church's long-standing political influence interfered peremptorily in the life of the European nation states (although unevenly so, more in countries like Italy than France or Spain, also because in Italy there was a historical territorial competition between the lay and the religious state). Nor should we overlook the concordats or treaties signed between the Vatican State and the national governments establishing Catholicism as the state religion (with the numerous privileges that come with it). Hence, in this respect also Europe has been quite distant from America, where the status of citizen has never been equated with that of believer. Still, the distinction between public and private sphere, which is constitutive of any open society, has permitted America to preserve its multicultural and multi-religious character, even in the face of repeated attempts to overstep this distinction, with the intention of imposing the hegemony of a specific culture or a religion. Although one has to remember that, to quote Fredrickson, American liberal tolerance "stopped at the color line,"[56] that is, it did not apply to African Americans.

Catholic anti-Americanism has grown deep roots in continental Europe, especially in the political elite that has governed countries with strong Catholic traditions (such as Italy, France, Belgium, Spain, and Germany) and that has continued to eye America with suspicion. Of course, the Cold War struggle of America against the "materialist" Soviet Union constrained the Catholic political elite to praise America's international role. However, this did not prevent that same elite from sympathizing with the strategic vision of the Holy See, which was frequently at odds with the American one (especially regarding the Palestinian-Israeli conflict). But above all, anti-Americanism has taken hold amongst militant Catholics engaged in volunteer work, pacifism, and international cooperation, for whom America still coincides with the culture of consumption and the empire at arms. Also here, the end of the Cold War has brought to the fore a new generation of Catholic politicians, more mindful of the liberal foundations of American democracy, and thus more interested in understanding the American political experience. However, all this has not yet been translated into an adequate interpretation of America.

Most likely the difficulty in seeing America for what it is, namely a contradictory experiment of liberal democracy in a superpower, is due to the influence that anti-modernist and anti-Western oriented currents of Catholicism continue to exert over both progressive and conservative Catholics. This Catholicism remains connected to the ecumenical inspiration of the church and to its expansion in the developing countries of the world, and this influence constitutes a significant obstacle to the comprehension of the most developed country. In fact, from the point of view of the poor countries, America is an opulent and militaristic country, unfair toward its population and arrogant toward other countries. The pauperist perspective of European Catholicism allows it to see only the vices but not the virtues of America. In brief, America may be less outwardly dangerous than other powers but nevertheless is not to be trusted.

1.6   Misunderstanding America

I am not interested to set the arguments of Americanism and anti-Americanism against each other in this book. Such a juxtaposition would not only be useless but also mistaken. In fact, there are valid arguments both for criticism and for praise of America. I am aware of the constant and widespread need to find new opposing arguments now that the end of the Cold War has claimed several ideologies that had previously served this purpose. But America is not and cannot be an ideology, despite what de Tocqueville and others after him wrote, exactly because it is the expression of an open society and a continuously evolving political system.[57] Nor is there an "American model" to emulate as some observers maintain. In fact, many elements of this "model," especially on the institutional level, would be quite difficult to export as they are part and parcel of a unique institutional experience, whereas other elements had better not be exported. In reality American democracy is a complex political system which needs to be studied and understood before subjecting it to criticism or singing its praise.

   Here I will employ the main criticisms advanced by anti-Americanism in order to launch such an investigation. These criticisms generally focus on four aspects of American democracy. Two of them are related to the institutional structure (system of government and electoral system) and the remaining two concern America's choices (in domestic and foreign policy). Of course, other criticisms can and have been leveled. I will thus seek to enter into a dialogue with the critics of America in order to show that the American system of government is not plebiscitary but personalized; that low voter turnout is not the result of the electoral system but of the characteristics of American electoral competition; that the social disparities are the outcome of political transformations that have led to the success of the neoconservatives as well as being the outcome of a market democracy; and that America's post-Second World War foreign policy aimed to construct an institutionalized hegemony instead of an empire. Implicitly, I will also seek to engage in a dialogue with pro-American observers, demonstrating that they commit errors in the interpretation of America similar to those of the critics, although they start from a different point of view.

Still, it is worthwhile trying to understand why America continues to evoke such widespread sentiments of hostility amongst numerous European political and intellectual elites and the public at large. It would seem that, with its behavior, America does its best to provoke hostile reactions, including in allied countries. Nevertheless, it should be pointed out that unlike any other country, the verdicts pronounced on America tend always to have a holistic nature. Rather than criticizing a particular state decision (for example the unilateral military intervention in Iraq or the use of the death penalty by state governors who care more about opinion polls than about their own civic conscience), individual decisions instead provide occasion for a verdict to be pronounced on the entire American democratic experience (as if it existed in a manifest and completed form). Nobody in Europe would accept a generalized definition of their country informed only by a particular decision of their government or of one of the numerous courts. Yet, such a general definition is regularly imposed on Americans. In sum, even today, the criticism of what America *does* is always combined with some kind of disdain for what America *is*. And it is always difficult to establish where the latter stops and the former starts.

Why does this happen? First of all, for the historical reasons I discussed above. As Lipset has reminded us America was the first nation of a new type,[58] and still today the old nations of Europe have not managed to understand the novelty of its arrival on the global scene (novelty, here, should be understood in relative terms, given that America has been a global power since the beginning of the twentieth century). Although it is true that America is capitalist, it is also a country which has provided an opportunity for economic betterment to millions of immigrants. Although America is racist (and a part of it has been, for a long time, even a slave-owning society), it is also true that it is liberal and tolerant. Although it is true that America is a hegemonic and sometimes aggressive power, it is also an isolationist if not pacifist country. Whereas it is true that its federal elections are marked by low voter turnout, yet it also boasts a vibrant grassroots democracy. It is true that its federal democracy is frighteningly costly (in the sense that truly large amounts of money are required in order to get elected to the Senate, the House of Representatives, or the presidency), yet it is also true that the electoral system has a sufficiently competitive character so as not to transform the country into an oligarchy. Above all, America is not the arithmetic sum of its parts, but rather the contingent and unpredictable outcome of the conflicts and tensions brought about by such contradictory characteristics.

The second set of reasons is of a cultural nature. Europe finds it difficult to understand America simply because from the outset the latter has embarked on a politico-economic trajectory distinct from the European one. In fact, in its relation with economic power, America has taken the road of regulation of the market, whereas Europe chose nationalization. In its relation with political power, America has taken the road of the separation of powers, whereas Europe chose the fusion of powers. In its relation with the power of the state, America took the road of federal decentralization, whereas Europe chose centralization, albeit mitigated by forms of regionalism and municipalism. It should be noted that (looking at the historical experience of Switzerland and the recent experience of Belgium), the only countries to adopt a federal model after the Second World War were Germany and Austria, who did so strongly conditioned by the American military occupation forces. The point is that European public culture has come to assume that Europe constitutes the natural order of things political, thus relegating America to the status of an exception to the rule. This, of course, tends to the great satisfaction of America's public culture, which has traditionally referred to its exceptionalism in order to celebrate America as the natural order of all things political.[59]

Being held prisoner by the myth of exceptionalism, European public culture continues to perceive America as a different world, "the veritable Other of our era."[60] Yet, many changes have occurred on both shores of the Atlantic. Being marked originally by the choice to create a compound sovereignty, America subsequently experienced the need to equip itself with a more pronounced institutional coherence, once it had become a crucial actor in the international system. After all, war (whether cold or hot) continues to exert irresistible pressures toward more centralized decision-making regimes, as has been the case in Europe during the last five centuries.[61] In their turn, the individual European countries, having been pressured to pool their own sovereignty at the supranational level after two dramatic world wars (which can more appropriately be considered European civil wars), have created a European Union (EU) which has the compound features of the American republic.

Thus, the process of European integration is promoting the formation of a political system that displays many more similarities with the American one than with the systems of the individual member states of the EU. Between Brussels and Strasbourg a sort of separation of powers is becoming institutionalized (instead of a fusion of powers as in the EU member states) between the Commission, the Parliament, and the Council of Ministers; with a European Court of Justice invested with the power of judicial review; with European political parties that are bland federations of national parties; and with interest groups that play a growing role in the process of policy-making.[62] At the same time, the process of European integration is promoting a market system at the continental scale that has the regulatory features of the American one. The strategy of market-substitution has been replaced by a strategy of market-support designed to create a private competitive, rather than a public controlled, economy. A system of regulatory capitalism has come to assert itself that is not very different from the one America started to experiment with in the 1890s, when the first anti-trust laws were passed.

1.7 Conclusion

Notwithstanding such tendencies, America continues to be misunderstood and little known in Europe. Given its international importance and its political and economic weight, such misunderstandings are not without relevance. They undermine the legitimacy of criticism, when it is necessary to advance it, but likewise they undermine the credibility of America's praise, when it is necessary to sing it. It would be desirable to try and approach America less emotionally and to study it with more precision. This book aims to provide a contribution in this direction.

2

A Plebiscitary Democracy?

2.1 Introduction

It is widely held that the American democracy is a plebiscitary one. As some have argued, America represents the

> brilliant victory of *soft* bonapartism, at whose center stands a leader, powerful because of his popular plebiscitary investiture, because of the very extensive powers he exerts and can magnify out of all proportion during a state of emergency, because of the holy halo he wears as the prophet of a sacred mission of liberty; because of his authority to wield this gigantic incomprehensible propaganda machine.[1]

For many observers, America is technically "a plebiscitary democracy," as only the president controls the political power, with the help of his own "Camarilla."[2] America simply is its president. In fact "Americans have no idea of what happens in Congress . . . There are no open debates . . . This is no longer a democracy . . . It is practically speaking an authoritarian system."[3] The emphasis may change, yet the view that the American government is identical to the president is widely shared. Is this really so?

A plebiscitary democracy may be defined as a democracy that satisfies (at least) two fundamental requirements: (1) governmental power is concentrated in the hands of a single leader; (2) that leader is elected by the citizens and maintains a direct relationship with them. In order to be considered plebiscitary, the American system of government would have to be controlled by the president, with Congress (composed of the House of Representatives and the Senate) relegated to a subordinate role. Moreover, no third power, like the Supreme Court or the judiciary, should be able to exert influence over the president, because the former do not enjoy the same degree of popular legitimacy. Simultaneously, the president would have to be chosen by means of a direct and general election, in which political parties and other organizations only play a limited role. The absence of such structures of intermediation should thus allow the president to address himself directly to the citizens during the exercise of his office.

In reality, the system of American government cannot easily be fitted into such a mold. Certainly, the presidency has become more personalized, in particular from the 1970s onward, but this should not be mistaken for a plebiscitarian transformation of American democracy. The American democracy, in fact, is institutionally anti-majoritarian, as it is an expression of liberal political thought distrustful of the concentration of power and, hence, preoccupied more with controlling power than with exercising it. Democracies with strong anti-majoritarian constraints cannot easily become plebiscitarian, even though America is not alien to phenomena of political mobilization typical of a mass society with a well-developed system of news media. But if America is not plebiscitarian, what kind of democracy is it? My answer is that it is a compound democracy, since it is based on a multiple separation of powers, both at the vertical level (between the federal state and the federated states) and the horizontal one (within the institutions of the federal government).

A compound democracy, hence, is a democracy with *fragmented sovereignty*, as institutional power is fragmented (on the governmental level) in the separated institutions of the federal center and in the federated states, whose system of government in turn is separated like the federal one. Here, I will discuss only the federal system of government. Federal decentralization constitutes an additional constraint on a plebiscitarian transformation of American democracy. Systems of government are separated when the government does not coincide with an institution (the executive) but with a set of institutions that share the decision-making power. One might say that a separated system is *governed without a government*, but by the collaboration (and frequently discord) of (and between) a number of separated institutions, which, however, are all equally legitimated to take part in the decision-making process.

It is, therefore, a democracy in which no institution can claim the monopoly of decision-making (as the Cabinet can in the European parliamentary democracies, be they majoritarian or consensual).

This chapter is structured as follows. First, I will revisit the central themes of the political theory of the compound republic, as it was defined in Philadelphia in 1787 (during the deliberations that led to the drafting of the federal Constitution), in order to re-examine the way it constrains the exercise of political power so as to prevent its abuse by individual office holders as well as by a majority of citizens (or by a combination of the two, as is typical of plebiscitary regimes). Next, I will discuss the evolution of the American system of government, from the era of pre-eminence of Congress (congressional government), to its decline and the subsequent rise of presidential government. Finally, I will discuss the institutional and political reasons (in particular the introduction of direct primaries as the general method for selecting the presidential candidate, and the related decline of the electoral role of political parties) which have led since the 1970s to the transformation of presidential government (which was the government of a leader who could rely on a party to connect the presidency with the congressional majority) into a personalized presidency no longer linked to Congress through a party.

It is this personalized presidency that has engendered the plebiscitary misunderstandings of the American democracy. The personalization of the presidency does not imply (and cannot imply) presidential control of the entire government, while plebiscitary regimes necessarily require the centralization of political power in the hands of the president. The president is the indisputable leader of the executive branch, having been elected on a personal basis, frequently without the organizational help of his party (and, for this reason, free from the latter's political constraints). Nevertheless the control of the presidency does not coincide with the control of the two chambers of Congress. Rather, the personalized presidency has weakened the president on the institutional level, because it has deprived him of those partisan links with Congress that, during the period of 1930s–1960s, allowed him to promote his own legislative agenda. The president's rhetorical emphasis on his popular leadership constitutes an attempt to counter-balance the weakness of his governmental leadership.[4] However, in order to prevail, popular leadership is much more in need of a continuous dramatization of the domestic and international situation than governmental leadership.

2.2   The Origins of Separated Government

2.2.1   *The compound republic: The debate of 1787*

The American Constitution represents one of the most sophisticated expressions of western enlightenment thought. The 55 founding fathers of the American republic, i.e. the political leaders of the 13 American states who, with some difficulties, congregated in Philadelphia in the torrid summer of 1787, displayed many differences of opinion, which in turn reflected different territorial and economic interests, on how to build the new federal republic. On one point though, they collectively agreed, namely that it was possible to respond in the affirmative to the important question posed by Alexander Hamilton in *Federalist* no.1, when he asked "whether societies of men are really capable or not of establishing good government from reflection and choice, or whether they are forever destined to depend for their political constitutions on accident and force."[5] Choice and reflection: these are the two criteria crucial to understanding the American constitutional debate. Choice is possible only when supported by adequate reflection, and the reflection of the founding fathers was nourished by two sets of considerations: an anthropological-philosophical one and a historical-comparative one.[6]

The first set of considerations boils down to the question: What is good government for a union of states and citizens? The drafters of the Constitution at Philadelphia did not have a common view of what constituted a good government. Rather, different schools of thought can be traced in the documents and discussions accompanying the intellectual formation of the new republic, from the Jeffersonian Declaration of Independence of 1776 to the Madisonian Constitution of 1787. According to the (liberal) Whig Theory of Lockean inspiration, good government coincides with a government based on the consent of the people and designed to preserve the constitutive trio of civil society (life-property-liberty). The (republican) radical theory of Machiavellian descent, instead holds that good government can be considered such only if it is able to bring about public virtue.[7] Although accepting many of its conclusions, the radical view goes beyond the traditional theory, as here the government sets itself more ambitious goals: to educate the citizens in the exercise of virtue, which coincides with the ability to reconcile private interests with the common good. But also the Unionist theory, with its roots in the federative Grotian tradition, and according to which the new republic represented an alternative to both "international anarchy" and "universal empire," can be detected in the constitutional debates. As Hendrickson wrote, the conventional ways of describing the American political inheritance, focusing on its "liberal" or "republican" character, need to be supplemented by recognition of a third paradigm of thought (the unionist paradigm), one centered on the problem of cooperation among the "several states in the union of the empire."[8]

Although those schools of thought (limited government, virtuous government, and compound government) were present in the debates at Philadelphia and have accompanied the political evolution of the country, nevertheless it was their combination which has informed the birth and the development of the American experiment with democracy.[9] So much so, that nowadays it is difficult to tell them apart. This combination has given rise to the so-called Madisonian or compound democracy, which is a democracy that seeks to hinder the permanent formation of political hegemonies and stable institutional hierarchies. One might say that the American Constitution of 1787 is the only truly liberal constitution still in force today, as it is concerned with checking the use of power even more so than with promoting its virtuous use. Their direct experience with the public affairs of the period 1776–87 had led many of the founding fathers to believe not only that the virtuousness of the governing and the governed could not simply be anthropologically postulated and could only be encouraged institutionally; but also that keeping together asymmetrical states (because of their different demographic size and economic capability) requires a diffusion of decision-making power and not its concentration.

This led to the elaboration of a sophisticated political theory based on the concept of political constraints. For the first time these constraints were no longer understood as a vertical form of political obligation, but rather as the horizontal structure of incentives and disincentives through which separated branches of government and distinct individuals (i.e. the components of a compound republic) succeed in solving the problems of collective action while pursuing divergent goals. Madison summarized the concept thus in *Federalist* no. 51:

> But what is government itself, but the greatest of all reflections on human nature? If men were angels, no government would be necessary. If angels were to govern men, neither external nor internal

controls on government would be necessary. In framing a government which is to be administered by men over men, the great difficulty lies in this: you must first enable the government to control the
governed; and in the next place oblige it to control itself.[10]

Concerning the historical-comparative reflections, the drafters of
the Constitution doubtless were negatively influenced by the post-
revolutionary history of the Confederacy. The articles of Confederation (i.e. the Constitution that the republic had given itself in 1781,
five years after having declared independence from Great Britain)
had abundantly shown that a limited government, dominated by
the legislature, cannot be a good government; instead, it risked
becoming a non-government. It was received opinion, in the
13 colonies now become states,[11] that the principle of liberty
coincided with the principle of representation and thus, with the
central role of the legislature in the organization of the state. The
first legislature on American soil was already established in 1619,
when the Virginia Company consented to the Constitution of a
House of Burgesses, which early on demanded, in addition to the
power to legislate, the power to deliberate on taxation. The hostility
of the colonies toward the British monarch, and his abuse of
power, was soon translated into hostility toward the executive,
which was considered a source of constant intimidation of the
elective institutions. Thus the Continental Congress progressively
came to assume a central role, before, during, and after the War of
Independence.

   After the revolution, all the powers of the states and of the Confederation were invested in the state legislatures and the Continental Congress, respectively. The articles of Confederation even
resolved to unite the three fundamental constitutional powers
within the legislature. Executive power was placed in the hands of
an executive committee of the confederated states that could operate
only when the Continental Congress was in recess, and that was
chaired by one of its members for a maximum term of one year.
But this constitutional apparatus, like its equivalents in the 13 individual states, soon revealed its limits. The state legislatures as well
as the continental one would soon fall prey to factions of particularistic interests, to popular moods, and to personal ambitions,
which on several occasions had conspired to paralyze its activities,
thus degrading the Confederation's decision-making capacity. This
experience prompted Hamilton to open *Federalist* no.1 with the
following observation: "After an unequivocal experience of the

inefficiency of the subsisting federal government, you are called upon to deliberate on a new Constitution for the United States of America."[12]

Hence, Philadelphia sought to draft a new system of government able to promote the pursuit of two mutually contradictory goals, namely the effectiveness and representativeness of the government. In short, Philadelphia constitutes the first example in history of the search for and deliberation on the constituent foundations of the political order for a democratic society (based on states and their citizens). The Constitution thus does not list a set of moral principles: but rather is the formalization of a system of decision-making structures entrusted with the task of promoting effectiveness and democracy in the context of a compound republic. Since then, the distinction between Constitution and system of government acquired fundamental importance: the Constitution embodies the will of the people (as they are organized in their states) whereas the system of government embodies the will of its representatives (chosen within the boundaries of the states). This distinction is impermeable: through its regular activities the government shall never alter the constitutional environment under whose constraints it operates. Government derives from the Constitution and not vice versa, just as the representatives express the will of the represented. Thus, sovereignty is neither unlimited nor unified, but rather constrained and fragmented. It is constrained by its own rules and governed by the institutional forms through which it expresses itself. But, of course, no institutional device as such can provide a sufficient guarantee of the legal integrity of a Constitution. The latter can only be upheld as long as the governed are willing to challenge possible unconstitutional acts of those who govern. To use Jefferson's words, "The tree of liberty must be refreshed from time to time, with the blood of patriots and tyrants. It is its natural manure . . ."[13]

2.2.2   *How to prevent the double abuse of power*

Whereas democracy needs virtuous citizens to protect it from itself in extraordinary circumstances, under ordinary circumstances, instead, its institutions are entrusted with this task. The *Federalist* constitutes the essential reference that helps us understand why America instituted a separated government. James Madison is the architect of separated government. His anti-populism had led him to (logically) emphasize ways to control the citizens, but his liberalism immediately led him to reflect on how to control the government. If the citizens are checked by the rule of law, government needs to be checked by a particular Constitution.

Why particular? Because the Constitution must succeed in opposing one power to another power, such that the overall outcome is one of reciprocal control between those who wield public power. As *Federalist* no. 51 notes, "Ambition must be made to counteract ambition."[14] Therefore powers needed to be separated, rather than merely divided, as was advocated by the French Enlightenment thought of Montesquieu. America not only resolved to separate the executive, legislative, and judicial powers, but the legislature was further separated into the House of Representatives and the Senate, because it was considered the most important, and thus potentially the most dangerous power. As Huntington argued some time ago, America chose the path of the separation of powers with Tudor England in mind, at the same time when Europe (post-Tudor England) was abandoning the traditional separation in favor of a move toward the fusion of powers (between legislature and executive with the formula of the *King in the Parliament*).[15] In America, separated powers mean reciprocally independent powers, both on the electoral and the institutional level; powers, therefore, that have been enabled to reciprocally control each other. To use Neustadt's words, in America there is a situation of "separated institutions sharing power,"[16] whereas the parliamentary systems of Europe are characterized by fused institutions (the executive depends on the legislature) that exercise distinct powers: government, by the executive and its parliamentary majority, and opposition, by the parliamentary minority or minorities.

The separation of powers is guaranteed not only constitutionally but first and foremost electorally. Whereas the members of the House of Representatives are elected directly by the voters of the various state districts, the senators for a long time were selected by the state legislatures and later by the state electors, and the president continues to be chosen by the Electoral Colleges of the various states. The presidential election is an indirect one (as the election of the senators was) because the winning contender is chosen by ad hoc candidates who gather in the capital of their respective states after having been elected. Those ad hoc candidates were subsequently known as the presidential electors and are elected only to perform this task. Each state is entitled to a number of presidential electors equal to the number of representatives plus senators that state has in Congress. Hence, there is no national college of presidential electors, but only state colleges of electors, in the sense that the presidential electors convene in the capital of the state where they were elected. The outcome of their voting is then communicated to the federal Senate in Washington, DC.

This method of apportionment of the presidential electors obviously favors the small states over the big ones. In fact, whereas the number of representatives is proportional to the size of the population (nowadays each member of the House of Representatives is elected in single member constituencies of about 600,000 inhabitants), the number of senators is completely independent of the size of the population (every state is entitled to two senators, irrespective of its demographic weight). This means that, due to the mechanism of the presidential electors, the smaller states carry a political weight disproportionate to their population in the election of the president. It goes without saying that this device was a price paid at Philadelphia in 1787 to keep the smaller states in the union.

Although separated, the institutions of government nevertheless have an equivalent power, as they all derive their legitimacy from the same source, namely the Constitution. Under the Constitution, all the federal institutions (whether elected directly or indirectly) are equal, which is to say that all are subjected to the authority of the Constitution as the exclusive depository of popular legitimacy, symbolized by the *We the People* with which the Preamble opens. However, the "deliberate effort (that) had been made during the Convention – led by Madison – to sink the foundations of the new union deeper than that of a conventional treaty" did not prevent "it from being considered from the start as a species of contract or compact." It was the political development of the compound republic that cleared the ambiguity, interpreting the Preamble as if "it had been made by 'one' people."[17] Accordingly, the judiciary can subject all the laws, passed by Congress and signed by the president, to judicial review, because it is invested with a power equivalent to that of the executive and the legislature, even if it lacks the popular legitimacy (direct or indirect) of the others. The Supreme Court, which stands at the apex of the judicial power, is thus entrusted with the task of guardian of the Constitution. Obviously here we have reached the opposite pole of the European national democracies in which the Jacobin principle of parliamentary supremacy has never seriously been called into question in the two centuries since the revolution of 1789. This is why the American system is anything but simply presidential.

As if this were not enough, to the vertical and horizontal separation of powers must be added the temporal separation between the various holders of public office. The president remains in office for four years (and, since amendment XXII of 1951, may serve two terms at most), whereas the members of the House of Representatives remain in office for two years and the senators six years (with the mandate of one third of the latter expiring simultaneously with the mandate of the representatives). To this temporal separation between the holders of public offices corresponds a likewise separation of the constituencies they are called to represent: the limited community of the district by the representative, the larger community of the state by the senator, and the still larger community of the country by the president.

These multiple separations are designed to promote competition between different (i.e. non-coinciding) institutional interests (or majorities). The system is anti-majoritarian not because it doesn't produce majorities (indeed, it does) but because the majority expressed by one institution is expected to be different from the majority expressed by other institutions, thus balancing one with the other. However, to ensure that this competition between different majorities will not lead to a paralysis of decision-making, a novel (and distinct) system of checks and balances was introduced into the separation of powers. In this system, cooperation between institutions is promoted by the fact that each one has a voice (or rather a veto power) in the functioning of the others. The president needs the "advice and consent" of the Senate in order to appoint the members of the presidency, and the (nine) life-time members of the Supreme Court, as well as to conclude treaties with foreign powers. At the same time Congress requires the signature of the president in order to turn an approved legislative proposal into law; a signature which the president may withhold, thus vetoing the bill in question. This obliges each institution to take into consideration the point of view (the interests and preferences) of the others, if it wishes to function adequately. Also presidential impeachment may be considered a form of check and balance of the presidential power, albeit an extreme one. The impeachment procedure, governed by article II, section 4, of the Constitution, envisages that a president can be removed from office when, following an allegation passed by the House, and thus voted by the Senate he is found guilty of "Treason, Bribery, or other high Crimes and Misdemeanors."

The American system is not only characterized by separated government, but it is also open to the possibility that different institutional equilibria may emerge over time.[18] In fact, since the adoption of the Constitution, different constellations of pre-eminence between the various branches of government have crystallized. However, the constitutional constraints of separated government render any such pre-eminence insecure. Because there is no predetermined center of power in a separated government, all the institutions have strong incentives to continuously attempt to redress the balance of their reciprocal relations. Each decision is the outcome of a process of negotiations between the actors of the different and separated institutions, who represent distinct electoral interests and institutional outlooks. It is a system designed to take decisions cautiously, with caution being guaranteed by the equilibrium and the reciprocal balancing between the institutions involved in the governmental process. Hence, in terms of its decision-making capabilities, the American government is a weak one, i.e. it is a government not designed to take good decisions but rather to prevent bad decisions. The system appears powerful because America is powerful, and not because it was designed to be so. Very much the opposite has been the case in Europe, where national democracies are guaranteed by a process of balancing between the political parties (and between government and opposition), instead of between institutions. This is why it is easier to govern in European nation states than in America; in the former stable majorities can be identified and formed, whereas they are institutionally fragmented in the latter.[19]

Historically, American separated government has achieved its goals. The government has been a virtuous one because the limits on the exercise of power by means of its multiple separation have thrown up an effective barrier to potentially anti-democratic threats that might originate from both the abuses of the governing and the governed. By distributing power amongst different institutions, the impetus for the formation of a single (across the board) majority has been fragmented. After the symbolic moment of the constitutional foundation of the republic, the people reunite only when called to approve or reject proposed constitutional amendments. The process of the formation of its political will has been institutionally scattered by channeling it into distinct and differentiated electoral environments. The virtues of separated government confirm the revolutionary revision of classical political theory wrought by the founding fathers who realized that democracy was safer in larger societies than in smaller ones. In a small democracy the spirit of factionalism may more easily prevail, contaminating the entire body politic and thus giving rise to the "tyranny of the majority." In a large and compound democracy, instead, it is more difficult to identify and form a majority. Yet, these virtues have also brought to light the existence of more than a few significant vices.

2.3 Congressional Government

The American system of separated government has witnessed different institutional constellations in its long democratic history. From the foundation of the new republic to the 1920s, this constellation was marked by the primacy of the legislature (Congress); starting with the 1930s the executive (the president) has progressively come to assert its primacy. The different institutional constellations of separated government derived from the different ability of the branches of government (president, presidency, and Congress) to respond to the challenges of the domestic and international environment and, thus, to their different ability to represent the coalition of interests and values that had gained prominence at any time in society and politics.

Notwithstanding the fears of the founding fathers at Philadelphia concerning possible abuses of the legislative power, and notwithstanding their deliberate choice to counter-balance the legislature with an independent executive, for all of the first century of the life of the republic, Congress maintained its position as the privileged locus of political decisions, on both the small and large problems that preoccupied the country or parts of it. The contradiction between the two presidential roles (the president, on the one hand, is the leader of a faction as head of the executive and, on the other hand, the leader of the whole nation as head of state) was resolved in favor of a ceremonial role for the president as head of state, as well as by means of a narrow interpretation of the provisions of the Constitution, which implicitly recognized Congress as the main branch of the American government (devoting to it the first article of the Constitution). Thus, the president was prevented from becoming a true popular leader, to such an extent that both amongst the public and the governmental actors, the president was widely perceived to hold a lesser authority than the Speaker of the House, or even some particularly influential senators. The characteristics of the system for the election of the branches of government were such as to make Congress (and especially the House of Representatives) appeared to be the only representative body, since the legislature was legitimated by popular will, whereas the president could only refer to the text of the Constitution to justify his own institutional salience.

In fact, the system for selecting the presidential candidate was entirely controlled by the congressional elite in the initial phase of the republic (the party caucus selected the candidate[20]), and subsequently by the party elites with a base in the state legislatures (the national convention, composed of the state and local party leaders, selected the candidate). The election of the presidential candidate instead, which according to the Constitution must take place by means of each state's Electoral College, was entrusted to the presidential electors chosen by the party leaders of the state legislatures. The point is that, during the phase of congressional government, the presidential electors generally were selected by the legislatures of the individual states, i.e. by the state parties in control of the legislatures. In this way, the state parties could keep a tight grip on the election of the presidents, both during the selection of the candidates and the election itself, making sure that they would not threaten the primacy of Congress. Congress, in turn, was also in their grip, as the state party leaders controlled both the direct elections of the House of Representatives and the indirect election of the two senators for each state. One might say that congressional government provided a tremendous opportunity for the assertion of the interests of the states over national interests.

Congress has sought to translate its representativeness in governmental capabilities by means of two main organizational devices: the committee system and the system of party caucuses. Concerning the former, as of 1825 in both chambers a system of permanent committees was institutionalized through which Congress not only succeeded in organizing its representational activities more rationally, but also to support its governmental activities. For this reason, congressional government, which consolidated since the 1820s, should more appropriately be defined as committee government, as Woodrow Wilson wrote in 1885.[21] The system of party caucuses developed alongside the committee system, with both mutually reinforcing each other. Ever since the first session of the first Congress, its members coalesced around two alternative political groupings on the main policy problems of the day. These groupings reflected different political preferences and were subsequently organized in the more permanent form of congressional caucuses. From this point of view, it would seem appropriate to maintain, as Lowi and Ginsberg have done, that for a century a party government existed within Congress, exercised through committee government.[22] The link between the committee government and the party caucus government for all of the nineteenth century has been the Speaker of the House. As Polsby has written, the chair of the House has been the institution that has sought to coordinate the parties and the committees.[23]

Although congressional government was able to mitigate the separation of powers between the legislature and the executive (limiting the presidency to its constitutional role), it nevertheless should not be confused with a parliamentary government. In fact, the separation of powers has manifested itself within Congress, through the committees' structure, which has made it particularly difficult to centralize decision-making. The committees, which represented the interests of specific and differentiated constituencies, have been able to exercise their veto powers to block unwelcome decision or to promote welcome ones, and in any case to protect their specific interests. During the period of congressional government, therefore, decision-making was the shared responsibility of various actors, i.e. the leaders of the state parties, committee chairmen, particularly influential senators, and the Speaker of the House and the Senate majority leader.

The primacy of Congress amongst the institutions of separated government would seriously be called into question, between the turn of the twentieth century and the Second World War, by two related but chronologically distinct fundamental processes of transformation: a radical change of the domestic and international environment and a pronounced democratization of the system of government. Once both processes had run their course, the revolutionary nature of the institutional innovations they progressively engendered became evident. At the end of almost half a century of change, the functional relations between the two institutions of government had been inverted. It was the president who now gained decision-making pre-eminence over Congress.[24]

2.4 The Crisis of Congressional Government

Major economic transformations were induced by the crisis of the 1880s, such as the formation of industrial and financial conglomerates (the first large corporations) of such dimension as to impose new rules on the working of the market; the emergence of well-organized interest organizations able to control in a quasi monopolistic way one or more resources of fundamental importance to the working of the economic system; as well as the changing production technologies and the emergence and successive development of standardized systems of mass-production. These and other processes have induced the federal government to play an increasingly active role in the economy and society. This was a transformation of historical dimensions of the American society; gradually the country came to define itself as a large industrial nation. Since the 1880s America saw itself confronted with a task of uncommon relevance.[25]

In this new structural context, congressional government soon revealed its limitations, both in terms of the slow process of policy formulation and its fragmented nature. Forced to operate within the constraints of representing consolidated interests, Congress had proven to be inadequate with respect to the task of swiftly defining strategic courses of action. While suited to the exigencies of congressional government, the weak administrative apparatus soon revealed its ineffectiveness in supporting the expansion of the federal government. Those evident limitations of Congress, together with the growth of the administrative apparatus, facilitated the progressive assertion of the presidency as the pre-eminent branch of the separated government. At the same time, domestic economic and social transformations created an opportunity for the presidents to redefine their role, both in terms of a more representative nature of their office and a more pronounced governmental interpretation of the prerogatives entrusted to them by the Constitution. In the new context, only the presidency could bring about a degree of administrative cohesion sufficiently high to guarantee the effective regulation of the market; and only the president could put himself forward as the representative of the general interest and, thus, as the symbol of national unity, precisely because the presidency was not burdened by a particularistic nature.

The experience of the First World War, together with the violent economic crisis of 1929, brought about a radical change of the institutional equilibria in favor of the executive. Obviously, the process was neither linear nor without its contradictions. The first two presidencies of Franklin D. Roosevelt (FDR) (1933–40), the true founding father of the modern presidency, were marked by a permanent conflict with both Congress and the Supreme Court, at least until one year before the outbreak of the Second World War. What was explicitly at stake here was the definition of a new hierarchy of power between the institutions of separated government. The outcome of this conflict was a dramatic shift of the separated government in the direction of presidential government: it is not by chance that, in this respect, scholars have talked of a *Roosevelt Revolution.*[26]

While having emerged under the pressures of domestic transformations, the new hierarchy of powers in favor of the executive became further consolidated due to the dominant role that America came to play in the international system with the Second World War. For all of the nineteenth century, the international involvement of the country was limited, although by no means insignificant, especially in the western hemisphere. In fact, the country had early on established its dominant position in Central and South America. Nor did America renounce playing a role in Asia, involving it in a military confrontation with Spain over the control of the Philippines at the end of the nineteenth century. The victory over Spain would transform America into a colonial power, albeit for a limited period. Yet, its geographic distance from Europe, the progressive downsizing of the European powers' territorial ambitions in North and Central America, the limited military capabilities of its neighboring countries, and the limited fighting power of the native-Americans, all conspired to shield Washington, DC from the forces that elsewhere would have urged the centralization of political power and its control by the executive.[27]

In other words, the imperatives of international politics and its fiscal and military corollaries had not gained a hold over American politics. It is not surprising, therefore, that America, similar to Great Britain, but in contrast to the countries of continental Europe, was able to develop the political and institutional structures of a democratic mass society without the constraints of a centralized state. Indeed, only in the wake of the Second World War did America acquire a powerful and permanent military apparatus managed by the executive branch through a specific presidential department. The outbreak of the Cold War, between 1946 and 1948, would further heighten the international power of the country, thus further supporting the presidential claim to pre-eminence in the decision-making process; a pre-eminence owed to objective but also symbolic reasons. After all, in the new international context, only the presidency could direct the gigantic military and diplomatic apparatus that had come into being, and only the president was able to represent the country in a unified way in the new bipolar international system.

These structural transformations of the country were accompanied by a significant democratization of its institutions of government. Many of the barriers erected by the founding fathers in order to keep the impact of the people on the federal decision-making process under control were called into question. They had become hard to justify in view of a progressive nationalization of politics which came to entrust the federal institutions with ever more important decisions. Thus, the bastion of the Electoral College started to crumble with the introduction of the election by general suffrage of the state presidential electors. The hold of the state parties over the selection of the presidential candidate was loosened by the experimentation with direct primaries in the first decades of the twentieth century. The elitist principle of the indirect election of the senators by the state legislators collapsed, with the approval in 1913 of amendment XVII of the Constitution which entrusted the election of the senators directly to the voters (albeit, by that time, more than half of the states had already introduced some kind of functional equivalent of direct elections).

There is no doubt that these processes of democratization were managed by the parties. The democratization of the Electoral College, of the system for the selection of the presidential candidates and of the senatorial elections did not call into question the role of the parties, especially in governmental politics. Their role, however, was seriously threatened at the electoral level. In fact, the criticism of the abuses of the party machines prompted legislation that introduced severe legal restrictions on the exercise of the vote (the so-called "system of 1896"), which in turn created the conditions for a weakening of the political parties as electoral organizations. Of course, American political parties, including those of the golden age of the nineteenth century, cannot be equated to their European counterparts: in America, the double (vertical and horizontal) separation of powers has continuously constrained their ability to maintain organizational and programmatic cohesion, whereas in Europe the system of fusion of powers (also in its federal variants), has instead consistently supported this ability.

Nevertheless, the progressive democratization of national politics, together with the modernization of the administrative apparatus of the federal government (e.g. the decrease of the spoil system through which the parties placed their supporters in public offices) had led to a gradual withering of the political parties in the institution that had heightened their power, i.e. Congress. The measure that symbolized this decline was that of the seniority system, introduced in the House in 1910, in the wake of the revolt of legislators (many of whom were of progressive leaning and elected for the first time in 1908) against the centralist methods of the then Speaker, known as Czar Cannon. Under the seniority system, the nomination of the congressional committee chairs was no longer at the discretion of the Speaker, but the chairmanship would instead accrue automatically to the member with the longest tenure. Although still important in the legislature, the gradual weakening of the parties was also confirmed, during the 1920s, by a decline in voting discipline of their congressmen.

In sum, whereas the changes in the external environment have spurred the rise of the presidency, the process of democratization progressively liberated the president from the influence of the congressional elites. One might say that, with the assertion of the presidency, the system of government has truly become separated. The turning point, in the history of the federal government, is marked by the presidencies of FDR. His first two presidencies (1933–40) provided the representation of a set of political and social forces which had acquired a growing national influence in the previous 50 years, but which had to await the Great Depression of 1929 in order to gain control of the federal government. Roosevelt's successive presidencies (1941–5) led America to fill the void left in the new international system by the decline of the European powers. Thus, a mutually reinforcing relation between the international rise of America and the domestic rise of the presidency was established.

2.5 Presidential Government

2.5.1 *The rise of the presidency*

Although it is true that the ascent of the presidency was prompted by changes in the domestic and international environment and the democratization of the system of government occurring between the 1890s and the Second World War, it is also true that this did not encounter insurmountable obstacles in the Constitution. Article II of the Constitution, devoted to the definition and organization of the executive power, has been defined by Corwin, one of the major twentieth-century scholars of the presidency, as "the most loosely drawn chapter of the Constitution."[28] The unclear constitutional definition of the executive has turned out to be crucial for the development of presidential government for two main reasons. First, it did not obstruct the president's claims to provide his office with a stronger constitutional underpinning. Secondly, it has justified the congressional renunciation of trying to provide its activity with an appropriate institutional underpinning. Thus, presidential government, which came into its own in the 1930s, should be interpreted as the result of the interaction between "presidential claims" and "congressional renunciation."

It is known that the founding fathers at Philadelphia wanted an independent executive and we also know, from the notes of their debates, that nobody (not even Hamilton) wanted an institutionally predominant executive.[29] But, whereas they agreed in principle on the need to defend the executive from the hegemonic aspirations of the legislature, they were rather less in agreement on how exactly to mount this defense. Thus, the final draft of the Constitution fails to provide an accurate definition of the president's role.[30] It could not have been otherwise, given the differences among the states of the new republic. As a result, the legal texts that form the backdrop for the interaction between presidential claims and congressional renunciation leave room for different outcomes.

Consider the debate on the so-called inherent powers of the executive. The ink on the Constitution had not yet dried when the theory of the inherent powers of the executive came to divide the same political elite that had written the Constitution. The heated debate, which pitted Hamilton against Madison during Washington's second presidency (1793–6), involved the following issue: whereas Hamilton held that if the Constitution did not explicitly prohibit the president from doing something, then he had the right to do it. Madison, in contrast, was convinced that such an interpretation rather reflected a monarchist vision of the presidency. But what is peculiar about this story is the behavior of Jefferson who, as Hamilton's main adversary on this issue, had solicited Madison to intervene against Hamilton,[31] but would show no hesitation to invoke that same theory of inherent powers, once having become president (1801–8), in particular to justify his foreign policy decisions.[32]

Even if Jefferson's conduct in office proved Hamilton's theory to be correct, and particularly determined presidents had demonstrated the potential for expanding presidential power on a limited number of other occasions, for all of the nineteenth century conditions had been anything but favorable for asserting the primacy of the presidency. Only in the twentieth century did presidential power structurally change. All the presidents since Theodore Roosevelt,

Woodrow Wilson and, above all, Franklin D. Roosevelt, have used the new domestic and international conditions to claim for themselves uncodified powers that allegedly "come with the territory." This change owes much to the judiciary.[33] Two decisions of the Supreme Court have proven to be of particular importance in establishing the legal basis of this recourse. The first decision, *In Re Neagle* of 1890, provided an extensive interpretation of the executive duties of the president also in domestic politics; whereas the second, *United States v. Curtiss-Wright Corporation* of 1936, established that the president is the sole organ in the field of foreign policy. The theory of "inherent powers" did not have only external implications, even if it has been in the field of foreign policy that the modern presidents have principally claimed their autonomy from the institutional constraints of separated government. In this respect, one should recall the ever more frequent recourse of the presidents to two executive instruments par excellence: executive orders (in domestic policies) and executive agreements (in foreign policy).

This presidential claim was spectacularly challenged in the famous *Steel Seizure Case* of 1952, in which the Supreme Court intervened in order to impose a limit to the assertion of the presidential prerogatives. On this occasion, the Court declared unconstitutional Truman's executive order that had placed the steel industry under the control of the federal government with the justification of the military exigencies of the country's engagement in Korea. But, although this decision helped prevent the abuse of the executive order by imposing constraints on its use, it did not have the strength to halt the expansion of the presidency. The same holds for executive agreements in foreign policy. Also here, although with the opposite result, there is an important decision of the Supreme Court, *U.S. v. Pink* of 1942, which had ruled as constitutional the choice of the executive to have recourse to agreements instead of treaties with foreign countries, an instrument preferred by the president in order to circumvent the procedure of advice and consent on the part of the Senate, which is required for the case of diplomatic treaties. This decision opened unprecedented possibilities for autonomous action of the president in foreign policy.

Now let us turn to the issue of congressional renunciation. The key historical turning point takes place during the 1930s, but already since the end of the First World War it seemed clear that Congress wanted to restrict itself to legislation of a general nature, because it was unable to govern a complex and ever-changing society by legislative means. A decade before the New Deal, in fact, Congress created the conditions for a larger presidential role in national politics with the passing of the Budget and Accounting Act of 1921. This act symbolized the process of delegation of powers from Congress to the presidency. Section 3 of article II of the Constitution establishes that the president "shall from time to time give to the Congress information of the state of the Union, and recommend to their consideration such measures as he shall judge necessary and expedient." Now, that same formulation has managed to justify diametrically opposed presidential actions.[34] For all of the nineteenth century, it had been used by Congress to confine the president within a completely secondary role in legislative matters. It may suffice to recall that, on most occasions, the president would not even care to venture to Capitol Hill to deliver the State of the Union address, sending instead a written message, which would be read out by the Speaker of the House, by the vice-president, in his capacity as chairman of the Senate or by one of their officials. During the next century, in contrast, it was Congress that would invite the president to take, on the basis of this formulation, the power of legislative initiative by means of setting the parameters of the federal budget.

Certainly, with that act Congress did not renounce its essential power to control the purse strings. Nevertheless, the president's budget proposals have defined the terms on which that power can be exercised. More generally, that act formalized an (unprecedented) legislative leadership role of the president, without which it would be inappropriate to talk of presidential government. Of course, the president was guaranteed to succeed in the exercise of this new role because he was the recognized leader of his party in Congress. Moreover, the assertion of this new presidential role has given rise to a re-interpretation of the old instruments at the disposal of the president, and one of them in particular, namely the veto power.[35] By means of the full use of his veto power, the president was able to become an actor in the legislative process, allowing him to influence the decisions of the legislature and to impose his own agenda. Article I section 7.2 of the Constitution states that:

> Every bill which shall have passed the House of Representatives and the Senate, shall, before it become a law, be presented to the President of the United States; if he approve he shall sign it, but if not he shall return it, with his objections to that House in which it shall have originated.

The president's veto, however, is not an absolute one, because a bill may nevertheless be re-approved if it obtains the support of a two-thirds majority of the members of both chambers of Congress. It goes without saying that such a qualified majority is not easy to obtain, and the presidential veto (or the threat of it) therefore may reveal itself as a formidable lever for exerting influence over the legislative decisions of Congress. Moreover, apart from the regular veto, the president has also come to use another type of veto, known as the pocket veto. The same article of the Constitution stipulates that:

> If any bill shall not be returned by the President within ten days (Sundays excepted) after it shall have been presented to him, the same shall be a law, in like manner as if he had signed it, unless the Congress by their adjournment prevent its return, in which case it shall not be a law.

Thus, occasionally, it has been sufficient for the presidents to postpone putting their signature to an unwelcome bill in order to block its passage, knowing Congress would be adjourned within ten days. The use of the presidential veto (both the regular and the pocket veto) had grown dramatically with FDR, was stable under Truman, and has become established as a regular weapon in the offensive of the executive against the legislature since the 1960s. Only the unusually strong unified party government of post-9/11 (in particular in the period 2003–5) registered a quasi absence of presidential vetoes, although the situation has changed with the renewed divided government of the period 2007–8 (see table 2.1). With the increasing use of the veto, the president also acquired a greater threat-potential with respect to the legislature. At the same time, congressional overrides of presidential vetoes have been infrequent. This increasing use of the presidential veto can only be understood in the framework of the legislative role Congress has awarded the president.

2.5.2   *The adaptation of Congress*

It would not have been possible to create the preconditions of presidential government without the complicity of Congress, especially in the field of legislative powers. In this way, an even more pronounced sharing of decision-making power between the three branches of the separated government came to be established between the 1930s and the 1960s, even if the presidency has seen

Table 2.1 Presidential vetoes, 1961–2008

Period	President	Total vetoes	Regular vetoes	Pocket vetoes	Vetoes not overridden	Overridden vetoes
1961–63	John F. Kennedy	21	12	9	21	–
1963–69	Lyndon B. Johnson	30	16	14	30	–
1969–74	Richard M. Nixon	43	26	17	36	7
1974–77	Gerald R. Ford	66	48	18	54	12
1977–81	Jimmy Carter	31	13	18	29	2
1981–89	Ronald R. Reagan	78	39	39	69	9
1989–93	George H. W. Bush	44	29	15	43	1
1993–2001	William J. Clinton	38	37	1	36	2
2001–03	George W. Bush*	0	0	0	0	0
2003–05	George W. Bush	1	1	0	1	0
2006–08	George W. Bush	8	8	0	7	1

*The absence of presidential vetoes can be explained by the very high ideological concord between the president and the majority of the House of Representatives.

Source: Adapted and updated from US Census Bureau, Statistical Abstract of the United States.

its pre-eminence recognized in some policy fields (foreign policy and defense, in particular), whereas the House and the Senate have sought instead to maintain their control over the policies that exert a direct impact on their respective constituencies. Congress' renunciation of some of its legislative prerogatives has come to intermingle (in the sense that it was both cause and effect) with the president's expansion of his traditional executive powers. Under presidential government, the president has sought to transform his prerogatives as head of state into the prerogatives of the head of the government, and has used the party as an instrument to mobilize his supporters in Congress.

But of course, aspirations are one thing and reality is another. Although both the presidency and Congress identified with the New Deal coalition that had durably congealed around the Democratic Party, there was no lack of policy conflicts between them. These conflicts were due to the fact that the congressional leadership was marked by the presence of strong committee chairmen (the so-called "barons" or "old bulls"), whose strength derived from the seniority system, which, by favoring the seniority of service, caused the secure, single-party and conservative regions of the (rural) Democratic South and the (rural) Republican plain states to be over-represented. This veritable oligarchy stood at the center of a cross-party conservative coalition, and repeatedly managed to tone down or block progressive policy innovations promoted by the president and his supporters in Congress – especially in the field of civil rights and gender equality – even when these proposals enjoyed the support of the majority of the country. The system of separated government, which implies multiple veto positions in the legislative process, permits particularly well-organized minorities to occupy vital nerve centers of the decision-making system (such as the congressional committees), thus allowing them to guard their interests, even if these are not shared by the majority. As a result, the seniority system de facto facilitated the opposite tyranny from the one feared by the founding fathers, namely the "tyranny of the minorities."

Hence, presidential ambitions were not able to challenge the constraints of the separation of powers. Presidential pre-eminence has been recognized by Congress, in particular in the field of foreign policy and defense (also because the Cold War did not permit other alternatives), but the presidential position remained one of pre-eminence and not of dominance. One might say that until 1968, or rather until the crisis of the imperial presidency brought about by the military defeat in Vietnam, Congress has accepted the new institutional equilibrium favorable to the presidency, in particular in foreign policy, but most certainly did not renounce its powers.[36] In view of the shared new international and national strategies of the country, Congress has adapted to the new role of the presidency by redefining its own institutional role. Since the primacy of the presidency manifested itself in the progressive erosion of congressional control over the legislative competences, Congress has countered this erosion by strengthening the powers of information (and specifically those defined as powers of oversight). Hearings and investigations in particular have become two effective procedures of the oversight of the policies of the presidency and its numerous regulatory agencies. Of course, the effectiveness of congressional activities in this field was also related to the fact that the committees and subcommittees have the power, directly or through the courts, to subpoena any government official not willing to collaborate loyally with Congress.

The congressional attitude toward the presidency changed noticeably with the crisis of 1968.[37] It could not have been otherwise, given that the massive mobilization against the war in Vietnam had challenged especially the pre-eminence of the presidency, accused of having become an "imperial" institution with respect to the other institutions of government, in addition to being accused of "imperialism" in the foreign policy it pursued. Thus, Congress, together with the judiciary and the media, became the institutional tool with which the opponents of the war halted the "imperial drift" of the Johnson and Nixon presidencies. This goal, as is well known, was effectively achieved. Between 1968 and 1974 the crisis of the "imperial presidency" unfolds. The starting point was marked by Democratic President Johnson's decision not to run for a second term. The crisis of the "imperial presidency" culminated six years later, in 1974, when Republican President Nixon was forced to resign in the face of possible impeachment by the Senate for his involvement in the burglary at the Democratic National Committee in the Watergate Hotel, i.e. the so-called Watergate Affair. This crisis will prompt a renewed congressional activism, with the approval of a panoply of bills (such as the War Powers Resolution, Campaign Finance Act, Budget and Impoundment Control Act, Ethics of Government Act, Freedom of Information Act, Foreign Commitments Resolution) that attempted to recover some of Congress' lost legislative powers, in addition to strengthening the powers of oversight and control. The attempt, however, was successful only in part because the primacy of the president continued to rest on apparent systemic reasons.

2.6 The Difficulties of Presidential Government

2.6.1 Direct primaries: Origins and development

Several processes have strained presidential government since the 1970s, but two in particular stand out: the diffusion of direct primaries for the selection of the presidential candidates and the institutionalization of divided government. Starting from the first, the diffusion of direct primaries has brought about an opening of the parties toward the electorate, but also their weakening as organizations expressing a collective identity. With the direct primaries, the electoral process has become ever more centered on the candidates, especially the presidential ones.[38] Without the constraint of the parties, the presidency has become personalized, but also isolated from the other institutions of government. Bereft of partisan links with Congress, the president no longer can succeed in carrying out fully and coherently his governmental activity, i.e. to promote his own legislative agenda. Thus, presidents were forced to have recourse to the rhetorical mobilization of the public in order to put pressure on a Congress hostile or indifferent to them.[39] Put differently, the president has been forced to dramatize domestic and international crisis situations in order to construct cross-party majorities in Congress or to neutralize opposition.

Why did the adoption of direct primaries contribute simultaneously to the personalization and the political weakening of the presidency? The method of the direct primaries was established at the beginning of the twentieth century but made a definitive breakthrough only with the presidential elections of 1972. Direct primaries are a method for selecting the candidates that will subsequently compete for institutional offices. Selection does not imply election; the former precedes the latter. Actually, primaries derive their name from the fact that they are held prior to the elections that will assign government office (the president) or seats of representation (in Congress). They are more appropriately named direct primaries, because they envisage the direct involvement of the voters in the selection of the candidates for whom they subsequently may vote. Direct primaries are a peculiar feature of American politics.[40] No other democracy has ever adopted a similar method to select candidates for public office.

The direct primary is a typical example of how the reform cycle plays out in America. At first, the innovation is put to the test in one state, due to some circumstances that make this necessary or possible. Next, other states copy the innovation, adapting it to the specific circumstances of their political system, or re-interpreting it on the basis of their predominant political culture. In our case, the first states to adopt legislation requiring that parties employ direct primaries were South Carolina in 1896, followed by Wisconsin in 1903. As V. O. Key Jr masterfully explained at the end of the 1940s, initially the direct primaries were adopted by the southern states for systemic reasons.[41] Since these states had become single-party constituencies after the Civil War (as is well known, the Republican Party could not legitimately compete in the elections in the states of the former Confederacy), some device needed to be found to make the selection of the candidates of the only legitimate party (the Democratic one) more competitive. Moreover, being the only party, the Democrats came to represent a host of frequently conflicting social and ideological interests. How to choose between them, or rather, how to choose between candidates from the same (Democratic) party who, at times, held antagonistic views?

The direct primaries provided a practical solution to this problem, as they allowed a one-party system to become more competitive and open. Yet, the characteristics of the primaries also proved useful for the pursuit of a different objective, namely to overcome the traditional party machines, which, at the turn of the nineteenth century, controlled municipal and state politics, frequently employing not very democratic methods.[42] Thus, from its inception, the reform movement that advocated the direct primaries has pursued a twin goal: opening up the parties and overcoming them. Soon, however, the second objective gained in importance. In any case, the direct primaries were so successful that, by 1916, almost half the states (20) used it for the selection of the candidates for the federal presidency. However, the economic crisis and the new threats of war would soon put a stop to the reform movement. The parties, even though diminished in importance, retook control of the selection of their own candidates, returning to their preferred instrument of the caucus. Being a party convention, the caucus is, in fact, more easily controlled by county and state leaders.

Accordingly, between 1916 and 1972, the number of states holding direct primaries declined inexorably (on average one third of all states), whereas the number of states resorting to party conventions grew. The party bosses nevertheless tolerated the primaries since they provided an opportunity to gauge the popularity of less well-known candidates. In fact, it was no doubt due to his success in the Democratic primaries that John F. Kennedy managed to overcome the resistance of the Democratic leaders to nominating an Irish Catholic as the party's candidate for the presidential elections of 1959.

It was not until the major conflicts of the 1960s that the direct primaries would be revitalized as a method for democratizing the parties. The nomination of a candidate (Hubert Humphrey) who supported the war in Vietnam at the 1968 Democratic Convention in Chicago unleashed such a storm of criticism of the method of the party caucus that, starting in 1972, the direct primaries were adopted as the principal way of selecting Democratic candidates. The Republican Party would eventually follow the Democrats down the same path, if only because the legislatures in states with a Democratic majority left them no choice. The direct primary thus became the main method for selecting candidates for public office (see figure 2.1). In 2000, the two major parties had recourse to a party caucus in only five states, whereas in 2004, they were used by the Democrats only in nine states (with an incumbent president running for a second mandate, the Republicans did not need to select a new presidential candidate) in 2004. In any case, also in the reform process launched in the 1970s, the direct primary continued to serve a double purpose, namely to open the political parties and to overcome them (see figure 2.1).

2.6.2   Types of direct primaries and their consequences

The direct primaries are a genus with several species, in the sense that the term "direct primaries" refers to a number of methods of selection, albeit each of these methods involves the direct participation of the voters in the selection of the candidates. The differences between the various species are not insignificant. Rather, the different ways of organizing primaries impinge on the outcome of the selection. The distinguishing criterion is registration for a party, not to be confused with the membership in a party. Registering for a party does not (necessarily) have financial or ideological implications. It is a public, non-private, act in the sense that it is governed by state law and not by party statutes. In short, in America one registers for a party, whereas in Europe one joins a party.

The political parties (and in particular the two major ones) have employed (mainly) five different types of direct primaries. The first

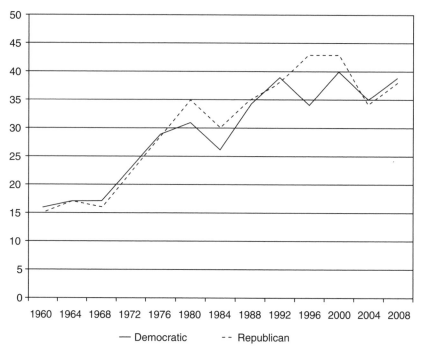

Figure 2.1 Number of states' presidential primaries by party, 1960–2008
Source: My elaboration and updating of S. Wayne, "Presidential Nomina-
tions and American Democracy" (2004), at http://usinfo.state.gov/
products/pubs/election04/nominate.htm

(and most widespread) type is the *closed primary*. In a closed primary
only those voters may participate who have registered in advance
for a party. The registration is public in the sense that it is deposited
with a public office, which also counts the ballots. The voters are
given a ballot sheet that lists only the candidates of the party in
question running for a given political office. Also within this type
of primary there are some significant differences concerning the
effective deadlines for registering or changing party affiliation,
which may range from having to register anywhere from one year
to three months, or even 15 days prior to the date established for
the direct primary.

The second type is the *semi-closed primary*. As in the previous
primary, those voters who have registered for a party may cast
ballots. Yet, in contrast to the closed primary, independent voters
may participate, but they can vote in the primary of one party only.

Generally, independent voters are registered for a party on the day in which they present themselves at the polling station for the direct primary of that party. Also in this case there are some significant differences. In some primaries, independent voters may take part in the direct primary of a party if this is the only party holding primaries; in others the independent voter may ask to be removed from the register of the party immediately after having voted in its direct primary; in others still the independent voter is automatically removed from the registry of the party once having voted in its direct primary.

The third type is the *open primary with public declaration of party affiliation*. In this direct primary those voters may participate who declare their choice of party on the day of the selection and at the place where it is held. Here no registration is required in order to take part in the direct primary. The primaries of the competing parties are held simultaneously at the same polling station, and in order to declare their affiliation voters take the ballot sheet of the party of their choice, mark the preferred candidate, and return it to the representatives of that party. Here there are some minor differences. In some states, the decision to vote in the primary of a party is considered the equivalent of an informal registration for that party and therefore valid also for the next year (in the sense that the voter may automatically participate in other direct primaries of the same party during that period of time). Conversely, in other states, this decision will have no consequences. Thus, a voter may vote in the direct primaries of another party, obviously to select candidates for a different public office.

The fourth type is the *open primary with private declaration of party affiliation*. All the voters who present themselves at the polling station where the primaries of the various parties are held may take part. Here, the voters receive the ballot sheets of all the parties, with the names of the candidates competing in the primaries of each of them. The voters may choose in the secrecy of the voting booth in which primary to participate, marking their preferred candidate on the appropriate sheet, and returning it together with the sheets of the other parties. In short, no declaration is required. Also within this type of primary the differences are many. For example, in some states, the Democrats, contrary to the Republicans, do not consider the outcome of this type of primary binding.

Lastly, the fifth type is the so-called *blanket primary*. Here the voters receive a single sheet with the names of all the candidates of all the parties that wish to run for the office in question. The two candidates receiving the highest number of votes, irrespective of their party affiliation, will contest the subsequent elections for the office at stake. As there are generally a number of offices to be filled, the voters will receive a ballot paper with the candidates of the respective parties for each of them. The voters choose the preferred candidate without any party constraint, which is to say that they may choose candidates from different parties for the different offices to be filled. This type of direct primary continues to be the subject of a heated public debate. So much so that in 2000 the California Democratic Party appealed to the Supreme Court, which subsequently ruled this type of primary unconstitutional (*California Democratic Party v. Jones*). The Californian Democratic Party argued, in fact, that this type of direct primary (required by California law) negated its right to preserve its organization, a right guaranteed by the first amendment of the constitution (on the freedom of assembly).

Although it is necessary to distinguish between selection by means of primaries (hardly controlled by the parties) and selection by the caucus (more easily controllable by the parties), it does well to also keep in mind that the various types of primaries display significant differences. Starting in the 1970s through the 1990s, the tensions between opening and overcoming the parties were resolved with the latter's transformation into tremendously efficient service structures for the victorious candidates. In short, the parties adapted to an electoral process that became ever more candidate-centered, in the sense that the candidates shaped the outlook of the parties and not vice versa. The parties provided no more than guidelines, i.e. generic expressions of the orientation of public policy. The program of the presidential party, or of the various local and state parties, instead, was defined by the winning candidates in the direct primaries. Indeed, at the beginning of the 1990s, some scholars even argued that with the direct primaries the parties were opened to such an extent as to have turned into some kind of "empty vessels" at the disposal of the victorious "commander."[43] However, with the Republican conquest of the majority of seats in Congress in the mid-term elections of 1994, a tremendous party-building process has started. Since then, the Republican Party especially has become more structured in organizational terms and more coherent in ideological terms. It has to be seen whether this process will continue after the disappearance of the George W. Bush leadership.[44]

Candidate selection by means of direct primaries has had two important implications. First of all, it has favored the growing influence of organized groups promoting specific issues (ideological and/or economic). In an ever more individualized polity, those are the actors (rather than the political parties as such) that can provide the candidates with (economic) resources and (political) objectives. In 1976, only 7 percent of the delegates to the Democratic National Convention, and 16 percent of the Republican Convention delegates were not affiliated with a group.[45] In 2000, one third of the delegates to the Democratic National Convention were trade union members whereas one fifth of the delegates to the Republican Convention were members of the National Rifle Association (the association defending the right to bear and use firearms privately, or rather the interests of those who manufacture firearms). Although those delegates were elected on an individual basis and not as representatives of their respective associations, nevertheless the latter have invested resources and activists in the direct primaries of the individual states, in order to promote candidates well disposed toward their preferences and interests.

Second, the direct primaries have also strengthened the political role of the media (and television in particular). By emphasizing the personal rivalries within the parties, the direct primaries have allowed the televised media to personalize the electoral campaign, exerting a strong influence over its outcome. The role of private television stations in particular has become so relevant in determining the winners of the direct primaries, that Polsby has identified their owners, the media bosses, as the present day functional equivalent of the traditional party leaders, the party bosses.[46] Whereas in the past the latter selected the candidates in smoke-filled rooms, after the 1970s the former did so on neat and tidy television screens. Candidate centered politics, therefore, has made it more difficult to link the branches of government. The president was no longer conditioned by the congressional leaders of his party, as once was the case, but at the same time he could no longer count on the support of his party in Congress (as Clinton had to recognize when the Democratic Congress of 1993–4 sabotaged his proposal to introduce a universal health system). Yet, neither the organized interest nor the media bosses were able to connect the institutions of separated government with each other.

2.6.3 *The personal presidency and the divided government*

In addition to the primaries, the institutionalization of divided government (i.e. the formation of opposing party majorities in Congress and the presidency) at the federal level has helped to call into question the presidential government inaugurated by FDR. Divided government has its roots in the elections of 1956, even though its official date of birth is the elections of 1968. It becomes institutionalized with the Republican presidencies of Ronald Reagan (1981–8) and George H. W. Bush (1989–92); is confirmed under the successive presidencies of the Democratic Bill Clinton (1993–2000, apart from the brief parenthesis of unified party government of 1993–4), and it extends into the first two years (2001–2) and the last two years (2007–8) of the presidencies of George W. Bush.

Such an experience is unprecedented in the history of the country. It is sufficient to recall that between 1832 (the year in which the modern party system came of age) and 1956, only three presidents have had to face a House or Senate controlled by the rival party at their inauguration: the Whig President Zachary Taylor in 1848, when both the House and the Senate were controlled by Democrats; the Republican President Rutherford B. Hayes in 1876, when the House had a Democratic majority; and the Democratic President Grover Cleveland, in 1884, who had to govern with a Republican majority in the Senate. Thus, the year 1956 represents a veritable turning point, with respect to the practice that had developed since 1884. This new constellation consolidated with the elections of 1968. Whereas the same party had been in control of the two institutions of government for 75 percent of the time between 1796 and 1945, and at least 50 percent of the time between 1945 and 1968, this was so only 25 percent of the time between 1969 and 2008 (in a 40-year period unified party government existed only for 10 years, i.e. in 1977–80, 1993–4, and 2003–6). In sum, from 1969 to 2008, for 75 percent of the time the federal institutions of government have been controlled by different parties (see table 2.2).

Party-divided government has given rise to an extraordinary level of conflict between the two branches of government, with the overall outcome of confusion in the decision-making process,[47] and, above all, the progressive transformation of the institutional resources (of both Congress and the presidency) into instruments of political warfare.[48] Whereas the majority of Congress has used hearings and investigations to question the legitimacy of presidential decisions, presidents in their turn did not hesitate to use the agencies they controlled to spread information casting doubt on the moral integrity of their adversaries in Congress. The institutional conflict continued even under the conditions of the highly unified government in the years 2003–6. For example, notwithstanding its Republican majority, Congress launched an investigation into the

Table 2.2 Political majorities in Congress, 1969–2008

Year	Party and president	Congress	SENATE			HOUSE		
			Majority party	Minority party	Others	Majority party	Minority party	Others
1969–70	R (Nixon)	91	D-58	R-42	–	D-243	R-192	–
1971–72	R (Nixon)	92	D-54	R-44	2	D-255	R-180	–
1973–74	R (Nixon)	93	D-56	R-42	2	D-242	R-192	1
1975–76	R (Ford)	94	D-61	R-37	2	D-291	R-144	–
1977–78	D (Carter)	95	D-61	R-38	1	D-292	R-143	–
1979–80	D (Carter)	96	D-58	R-41	1	D-277	R-158	–
1981–82	R (Reagan)	97	R-53	D-46	1	D-242	R-192	1
1983–84	R (Reagan)	98	R-54	D-46	–	D-269	R-166	–
1985–86	R (Reagan)	99	R-53	D-47	–	D-253	R-182	–
1987–88	R (Reagan)	100	D-55	R-45	–	D-258	R-177	–
1989–90	R (Bush)	101	D-55	R-45	–	D-260	R-175	–
1991–92	R (Bush)	102	D-56	R-44	–	D-267	R-167	1
1993–94	D (Clinton)	103	D-57	R-43	–	D-258	R-176	1
1995–96	D (Clinton)	104	R-52	D-48	–	R-230	D-204	1
1997–98	D (Clinton)	105	R-55	D-45	–	R-226	D-207	2
1999–2000	D (Clinton)	106	R-55	D-45	–	R-223	D-211	1
2001–02	R (Bush)	107	D-50	R-50	–	R-221	D-212	2
2003–05	R (Bush)	108	R-51	D-48	–	R-229	D-205	1
2006–08	R (Bush)	109	D-51	R-49	–	D-233	R-202	–

D = Democrats; R = Republicans

Source: Adapted from School of Politics, Keele University, *US Government and Politics: The Legislative Branch*, at www.keele.ac.uk/depts/por/usbase.legis.htm; US Congress, Joint Committee on Printing, *Congressional Directory*, annual

possible responsibility of the presidency for the country's inadequate preparation for the terrorist attacks of September 11, 2001, an investigation which has caused more than a few difficulties for the president.

Within Congress, divided government has also led to an intensification of the conflict between the two party caucuses, with the effect of making separated government even more separated. The percentage of roll call votes (in the House and the Senate) in which the majority of one party has voted against the majority of the other party has systematically grown since the 1970s, from less than 30 percent in 1972 to a little less than 80 percent in the 1990s. The shock of 9/11 promoted a more bipartisan attitude and votes in Congress (indeed the number of partisan votes declined in 2002 to 43 and 45 percent in House and the Senate respectively).[49] However, the failure of the invasion of Iraq and the return to a divided government with the mid-term elections of 2006 have increased the opposition between the two parties in Congress. It should not come as a surprise, therefore, that the polarization of the vote has also put an end to the anomaly of the conservative coalition that united the Democratic representatives of the south with the conservative representatives of the Republican Party.

This institutional conflict has pushed the parties to coordinate on the level of Congress, in order to sustain the conflict with the rival institution (the presidency). In addition to strengthening the congressional organization of the two parties, this partisan conflict has also led to a re-evaluation of the role of the Speaker of the House, to the point that the latter has come to embody an alternative leader to the president. The most striking example, in this respect, is the one of the Republican representative Newt Gingrich, voted Speaker of the House on the wave of the extraordinary neoconservative success in the mid-term elections of 1994. In those elections, the Republican Party ran on a proper platform ("The Contract with America"), subsequently adopted by a large majority of its elected candidates and put into practice to a large extent from 1995–6. Indeed, from the start Newt Gingrich acted as a prime minister rather than as Speaker of the House.[50] This led him to pursue such an aggressive strategy toward the president to make him unpopular even amongst his own supporters, with the result that he was forced to resign from Congress in 1999 (although for moral misbehaviour).

As is well known, the conflict between the presidency and Congress during the 1990s culminated with the failed attempt of the Republican majority of the latter to impeach Democratic President

Clinton. In fact, in 1998 the House passed articles of impeachment. However, President Clinton was acquitted in the Senate the following year with 45 votes in favor and 55 against on the charge of perjury, and 50 against 50 on the charge of obstruction of justice, whereas a two-thirds majority of the Senate would have been required to return a guilty verdict in both cases. This episode testifies to the momentous deterioration of the institutional relations between the presidency and Congress. In view of the limited or non-existent constitutional relevance of Clinton's behavior, several scholars have even talked of a *coup d'état* by the neoconservative majority of Congress.[51] In a more than 200-year history there has never been a presidency so persistently besieged by its political adversaries as the two Clinton presidencies.[52] Clinton has been subjected to a permanent judicial inquiry (at considerable expense to the taxpayer) by two special prosecutors (Robert Fishke and Kenneth Starr), as well as a substantial number of congressional commissions. Moreover, the Supreme Court decision that an incumbent president is liable to civil prosecution has handed enormous opportunities to the president's adversaries.[53]

The open institutional conflict between the presidency and Congress, no longer mediated by parties, has pushed the president to seek a personal legitimacy independent of the legitimacy of his office. Since the clash between the executive and the legislature has led to a cyclical paralysis of decision-making, the president ever more frequently had to appeal directly to the public in order to try and promote his own legislative agenda. Rather than a plebiscitary president the country witnessed a rhetorical presidency. Accordingly, presidential government has shifted into the direction of a personal presidency, as effective on the symbolic level as it was ineffective on the operational level.[54] In fact, it is hard to try and solve personally the institutional problems of a divided government split along party lines.

Congress failed to re-establish its pre-eminence in the field of policy-making for comprehensible systemic reasons, i.e. it is impossible to govern a large democracy with the legislature. Yet, its challenge to presidential pre-eminence in domestic policies, ever more frequent in foreign policy, in combination with a quasi-permanently divided government and the inability of the parties to aggregate interests, has led to an increase of the inter-institutional level of conflict between the two branches. This is why it is incorrect to argue that the American government has a pronounced decision-making capacity.

In any case, the quasi-permanent institutional conflict between the president and the two chambers of Congress has promoted a growing politicization of the judiciary. Since the 1970s American politics has turned into a vast and permanent legal proceeding, in the sense that the judiciary has come to play an ever more relevant political role. This role culminated in the ruling that decided the presidential elections of 2000. Such an episode, in fact, was akin to a laboratory experiment for understanding the nature of the American democracy, if only because it has shown that the procedure to elect the president is anything but plebiscitary. The Supreme Court's decision not to allow a recount of the ballots in some Florida electoral districts testifies that the American democracy is a compound one. It is a democracy which, not placing too much trust in the voters, has entrusted non-elected institutions, and in particular the judiciary, with crucial decision-making prerogatives. Although this was the first time the Supreme Court intervened in a presidential election, it nevertheless has played a governmental role for nearly two centuries, ever since the Chief Justice of the Supreme Court John Marshall managed to establish (with the famous *Marbury v. Madison* decision of 1803) judicial review of the bills approved by Congress and signed by the president, in order to ascertain their constitutionality.

This could come about because the American democracy is not based on the primacy of a particular governmental institution but on the primacy of the Constitution. No governmental institution can claim primacy because none of them is the exclusive representative of the will of the voters. In America, the will of the voters is separated, as is the system of government. No institutional power, or rather no representative of any of the institutional powers, can claim to possess a superior legitimacy or to be above the Constitution. Of course, when powers are separated, both horizontally (at the center) and vertically (between the center and the periphery), permanent occasions for conflicts between them are created. This situation has favored the growing influence of the judiciary, which is called upon to regulate this conflict. If the Constitution is the casing of politics, it is not surprising that it falls to the guardians of the Constitution (the nine justices of the Supreme Court) to have to solve a possible paralysis. Hence, while having invented electoral democracy, America continues to be the country that most retains the democracy of the guardians. However, both types of democracy (the electoral and the guardian democracy) are not always easy to separate.[55]

2.7　Conclusion

The American government is a separated one, as several distinct institutions must participate in the decision-making process. In its more than 200-year history, separated government has witnessed diverse institutional equilibria, i.e. the pre-eminence of different institutions. The long phase of the pre-eminence of Congress was followed by a phase in which the presidency enjoyed pre-eminence amongst the institutions of government. In response to relevant reforms of the procedures for selecting presidential candidates, and to the diminishing role of the parties, the presidency was progressively transformed into a government of the personal president; as imposing on the rhetorical level, as it was weak on the institutional level. In short, the presidency has become ever more personalized but this did not imply a turn to a plebiscitary democracy: not only because the president continues to be elected indirectly and to operate in the context of a separated government that he cannot control unilaterally, but also because the personalized presidency, made possible by the weakening of the parties, has no guarantee of being supported in Congress (in particular when Congress is controlled by a political majority different from his own). The president may benefit from objective and dramatic threats to the country, like the terrorist attacks of September 11, 2001, to establish himself as "commander in chief of the country," but the normal functioning of the separation of powers is bound to constrain his room for maneuver in any case.

The separation of powers does constitute a powerful insurance against the abuse of power by the president and against the possibility of a majority faction taking control of the entire system of government, thus threatening the rights of the various minorities. Yet, the separation of powers has also generated a fair number of vices. First of all, it has made it difficult to identify where responsibility lies for the decisions taken. When decisions are the outcome of the actions of various institutions and the multitude of actors that operate within them, how can one establish who is responsible for these decisions? The separation of powers hampers the abuse of power, but it also makes it more difficult to hold responsible those who exercise those powers. Second, whereas it is true that a possible tyranny of the majority has been avoided by providing the various minorities with veto powers that enable them to obstruct decisions, it is also true that such a distribution of veto powers has ended up producing (in the most controversial policies) the opposite outcome, namely the tyranny of the minorities. Thus it was possible, for example, for a minority of congressmen from the southern states to obstruct for a long time legislation promoting the granting of full civil rights to African-American citizens, through their control of the chairmanship of crucial congressional committees. Third, the separation of powers promotes competition between institutions but obscures competition between the parties. If there is no government, there is no opposition either.

It is striking to note that all these three vices also manifest themselves in the functioning of the EU. In Brussels it is difficult to establish who is responsible for what; there too one can witness a certain tyranny of the minorities and there too the institutional dynamics do not allow for competition between government and opposition. The American rose may have its thorns, but the European rose is not without them either.

3

A Democracy without the People?

3.1 Introduction

Since the 1930s only half (or a little more) of the American electorate has turned out at the voting booth to elect the presidential electors (see table 3.1). Even if that percentage did rise to 60 percent during the crucial 1960s, the low voter turnout, nevertheless, meant that the support of one quarter or one third of the electorate has been sufficient to gain the majority of votes in the Electoral College. At the same time, the congressional elections have seen an even lower voter turnout in particular for the mid-term elections, at little more than one third of the voters, implying that the elected candidates represent an even lower percentage of voters. It is obvious that such a low voter turnout cannot be played down by pointing out that turnout is higher when calculated as a percentage of those who have registered as voters, as some American scholars have done. In fact, even when one uses this definition (see table 3.2) voter turnout remains rather low. It is no surprise, therefore, that the low electoral participation has attracted the attention and criticism of many observers. Claus Leggewie, commenting on the American elections of 2000 in *Die Zeit*, raised the question: "Why should Europeans show interest for an electoral campaign to which the majority of US citizens prefers a football match or a soap opera? Why should we have to appreciate an election where half of the entitled voters don't show up?"[1] Indeed, not only for Europeans but also for many Americans,[2] the low electoral turnout constitutes the Achilles heel of American democracy, the proof of its transformation in a truly oligarchic if not dynastic regime.[3]

Table 3.1 Voter turnout in presidential and congressional elections, 1932–2006

Year	Resident populations (including foreigners) with the right to vote (millions)	Presidential elections (%)	Congressional elections (%)
1932	75.768	52.5	49.7
1934	77.997	–	41.4
1936	80.174	56.9	53.5
1938	82.354	–	44.0
1940	84.728	58.9	55.4
1942	86.465	–	32.5
1944	85.654	56.0	52.7
1946	92.659	–	37.1
1948	95.573	51.1	48.1
1950	98.134	–	41.1
1952	99.929	61.6	57.6
1954	102.075	–	41.7
1956	104.515	59.3	55.9
1958	106.447	–	43.0
1960	109.672	62.8	58.5
1962	112.952	–	45.4
1964	114.090	61.9	57.8
1966	116.638	–	45.4
1968	120.285	60.9	55.1
1970	124.498	–	43.5
1972	140.777	55.2	50.7
1974	146.338	–	35.9
1976	152.308	53.5	48.9
1978	158.369	–	34.9
1980	163.945	52.8	47.6
1982	169.643	–	38.0
1984	173.995	53.3	47.8
1986	177.922	–	33.5
1988	181.956	50.3	44.9
1990	185.812	–	33.1
1992	189.493	55.1	50.8
1994	193.010	–	36.7
1996	196.789	48.9	45.7
1998	201.270	–	32.7
2000	205.813	51.2	47.2
2002	215.077	–	34.7
2004	220.377	55.5	51.4
2006	207.337*	–	40.2

*M. McDonald, The United States Elections Project, George Mason University, Department of Public and International Affairs, last updated 7/03/07, at http://elections.gmu.edu/Voter_Turnout_2006.htm. Note that these data provide preliminary estimates of the voting-eligible population for the November 2006 election.

Source: US Census Bureau, *Statistical Abstract of the United States* (2007)

Table 3.2 Voting age population, percentage reporting registered and voted, 1980–2004

Year	Voting age population (millions)	Reporting registered		Reporting voted (%)	
		Presidential elections	Congressional elections	Presidential elections	Congressional elections
1980	157.1	66.9		59.2	
1982	165.5		64.1		48.5
1984	170.0	68.3		59.9	
1986	173.9		64.3		46.0
1988	178.1	66.6		57.4	
1990	182.1		62.2		45.0
1992	185.7	68.2		61.3	
1994	190.3		62.0		44.6
1996	193.7	65.9		54.2	
1998	198.2		62.1		41.9
2000	202.6	63.9		54.7	
2002	210.4		60.9		42.3
2004	215.7	65.9		58.3	

Source: US Census Bureau, *Statistical Abstract of the United States* (1996), p. 286; (2003), p. 269; (2007), p. 256

However one may wish to interpret these figures, there can be no doubt that the limited electoral participation deserves particular attention, if only because America was the first country to have introduced universal male suffrage and thus to have developed as a truly electoral democracy. It is true that women were excluded for a long time from the democratic vote, at least until the 1920s, and longer still African-American citizens, at least until the 1960s. Nevertheless, it is also true that America has been far ahead of the European countries in terms of electoral participation of the entire adult population in the process of staffing and shaping the institutions of representation and government.[4] Thus, America has acquired the traits of a post-electoral democracy, while remaining an unprecedented experiment in electoral democracy. American democracy has acquired post-electoral traits because the power relations between the parties and the coalitions of interests are established, in many cases, in relation to the capacity to use extra-electoral instruments, such as the resources at the disposal of the institution of government controlled by one or the other party and the alliances each governmental institution is able to activate with judicial bodies or the media.

However, America remains an electoral democracy because "elections are held more frequently than in any other modern society" and the number of electoral positions (local posts, state officeholders, administrative officials, and judges) is without equivalent in other democracies, as Lipset has reminded us.[5] At the end of the 1990s, according to the US Census Bureau, there were more than 550,000 elected public officials, which means one elected official for each 360/370 voters. The majority of them, 491,669, held local offices, 18,828 held state offices, half of whom were judges or administrative officers. This implies that, taking into consideration the primaries and all public offices, more than a million elections take place during each four-year electoral cycle, as many of these public offices have an annual or biannual mandate. The state and local governments submit for electoral approval bills, budget proposals, and constitutional amendments like no other democracy. In many states, the citizens may propose new bills by means of the citizen's initiative. What Ranney wrote disconcertedly after the presidential and congressional elections of November 8, 1988 still holds true today, namely that on that day, he was asked to "take no less than 61 decisions in total" in the polling booth.[6]

This being so, is it justifiable to claim that America is a democracy without the people? I will try to answer this question by proceeding in the following way. First, I will analyze the institutional characteristics of the American electoral system, with respect to the institutions of federal government. Next, I will discuss the developments of the electoral process within this framework of institutional rules. Then, I will reconstruct the scientific debate that has sprung up during the last 20 years around the problem of low voter turnout. Finally, I will try to sketch the main implications of the post-electoral transformations of American democracy.

3.2   The Characteristics of the Electoral System

The American electoral system is of the majoritarian type, both at the state and federal level. Here I will only analyze the electoral rules for the federal institutions. The Constitution provides for three different electoral systems: one for each of the main branches of government (the House of Representatives, the Senate, and the president). These three electoral systems reflect the raison d'être that led to the formation of the compound republic in 1787, namely to give birth to a system of separated government in which the members of each of the different branches would have to be elected according to different modalities, both in order to emphasize the different role assigned to each institution in the system of government and to foster different communities of interest within them.[7] The successive evolution of the American political system has brought about a progressive homogenization in a majoritarian direction of the electoral system's guiding principles. This evolution, however, has neither made inroads on the separated character of the system of government nor, above all, on its compound nature.

The result, therefore, is an anti-majoritarian democracy (i.e. obstructing the formation of a uniform majority across the various institutions of government)[8] with a plurality of majoritarian electoral systems to elect the member of those institutions.[9] Although this is rather paradoxical, nevertheless, it did not impede the functioning of the American democracy for more than two centuries. The reason lies in the role the parties have come to play right from the very start of the new republic. As we have seen, both during the long era of congressional government as well as in the shorter era of presidential government, the parties had managed to ensure the linkage between the separated institutions, without which the latter would have functioned only with difficulty.[10] The evolution of the electoral system in a majoritarian direction has accompanied the two main parties in the exercise of their strategic role of connecting separated institutions, and has further strengthened the two-party structure of the country. But the task of connecting separated institutions has proven to be as difficult to accomplish as it was essential. In practice, the separated nature of the system of government has consistently made life difficult for the parties, subjecting their capacity for institutional and programmatic cohesion to constant pressures.

The traditional approach to American parties interprets them as a three-level system, namely the party in the electorate, the party as organization, and the party in government. Adopting this approach, one can argue that the strong decline of the parties in the electorate (measured by the decrease of the number of voters identifying with either one of them) and of the parties as organization (measured by the weakening of their structures outside of the institutions), which we have witnessed during the 1970s through the 1990s, has served to emphasize the separated nature of the system of government, and has unearthed problems novel to the country.

But let's examine this in detail, starting from the electoral procedures of the three branches of government.

3.2.1   Congress: The House of Representatives and the Senate

The House of Representatives, according to article I, sections 2.1 and 2.2 of the Constitution, "shall be composed of members chosen every second year by the people of the several States." Such members must have attained the age of 25 years, they must have been a citizen of the country for at least seven years at the time of the election, and they must reside in the state in which they are elected. Section 2.3 specifies that "Representatives shall be apportioned among the several States according to their respective numbers, counting the whole number of persons in each State," on the basis of a census to be held every 10 years (the first was in 1790). In 1929 a law was passed establishing that the total number of the members of the House should remain fixed at 435. Since then each census implies a complex reapportionment of seats in relation to demographic changes. The fathers of the Constitution had defined the House as the popular branch of the federal government, and because of its popular character it was entrusted with exclusive competences concerning the federal budget. As article I section 7.1 of the Constitution states: "All bills for raising revenue shall originate in the House of Representatives," although the Senate may propose amendments.

The Constitution does not require the adoption of a specific electoral formula. In fact, the states have experimented widely with the modality for translating votes into seats.[11] They adopted a proportional representation system (list voting) at both state and district levels; and thus majoritarian uninominal systems with simple or absolute majority. With a federal Bill of 1842, however, some order was imposed on this experimentation, by requiring the adoption of single-member constituency ballots with simple majority, known as first-past-the-post system. In addition, the biannual elections were synchronized to take place in even years, and not in odd years, as some states had done up to then. Of course, the standardization of the electoral formula on the federal level did not imply an immediate and corresponding standardization of the electoral formulas adopted by the individual states for the election of their respective legislatures. The municipalities, in particular, have continued to experiment with various electoral systems: for example, between 1938 and 1947, the city of New York employed a proportional representation system (connoted by list voting) for the elections of the city council. The system was abandoned, after the outbreak of the Cold War, because it would have led to a significant number of Communist seats in the council (about 9 percent in 1945).[12]

Once the electoral formula and the number of representatives had been defined, the component of the electoral system that has become the subject of a furious partisan conflict is the drawing of the boundaries of the electoral districts.[13] In this respect, article I section 2.3 of the Constitution stipulated only one constraint: "each State shall have at least one representative." It is the task of Congress to establish how many representatives accrue for each state, on the basis of decennial census. But, here the power of the federal Congress ends. In fact, it is the task of the state legislatures to design the electoral districts in which the federal representatives apportioned to each state will be elected, just as the states are also responsible for designing the electoral districts for the election of the members of their legislatures. Accordingly, the decisive role in the redefinition of the districts is played by the state legislatures, rather than the federal legislature. It is worth recalling that these legislatures have not infrequently abused their powers in this field by designing districts that served the purposes of the dominant party in the state.[14] Eventually the Supreme Court – followed by the state courts – was forced to intervene with its famous decision of 1962 in *Baker v. Carr* that regulated the drawing of the electoral districts by the state legislatures on the basis of the constitutional principle of "one man/one woman, one vote."

As established by article I section 3.1 of the Constitution, the federal Senate "shall be composed of two senators from each State, chosen by the legislature thereof for six years; and each Senator shall have one vote." In order to be eligible for the position of federal senator, candidates must have attained the age of 30 years, must have been citizens of the country for at least nine years, and must reside, at the time of the election, in the state in which they run for office. To further emphasize the separation of powers within the legislature, the Constitution established not only that each chamber be elected by different constituencies (district colleges in the case of the House and state colleges for the Senate), but that the dates for the election of the senators would be differentiated. According to article I section 3.2 of the Constitution, the senators:

> shall be divided as equally as may be into three classes. The seats of the Senators of the first class shall be vacated at the expiration of the

second year, of the second class at the expiration of the fourth year, and of the third class at the expiration of the sixth year, so that one third may be chosen every second year.

Such an elitist method for electing the senators, and above all the staggering of their election in three phases, served the purposes of turning the Senate into a sort of cabinet of the president, in its quality of representation of the states. Its indirect election made it independent of the popular mood, whereas its staggered elections were intended to guarantee a certain continuity and stability of its institutional role. Accordingly, the Senate was invested with a special power: namely to provide *advice* and *consent* to the president in crucial areas of public policy. Thus the Senate was envisaged to play a crucial role in the Madisonian system of checks and balances, in particular in those areas that were of direct interest to the states, such as judicial policy (awarding the Senate a veto in the nomination of the members of the Supreme Court) and foreign and defense policy (giving it a veto in the ratification of international treaties). As if this were not enough, the Senate exerted influence on the composition of the presidency itself, since its advice and consent were required for the nomination of the secretaries of State and of the closest collaborators of the president. In this way, the Senate's powers were intended to counterbalance the exclusive competence of the House of Representatives over budgetary policies.

The democratization of the rules for electing the federal senators has altered neither the role nor the powers of the Senate. Moreover, the pressures for the democratization of the election of the senators did not originate with the beginning of the twentieth century. Already in the 1830s, a Jacksonian wind had blown over the practice of electing the federal senators by the state legislatures. In fact, in many states the candidates for the bicameral state legislatures (only Nebraska has become unicameral since 1934) were urged by the voters to make known which candidate for the federal Senate they would support in case they should be elected. Thus, early on the popular elections at state level came to exert an influence over the indirect elections for the federal Senate, even if they formally remained within the competence of the state legislatures. However, the full democratization of the elections of the federal senators had to await the wind of the progressive era. In 1913 amendment XVII of the Constitution, which entrusted the election of the senators directly to the voters instead of the state legislatures, was approved.

The aristocratic principle was definitively replaced with the democratic one.

In any case, the election of the two senators for each state still takes place on the basis of a state-wide Electoral College, with the seats being assigned to the two candidates that have received the most votes. Whereas the nature of the electoral system of the Senate has undergone profound changes, the nature of the elections for the House, in contrast, has witnessed a substantial continuity, the reform having altered only its formula. In short, in the first case, we are faced with a constitutional reform, whereas, in the second case, we are dealing with an institutional reform. Of course, there have been constitutional changes that have also had an impact on the electoral system of the House. Three in particular deserve a mention: amendments XIV and XV of 1868 and 1870 respectively, recognized African Americans as citizens having the right to vote; amendment XXIV of 1964 removed some of the administrative and legal obstacles (in particular the "failure to pay any poll tax or other tax") that de facto had prevented African Americans and other minorities from exercising the right to vote they had been granted a century earlier; and amendment XXVI of 1971 established that "the right of citizens of the United States, who are eighteen years of age or older, to vote shall not be denied or abridged by the United States or by any State on account of age." Thus, as one can see, all three amendments did not diminish but rather underlined the democratic nature of the electoral system.

3.2.2   The president: The transformation of the Electoral College

At Philadelphia it was decided that the president has to be elected by means of ad hoc Electoral Colleges in each of the states composed of electors selected by the state legislatures. The Constitution, after having specified, in article II section 1.1, that the president of the United States "shall hold his office during the term of four years," and after having established in section 1.5 of the same article that, in order to be eligible for the office of president the candidate must be "a natural born citizen, or a citizen of the United States" and have "attained to the age of thirty-five years" in addition to being "fourteen years a resident within the United States," stipulates, in section 1.2, that "each State shall appoint, in such manner as the legislature thereof may direct, a number of Electors, equal to the whole number of Senators and Representatives to which the State may be entitled in the Congress," specifying furthermore that such Electors should not hold an "office of trust or profit under the United States." Nowadays, the presidential electors number 538, i.e. equal to the number of senators (100) and representatives (435) plus the delegates from the District of Columbia (3), where the capital and the federal government reside. Only on this occasion is the capital granted the right to be represented. In fact, as such the District of Columbia still does not have any representatives in the Senate and has only one observer or non-voting delegate in the House of Representatives.

The Constitution does not envisage an institution called the Electoral College. In article II section 1.3 the Constitution only stipulates that "the Electors shall meet in their respective States, and vote by ballot for two persons, of whom one at least shall not lie an inhabitant of the same State with themselves." Hence, not only does the Constitution fail to establish a specific modality for the selection of the presidential electors, but it does not prescribe a specific modality either for counting the votes cast by them. The Constitution only states, in the same section 1.3, that "the person having the greatest number of votes shall be the president, if such number be a majority of the whole number of Electors appointed." As a result, the election of the presidential electors, though remaining indirect, has taken different forms. For example, in some states, the presidential electors were chosen by the plenary session of their legislative chambers; whereas other states did so by means of a concomitant vote of the two chambers of the state legislature; or in other states still through the vote of the state legislators from a list proposed by the voters. Concerning the tallying method of the votes cast by the presidential electors, different methods were adopted, from proportional to majoritarian methods, with the latter now having become predominant. Hence, the Constitution did not contain any provisions for some important features of the procedure for electing the president, even if it was determined to erect a series of barriers around the formation of executive power so as to facilitate a well-considered choice of the candidate to be president.

The institution known as the Electoral College, or college of presidential electors, constitutes one of those barriers. It has institutionalized the will of the drafters of the Constitution, namely that the presidential election should be an indirect one. How to organize such an indirect election was left to the states, which were granted the power to establish the modalities of the election of their respective presidential electors. But also the task of organizing the election itself was left to the states, with the outcome (as we have seen in

Florida in November 2000) that, even within the individual states, each county may employ different methods of recording the votes cast, to the extent that Congress saw fit to pass a bill in 2002 (Help America Vote Act) which requires each state to standardize its voting methods. Note, however, that voting methods do not need to be standardized between states. In sum, the founding fathers were concerned only to assert the principle that the president should be elected indirectly by ad hoc state presidential electors.

The barrier thrown up around the executive power did not hold as originally foreseen.[15] Already with the elections of 1800 the first (two) political parties emerged whose stated purpose was to organize the electoral competition for Congress. But above all with the presidential elections of 1828 party competition had fully matured. In fact, many state constitutions were changed so as to permit the voters, instead of the members of the state legislatures, to vote on the basis of competing slates for the presidential electors that were to make up the state Electoral College. At the root of these changes stands the controversial and impassioned presidential campaign of 1824, the first in which some states experimented with the popular election of the presidential electors. Since no candidate obtained the absolute majority of the electoral votes (that is the vote of the presidential electors), it fell to Congress to pick the president from amongst the top three candidates (it's been three since amendment XII of the Constitution of 1804, because the Constitution originally asserted in article II section 1.3, that "if no person have a majority, then from the five highest on the list the . . . House shall . . . chuse the President").

Congress preferred the insider John Quincy Adams (vice-president of outgoing President Monroe), to the outsider and famous war hero Andrew Jackson: even though the first had obtained only 30.5 percent of the popular vote (and 84 votes in the Electoral College) as compared to 43.1 percent of the popular vote (and 99 votes in the Electoral College) for Jackson. It was the reaction of the Jacksonians to this decision of Congress (or rather to the *King Caucus* of the Democrats-Republicans, as it was called) that triggered the process of democratization. Not only did many states remove the property qualifications (for white males) for the right to vote before the 1828 elections, but also the election of the presidential electors was removed from the state legislatures and was held between parties having expressed a commitment to vote for a certain presidential candidate: hence, the importance of slates of presidential elector nominees committed to vote for a given presidential candidate, competing with other slates of nominees pledging to vote for the rival candidate.

Thus, with the elections of 1828, a sort of twin method for electing the president emerged: the formal one of the vote in the Electoral College and the informal one of the popular vote. On the constitutional level, this did not create any inconsistency: because it did not alter the indirect nature of the presidential election. The ability of the political parties to structure the vote has made it possible to reconcile the two modalities: the presidential electors who gathered in their respective state capitals to vote for a presidential candidate generally voted on the basis of the commitments made to the voters who had elected them. However, the majoritarian character the electoral system has acquired, and according to which the candidate that polls the majority of the popular vote obtains all the votes of the state presidential electors, has produced several cases of political inconsistency between the popular vote and the vote of the Electoral College.[16] This inconsistency exploded in a spectacular fashion in the presidential elections of 2000, when Democratic candidate Albert Gore was defeated in the Electoral College (with 266 to 271 votes), although having polled more popular votes than his Republican rival George W. Bush (51,003,894 votes, as against 50,459,211).

It should be added that the founding fathers were not very enthusiastic about the ability of the Electoral College to act as a truly deliberative assembly. In fact, the Constitution envisaged a role for the House in choosing the president, a role further specified by amendment XII of the Constitution of 1804. This amendment, in fact, states that "in choosing the President, the votes [of the House of Representatives] shall be taken by states, the representation from each state having one vote; a quorum for this purpose shall consist of a member or members from two-thirds of the states, and a majority of all the states shall be necessary to a choice," thus confirming what article II section 1.3 of the Constitution had already provided for. This amendment reasserts the role of the Electoral College as a chamber where the popular moods that are inevitably aroused in elections for monocratic offices like the one of the president, are allowed to cool off. Thus, it falls to the Electoral College to temper the demagogy typical of a personal election. In fact, the same amendment requires that the presidential electors shall gather in the capital of their states and not all together in the federal capital.

Certainly, with the introduction of general suffrage for the elections of the presidential electors, the indirect character of the presidential election has been called into question. Moreover, the election of the presidential electors has set in motion a majoritarian logic that is hard to reconcile with the deliberative logic that should have characterized the state Electoral Colleges. With the progressive emergence of a two-party system during the twentieth century, most states have come to adopt the majoritarian criterion of winner takes all, according to which the slate of the candidate that has obtained most votes takes all the votes of the presidential electors apportioned to that state.[17] Thus, the presidential electors are selected on the basis of a party list (Republican, Democratic, or independent parties), composed of a number of electors' nominees equal to the number of Electoral College votes that accrue to that state. Naturally, the members of the Electoral College are not constrained to vote for the presidential candidate they had pledged to support during their campaign. However, this has rarely happened. Only a few noteworthy instances of presidential electors breaking their electoral promises have occurred, i.e. in 1960, 1968, and in 1972 a presidential elector refused to cast his vote for Nixon whom he had pledged to support.[18] However, although the rise of the parties in national politics has enfeebled (or rather neutralized) the cooling-off function of the Electoral College, this did not alter the indirect nature of the presidential elections. However, thanks to party competition the presidential elections have acquired a popular character.

3.3 The Development of the Electoral Process

3.3.1 *The electoral origins of divided government*

Electoral democracy and party competition have allowed for the social and ethnic tensions of the country to be integrated.[19] In addition, the political parties managed to progressively establish themselves as the only actors able to connect the various parts of the system of government, not only during the golden age of congressional government, but also in the era of presidential government, when voters increasingly identified with the president rather than a party. After all, as Milkis has written, with the leadership of Franklin D. Roosevelt the Democratic Party had sought to lessen the importance of the two-party system, establishing "a modern executive as the principal focus of representative government in the United States."[20] However, with the assertion of the governmental primacy of the president, the political parties have retained an important role in the political system because of their capacity to unite a separated government, i.e. to politically connect the president with his supporters in Congress. In the 1970s this institutional equilibrium dissolved. Since then, America, as Bruce Cain has noted, "has moved closer to the Madisonian/pluralist ideal of a large, extended Republic with numerous, flexible electoral interests and away from a system simplified by stable party factions."[21]

These transformations have had three main consequences for the electoral system. The first one has been the emergence of the divided vote. The vote is divided when a significant percentage of voters support the candidate of one party for a certain office and the candidate of another party for another office.[22] One may discuss how to quantify the adjective "significant": the divided vote, in fact, becomes a relevant concept for describing the history of electoral behavior only after 1945, in particular with respect to the presidential elections and the elections for the House of Representatives. Excluding the rather peculiar episode of the 1912 elections (when the Republicans, the dominant party for half a century, ran divided in the presidential elections), the divided vote was an altogether marginal phenomenon until the Second World War. Only in the elections of 1948, and since the elections of 1956, has it come to characterize the voting behavior of more than one quarter of the voters and by 1964 the share had increased to one third. In particular at the federal level, the divided vote may be said to lie at the roots of the institutionalization, since 1968, of a government divided along party lines.

The second consequence has been the increased importance of the personal vote, which in turn was the outcome of the increased importance of incumbency in the congressional elections. Since the elections of 1950 a striking electoral phenomenon has emerged, known in the literature as the *incumbency factor*, and referring to the competitive advantage enjoyed by a politician who holds a public office. Since 1950, the members of the House of Representatives running for another term have been confirmed in their office with very high percentages (generally around 90 percent, see table 3.3). This is less so for the senators because they run in a larger constituency, i.e. their state, and because the senatorial elections are more nationally oriented. Nevertheless, the percentage of senators re-elected remains rather high and only slightly lower than that of the representatives. Of course, some elections have brought about a turnover of the members of Congress, such as the elections of

Table 3.3　Members of Congress, incumbents re-elected, 1964–2002

	REPRESENTATIVES			SENATORS	
Year of presidential election	Retirements*	Total	Candidates re-elected (%)	Total	Candidates re-elected (%)
1964	33	397	86.6	33	84.8
1966	22	411	88.1	32	87.5
1968	23	409	96.8	28	71.4
1970	29	401	94.5	31	77.4
1972	40	390	93.6	27	74.1
1974	43	391	87.7	27	85.2
1976	47	384	95.8	25	64.0
1978	49	382	93.7	25	60.0
1980	34	398	90.7	29	55.2
1982	40	393	90.1	30	93.3
1984	22	411	95.4	29	89.7
1986	40	394	97.7	28	75.0
1988	23	409	98.3	27	85.2
1990	27	406	96.1	32	96.9
1992	65	368	88.3	28	82.1
1994	48	387	90.2	26	92.3
1996	50	384	94.0	21	90.5
1998	33	402	97.7	29	89.7
2000	32	403	97.8	29	79.3
2002	35	398	96.0	28	85.7

*Not including those deceased or that resigned before the elections.
Source: US Census Bureau, *Statistical Abstract of the United States* (2004)

1964 and 1966 (at the height of the Vietnam War), or the elections of 1992 and 1994 (at the height of the neoconservative revolution). But, as the figures show, the turnover was rather modest. In sum, a very large majority of the incumbents running for a consecutive term is confirmed in office by the voters, irrespective of their party affiliation. Simultaneously, the high rate of confirmed incumbents has promoted a growing hostility toward professional politicians.

The gradual assertion of the incumbency since 1945, and its relevance even in critical elections, seems to reflect a considerable tendency toward the individualization of congressional politics. The electoral decline of the parties has exacerbated this tendency, although it did not cause it. Probably this tendency is intrinsic to the system used for congressional elections. Majoritarian and single-member constituencies, in the context of a separated system in which the legislature is not held to support (with a vote of confidence) the executive, tend to emphasize the individual representative more than party or collective representation.[23] Hence, in America, the pressures toward individualization deriving from the electoral system, in the presence of parties that are weak both in electoral and organizational terms, have further underlined the separated nature of the system of government.

As we have seen, this tendency toward the individualization of the legislative process, not having encountered serious obstacles in Congress, has imparted an additional impetus for a further decentralization of the internal organization of the legislature, with the aim to augment the effectiveness of the individual representatives rather than the effectiveness of the institution as a whole. Only a decentralized legislative structure could allow the individual representatives to serve first of all their electoral district (and thereby their chances of being re-elected) and second the interests of their party. This tendency toward decentralization has been partially mitigated since the 1980s, with the transformation of divided government into a veritable institutional conflict. The congressional parties have since become the coordinators of the inter-governmental conflict (not to be confused, however with a strengthening of the party in the government, the one traditionally connecting the president with Congress). Still, the American Congress continues to be the most individualistic legislature of all the western democracies.

The third consequence has been the growing role played by particularistic groups in the electoral process, which is the outcome, not only of an increasingly fragmented political process, but also of its inadequate institutional regulation. In this respect, the reform of campaign financing has turned out to be crucial. The reform was launched in 1971, with the passing of the Federal Election Campaign Act, and subsequently consolidated by the successive amendments of 1974, 1976, and 1979.[24] Strongly influenced by the 1976 Supreme Court decision in *Buckley v. Valeo* that equated the right to financially support the campaign of a candidate with the right of free speech guaranteed in the first of the ten amendments known as Bill of Rights (i.e. the constitutional amendments I–X concerning individual rights, ratified by the states soon after the approval of the Constitution), such a system of campaign financing has benefited the individual candidates to the detriment of the respective political parties. So much so that Congress has had to recognize the need to assist the parties by introducing financing for their electoral mobilization activities (in particular those activities aiming to convince the voters to register).

This so-called soft money, however, was in the end used more by the individual candidates than by the parties, given the latter's organizational weakness. Thus, the candidates have found themselves in the position of being able to spend as much money as they wished (or were able to raise) on their electoral campaigns. Only when they accepted so-called federal matching funds did the candidates have to observe a spending cap. But the point is that the decision of the Supreme Court, ruling unconstitutional the limits imposed both on independent expenditures (i.e. expenses on a particular issue that marks the campaign of a given candidate, but made independently of that campaign) and on personal expenditures (i.e. the expenses incurred personally by the candidates), has ended up promoting an extraordinary growth of individual electoral expenditures in all the competitive arenas of the system.

In this way, favorable conditions were created for an unprecedented activation of interest, or better of particularistic groups (and of their Political Action Committees, or PACs), because the 1970s laws on political financing established that contributions from an individual to a candidate should not exceed $1,000 per election and should not exceed $5,000 in the case of groups like the PACs. An ever more individualized and highly capital-intensive electoral process, without spending limits, could only work to the benefit of those groups able to control resources of strategic importance for the political competition, such as funds, information and, obviously, support.[25] Naturally, an electoral process of this kind has served not only to further weaken the parties, but has also assigned a back seat to the importance of the direct mobilization of the voters for determining the outcome of the electoral competition. More so than elsewhere, in America votes count, but resources are decisive. This has also handed an additional advantage to the incumbents, exactly because the PACs have preferred supporting the candidates with the highest probability of being re-elected, irrespective of their party affiliation (see table 3.4). The parties have sought to respond to this challenge by rationalizing and modernizing their techniques for fund raising and the organization of electoral campaigns. Nevertheless, their weakening amongst the electorate did not permit the parties to counterbalance the influence of the PACs on the

Table 3.4 Contributions to congressional campaigns by Political Action Committees (PACs) by type of committee, 1993–2004 (in millions of $)

Type of committee	Total [a]	Democrats	Republicans	Incumbents	Challengers	Open seats [b]
House of Representatives						
1993–94	132.4	88.2	43.9	101.4	12.7	18.3
1995–96	155.8	77.3	77.7	113.9	21.4	20.5
1997–98	158.7	77.6	80.9	124.0	14.9	19.8
1999–00	193.4	98.2	94.7	150.5	19.9	23.0
2001–02	206.9	102.6	104.2	161.0	13.8	32.1
2003–04, total [c]	225.4	98.6	126.6	187.3	15.6	22.5
Corporate	68.2	23.6	44.6	59.7	1.6	6.9
Trade association [d]	57.2	23.0	34.2	47.1	2.1	8.0
Labor	44.4	39.9	4.3	31.5	5.2	7.7
Nonconnected [e]	32.2	14.0	18.1	18.5	4.8	8.9
Senate						
1993–94	47.2	24.0	23.2	26.3	5.7	15.1
1995–96	45.6	16.6	29.0	19.4	6.9	19.3
1997–98	48.1	20.7	27.3	34.3	6.6	7.2
1999–00	51.9	18.7	33.2	33.5	7.1	11.3
2001–02	59.2	25.4	33.8	37.0	14.2	8.1
2003–04, total [c]	63.7	28.4	35.3	39.3	5.6	18.8
Corporate	23.4	7.0	16.4	15.8	4.3	3.4
Trade association [d]	14.3	4.9	9.3	9.5	3.1	1.7
Labor	7.5	7.0	0.5	4.1	2.4	1.1
Nonconnected [e]	12.5	5.8	6.6	6.6	4.1	1.8

[a] Includes other parties, not shown separately
[b] Elections in which an incumbent did not seek re-election
[c] Includes other types of PACs not shown separately
[d] Includes membership organizations and health organizations
[e] Represents "ideological" groups as well as other issue groups not necessarily ideological in nature
Source: US Census Bureau, *Statistical Abstract of the United States* (2003, 2006)

individual candidates; instead they frequently transformed themselves into an additional interest group supporting the individual candidates.

3.3.2   The rising costs of electoral politics

Because the reform of campaign financing had set no limits on independent expenditures, not only by individuals but also by multi-candidate committees (if registered regularly), it ended up stimulating the multiplication of the PACs, political expressions of specific and particularistic economic and ideological interests. By means of the PACs, each interest group was able to assume autonomous political and party-like shape, representing themselves directly in the electoral arena. This implies a radical change of the traditional relation between interest groups and political parties, which in the past was guided by the principle according to which the former delegated to the latter the political (general) representation, while retaining the functional representation (particular). The electoral decline of the parties and the rise of the candidates has created a void of political representation, which the special (functional and/or ideological) interests have sought to fill by intervening directly in the process of representation.[26] The self-representation of groups, in turn, has made it even more difficult for the parties to regain the initiative in their own field, namely the political integration of the separated institutions. Hence, during the 1980s and 1990s, alongside divided government a "neo-factional political system"[27] or rather a "new political disorder" emerged,[28] which has made it difficult to form coherent and relatively stable programmatic majorities in the field of public policies.

In fact, this system for regulating campaign financing has contributed to inflate dramatically the costs of campaigns (see tables 3.5 and 3.6). In the 12 years between 1994 and 2006 the amount of funds raised by candidates for the House of Representatives and the Senate doubled (although more for being elected in the former and less in the latter). When considering the expenses incurred by the winning candidates in the congressional elections, which provide a more realistic measure of the effective costs of a seat in the legislature, one reaches disturbing conclusions. According to a report presented by Congress, the average costs incurred by a winning candidate "show an increase in the House from $87,000 in 1976 to $891,000 in 2002; a winning Senate race went from $609,000 in 1976 to $4.9 million in 2002 (not adjusted for inflation)."[29]

Table 3.5 Financial activity of General Election congressional candidates (House), 1994–2006

	Year	Number of candidates	Receipts (million $)	Contributions from individuals (% of revenues)	Contributions from other committees (% of revenues)	Candidate contribution & loans (% of revenues)	Disbursements (million $)
House	2006	837	677.92	55.02	37.31	4.46	563.81
	2004	824	543.72	57.43	35.72	3.99	432.68
	2002	768	468.14	50.70	37.10	8.23	389.57
	2000	732	472.84	53.47	35.43	6.58	384.40
	1998	772	357.11	53.97	35.73	4.41	281.90
	1996	873	370.60	56.31	33.92	6.10	297.61
	1994	822	292.68	52.55	36.44	7.42	242.35
Democrats	2006	447	322.04	58.48	34.69	4.30	266.98
	2004	408	242.81	57.96	35.13	4.43	198.91
	2002	377	233.19	47.52	37.54	11.25	196.34
	2000	371	235.30	51.10	36.91	7.44	192.16
	1998	380	162.05	51.48	38.76	2.12	126.15
	1996	434	167.98	50.86	36.89	8.73	138.39
	1994	403	158.60	45.47	45.74	5.03	134.43
Republicans	2006	390	355.88	51.89	39.69	4.61	296.83
	2004	416	300.91	57.00	36.19	3.64	233.77
	2002	391	234.95	53.85	36.67	5.24	193.23
	2000	361	237.54	55.83	33.97	5.73	192.24
	1998	392	195.06	56.05	33.21	6.31	155.75
	1996	439	202.62	60.83	31.46	3.92	159.22
	1994	419	134.08	60.91	25.43	10.26	107.92

Source: Adapted from Federal Election Commission, United States of America, at www.fec.gov/press/press2006/2006l102can/hselong12g2006.xls

Table 3.6 Financial activity of General Election congressional candidates (Senate), 1994–2006

	Year	Number of candidates	Receipts (million $)	Contributions from individuals (% of revenues)	Contributions from other committees (% of revenues)	Candidate contribution & loans (% of revenues)	Disbursements (million $)
Senate	2006	65	435.99	68.49	14.06	12.84	385.19
	2004	70	326.57	73.43	17.33	2.78	277.60
	2002	69	257.44	67.53	18.87	6.73	225.77
	2000	65	324.97	56.86	13.96	23.16	296.49
	1998	67	214.34	62.71	18.42	10.92	194.72
	1996	68	187.17	66.03	18.21	10.32	167.65
	1994	70	225.69	60.58	16.41	18.59	204.20
Democrats	2006	32	237.16	73.55	11.33	11.08	206.03
	2004	36	172.15	78.16	15.22	1.63	148.61
	2002	31	126.83	72.49	16.63	5.92	113.90
	2000	32	178.14	43.10	9.52	41.88	161.26
	1998	34	101.12	63.26	17.70	8.63	92.63
	1996	34	90.04	67.50	14.05	13.64	82.43
	1994	35	95.84	62.71	20.78	10.27	86.98
Republicans	2006	33	198.83	62.46	17.30	14.95	179.16
	2004	34	154.42	68.16	19.68	4.07	128.99
	2002	38	130.61	62.71	21.05	7.51	111.87
	2000	33	146.83	73.56	19.35	0.45	135.23
	1998	33	113.22	62.22	19.06	12.96	102.09
	1996	34	97.13	64.67	22.06	7.24	85.22
	1994	35	129.85	59.01	13.18	24.74	117.22

Source: Adapted from Federal Election Commission, United States of America, at www.fec.gov/press/press2006/20061102can/senlong12g06.xls

Thus, political activity has increasingly turned into an activity for the wealthy, or at least for those who are able to raise huge sums thanks to their personal connections.[30] Of course, in an electoral competition that privileges special interests, those that have benefited most are the interests of business and the corporate groups, as compared to the interests of trade unions or other associations. In fact, the business sector has established the most PACs (see figure 3.1), in addition to having raised the most funds, having spent the most, and having contributed the most to the electoral campaigns of the various candidates (see table 3.7).

Such an organization of electoral campaign financing was bound to provoke popular and institutional pressures for reform. Yet, a substantial part of the effort to regulate campaign financing was directed at the financing of parties. Accordingly, it has been sought to impose a cap on the use of soft money, i.e. those expenditures that should have benefited the activities of the parties (even if it had turned into a form of indirect support to the electoral

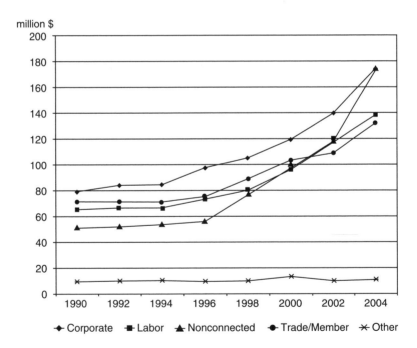

Figure 3.1 PAC receipts through June of the election year
Source: Federal Election Commission, United States of America (2004), at www.fec.gov/press/press2004/20040830pacstat/pacgrowthchart.pdf

Table 3.7 PACs, financial activity summary by committee type, 1997–2004

Committee type	Receipts (million $)				Disbursements* (million $)				Contributions to the candidates (million $)			
	1997–98	1999–00	2001–02	2003–04	1997–98	1999–00	2001–02	2003–04	1997–98	1999–00	2001–02	2003–04
Corporate	144.1	164.5	191.7	239.0	137.6	158.3	178.3	221.6	78.0	91.5	99.6	115.6
Labor	111.3	136.0	167.8	191.7	98.2	128.7	158.0	182.9	44.6	51.6	53.9	52.1
Trade/membership/health	119.6	142.9	166.7	181.8	114.4	137.2	165.7	170.1	62.3	71.8	46.3	83.2
Not affiliated	114.3	144.3	145.8	289.4	107.8	139.7	141.3	255.2	28.2	37.3	75.1	52.5
Cooperative	4.5	3.7	3.7	4.2	4.3	3.3	3.6	3.9	2.4	2.4	2.7	2.9
Corporation without stock	8.8	13.6	9.7	9.6	8.5	12.2	9.6	9.2	4.4	5.3	4.4	4.2
Total	502.6	605	685.4	915.7	470.8	579.4	656.5	842.9	219.9	259.9	282.0	310.5

*Including contributions to candidates, independent expenses and other expenses

Source: US Census Bureau, *Statistical Abstract of the United States* (2006)

campaigns of individual candidates), rather than on the use of the hard money of the PACs. After a rather tortuous legislative process,[31] Congress passed the so-called McCain-Feingold Act, named after the Republican and Democratic Senators who drafted and sponsored it in 2002. The act's passage benefited from the previously erupted Enron scandal that revealed the incredible ease with which the management of large corporations employed funds not entered in the corporate accounts to support the campaigns of the various members of the congressional committees. This concerned especially those in charge of drafting and approving the regulatory laws of the various sectors of the economy in which those companies were engaged, a not altogether disinterested contribution, one might suspect.

The opponents of the act did not hesitate to challenge its constitutionality in the Supreme Court. In its decision of December 2003, the Court, however, ruled the act constitutionally legitimate. Thus, rather than to constrain the activities of the powerful interest groups, the McCain-Feingold Act has sought to constrain the already weak political parties. But then again, it would hardly have been realistic to think that the members of Congress would be disposed to bite the hand that feeds them. Accordingly, the political parties have assumed the responsibility for an unjust electoral process that is exposed to corruption, albeit that evolution of the electoral process was not promoted by them.

3.4   Why Americans Don't Vote: The Debate

3.4.1   *The rational interpretation*

Having placed the low voter turnout in the context of the dynamics of the electoral system, it is now worth taking a look at how the phenomenon has been interpreted by American scholars. Since the 1980s, three main approaches have emerged. The first one is the rational choice school, which is in turn subdivided into a group that underlines the motivational reasons[32] and a group that instead emphasizes the instrumental reasons for not voting.[33] For the first group, the reasons for not voting must be sought in the nature of electoral competition, or better, in its inability to alter the utility calculus that each voter may be assumed to make before deciding whether to vote. For the second group, not voting is a rational decision when the cost of voting is perceived to be higher than the benefits one might derive from it. Both groups, however, apply the criteria of cost/benefit analysis to the study of electoral behavior. The costs of voting are high because America has a system of individual voting responsibility, i.e. a system that obliges the single citizen to negotiate a series of administrative obstacles in order to become an active voter. In other words, contrary to most western democracies, who have a collective system of voting responsibility in which it is the public authority's responsibility to register the citizens, in America exercising one's right to vote has implied, at least until the 1990s, the prior completion of a set of administrative practices by the individual citizen (going to a public office, at set hours of the days and set days of the week, in the span of a particular period prior to the election; proving to satisfy the requirements concerning residence, age, and sometimes acculturation; and, finally, entering one's name in the voter registry). Such practices inevitably discourage the less motivated citizens from becoming voters.

Considering the advantages the voters may derive from voting, one may understand, according to this approach, why many American citizens abstain from voting on election day. In a country as complex and vast as America, it is likely that the individual citizens will come to consider their vote irrelevant, in terms of the influence it may exert on public policies. This is why, according to this approach, not voting is understandable if the individual citizens consider their own vote irrelevant in terms of its influence on politics and public policies. In this case, the non-vote may be considered a rational decision. If the electoral competition is unable to furnish different motivations for individual behavior, and if the costs of voting are high and the benefits few, what reason is there to vote? According to some scholars who adhere to this approach, the non-vote straddles all social strata, but in particular the younger generation including those with a good education. Therefore it would be incorrect to say that the low voter turnout mainly penalizes the less well-off strata. Moreover, it is argued, when groups of non-voters decide to vote, the distribution of their political preferences turns out not to be different from the traditional voters.

Although this interpretation helps to address the problem of the low voter turnout in empirical terms, the analytical approach employed does not appear very convincing. In fact, it seems to be applicable exclusively to the context of the presidential elections, but rather less so to congressional elections. In the latter environment, voting preferences would not seem to be motivated (or decreasingly so) by party affinities, but rather by the voter's evaluation of the constituency service rendered by the incumbent congressman/congresswoman. Hence, the congressional vote displays the main characteristics of an exchange vote that tends to emphasize the individual benefits and therefore it should increase the willingness to vote of the citizens of the electoral district.[34] Yet, it is exactly in the congressional elections that the lowest voter turnout is recorded (and this is why the cost-benefit analysis does not seem convincing). Moreover, the decreasing costs of voting do not seem to have yielded significant results. In fact, despite the passing of the so-called Motor-Voter Act of 1993 (which allows citizens to register by mail when applying for a driver's license or some other public service or benefit), electoral participation did not increase during the 1990s. Hence, it is the limited motivation to vote, rather than the rational calculus of the costs and benefits of the decision itself, that should be taken into consideration. Finally, although this interpretation helps us to understand the social heterogeneity of the non-voters, it nevertheless seems to underestimate the fact that the decision not to vote tends to be concentrated amongst the marginal rather than the central strata of the population. This does not imply, however, that a mobilization of the marginal strata is bound to be beneficial for the Democratic Party.[35] Indeed, since the 1990s, the Republican Party has benefited more from electoral mobilization.

3.4.2   The radical interpretation

The radical approach, instead, arrives at a substantially different interpretation of the non-vote.[36] The radical scholars place themselves amongst the ranks of those who interpret the non-vote in terms of politico-institutional rather than socio-psychological or economic motivations. In other words, they trace the reasons for the low voter turnout to the political and institutional characteristics of the electoral arena, rather than to the calculus of the non-voters. Their criticism is primarily addressed to those who underestimate the salience of the low turnout, assuming it to reflect some kind of silent support to the political regime; a manifestation of an affluent and individualistic society whose members are interested in maximizing the use of their own resources (and their time, first of all) in order to increase their individual and family welfare. In short, low turnout is a reflection of a predominantly economic society that turns to politics only when necessary. At the same time, radical scholars aim their criticism at those who see the non-vote as the result of contingent behavior of socially and culturally marginal strata and groups: contingent, in the sense that economic growth and the spread of education are assumed to inevitably lead to an increase in electoral participation.

For the radical scholars this is not so, and has not been so. In fact, they ask why similarly marginalized groups and strata of other industrialized countries (mainly in Europe) instead continue to participate in the electoral process to a rather larger extent than their American counterparts; and why has the so-called passive support been associated so unilaterally, for all of the twentieth century, with the lower strata, instead of the upper and middle strata who have many more reasons to be satisfied with the functioning of the political system? Yet, these latter groups have actively participated in the electoral process. Hence, the explanation of the non-vote must be sought amongst those political and institutional factors that shape the electoral competition. The institutional (the administrative and electoral) devices that regulate the participation in the electoral process, rather than the political variables (the competition between the parties), should enjoy priority in the interpretative model. In line with the institutional-legal studies proper of a considerable part of the political research undertaken by radical scholars, the origin and subsequent evolution of the non-vote have been attributed to the long-term effects of particular devices, aiming to exclude sections of the working class and entire minorities (African-Americans in particular) from participating in elections.

Historically, the turning point came with the elections of 1896, which gave rise, as we have seen, to the so-called "system of 1896."[37] In fact, those elections mark the definitive defeat of progressive populism and the rise of the conservative wing of the Republican Party (the majority party at that time), i.e. of the wing most strongly connected with and influenced by business. As a result of the elections a process of electoral reform was initiated that developed along two main axes: the weakening of the local parties and the disenfranchisement of significant sections of the electorate (in other words, the negation of the right to vote to minorities, poor white voters, and sections of the working class). According to this approach, therefore, the reforms of the Progressive Era have ended up promoting the goal of business to shield the emerging public intervention in the market from the popular pressures that might have been able to express themselves through an open electoral competition. Those reforms, hence, conformed to the interests of the large corporations, in a crucial historical period of their industrial and institutional reorganization. The same efficiency criteria that guided these corporations led them to espouse a vision of the political system more akin to a political market than an electoral democracy.

Whatever may have been the reasons that led to the "system of 1896," they have engendered a diminished (quantitatively) and selected (demographically) electorate; and on this basis a specific organization of the electoral process subsequently took shape. The political parties have progressively come to tune their political message to the conditions of a diminished and selected electorate; between the elections of 1896 and those of 1920 voter turnout declined from 79 percent to 49 percent of the potential electorate. The political message of the parties (i.e. the values they uphold and the proposed policy program) has become ever more alien to the aspirations and expectations of those who do not vote, thus consolidating the low turnout. The electoral marginalization of more vulnerable groups of citizens has indirectly encouraged the main political parties to embrace a political culture largely unresponsive to the interests of these groups, and this, in turn, has pushed these groups to adopt attitudes even more strongly marked by political alienation and electoral abstention. Hence, the absence of a class-based and social-democratic version of the national political culture that has discouraged the lower strata from participating in elections must be understood as the result of a political evolution that was institutionally shaped by the administrative and electoral devices put in place after the elections of 1896 to the benefit of the upper strata of society.

The political parties have adapted to this environment, orienting their policies toward conquering a majority of the voting citizens. With reference to this electorate, they have built their connections, their know-how, and their organization. Needing to operate in a stable context, they have come to oppose (more or less openly) the various proposals to lower the hurdles to electoral participation. Nevertheless, on several occasions these hurdles were (at least partially) neutralized: during the New Deal period, when a vigorous political and electoral competition with strong class overtones developed; in the early 1960s, when an impetuous civil rights movement urged the Democratic presidencies and Congress to sponsor and pass an effective electoral legislation favorable to the minorities and social groups previously excluded from the electorate; and in the early 1990s, with the pressure of President Clinton on the Democratic Congress to pass the Motor-Voter Act. However, according to radical scholars, these changes did not affect the logic of the electoral process. First of all because the judicial lowering of the electoral hurdles is a relatively recent phenomenon. Second, because many administrative hurdles to electoral participation have survived. Still today, notwithstanding the Motor-Voter Act approved in 1993, few states have decentralized voter registration; few states and municipalities keep open the voter registry during weekends or extend their opening hours beyond the traditional office hours; or in many states the registration forms are unnecessarily complex and generally no assistance is provided to those who are not native English speakers. Third, because the institutionalization of incumbency has created an incentive for congressmen/congresswomen not to promote the expansion of the electorate, since such an expansion might create a conflict between the interests of the new voters and of the old ones, who are so well-represented by the PACs and their financial contributions.

But above all, the electoral hurdles (or rather the institutional and legal factors) are relevant, not only because of the direct effects they have had on voter turnout, but also because of their indirect effects. These hurdles have molded the culture of the (two) political parties to the extent that the middle and upper-middle classes of American society have progressively become their privileged interlocutors. Hence, the impact of institutional factors has been rather significant, even if non-quantifiable. For example, it has helped to institutionalize a common bias in favor of the interests and values of the middle classes in both major parties, thus contributing to their progressive political and programmatic standardization. This development has primarily penalized the Democratic Party, which – notwithstanding the episode of the New Deal – was never able to develop as an authentic social-democratic party exactly because of the consequences of these legal and administrative devices. The impact of institutional factors is not easily neutralized, as they give rise to a path dependency, reproducing their effects through the behavior of the political actors who adjust their expectations and perspectives accordingly. Hence, according to the radical scholars, and in contrast to what the rationalists maintained, the non-vote is to be understood as the long-term effect of a specific strategy of electoral demobilization of the lower social strata, initially pursued by the economic elites and subsequently adopted by the two main political parties. This strategy did not claim a high price in terms of the legitimacy of the system, because the prolonged practice of not voting has contributed to the diffusion of an underdeveloped political awareness amongst the lower classes and the minorities (i.e. amongst the non-voters). In conclusion, according to the radical approach, the principal actors of the American democracy have come to adopt the culture of the middle classes.

3.4.3 The party school interpretation

While being aware of the influence of structural factors, the so-called "party school" approach is rather more attentive to the political aspects of the electoral process.[38] This approach originated in the contributions of Walter D. Burnham in particular, which still today remain a point of reference for scholars of this approach.[39] According to this approach, the decision whether to vote or not is certainly guided by both emotional and instrumental motives. However, the decision not to vote may reasonably be seen to result from a declining identification between citizens and parties, or rather from the difficulty of the potential electorate to discern relevant differences between the various candidates. In this view, electoral participation is related to the inability of the parties and other political entrepreneurs to make the electoral competition susceptible to a differentiated utility calculus by the individual citizens. In fact, the substitution of the political parties (in their role as the main organizers of the electoral market) with the personal organizations of the candidates (and their sophisticated technologies) has engendered the disintegration of some of the criteria (such as historical memory, collective identity, emotional identification, perceived effectiveness) traditionally employed by the citizens to guide their electoral choices.

An electoral market characterized by candidate-centered politics, symbolic appeals and images, and increasingly sophisticated electoral technologies, would not seem to promote the ability of the individual voters to calculate the utility of the various alternatives, nor – what is more – does it allow for some form of stable political identification. Moreover, bereft of stable party support, the candidates live with the constant fear of not being re-elected.[40] As a result they engaged in a permanent electoral campaign in order to obtain funds and support. Accordingly they devote their time to those who control financial and organizational resources, rather than to the "simple" voters. When political competition comes to acquire the traits of personal competition (the candidates seem to be guided by the principle of each man/woman for himself/herself), it is inevitable that there should be a growing number of citizens who perceive their vote to be barely effective, or even ineffective, or who decreasingly feel that they belong to a collective entity. On the other hand, with the reduced pressure for the representatives to assume responsibility as part of a collective political organization, it is not surprising that notion of identity or collective belonging between elected officials and the citizens should have come to decline.

The consequences of this transformation of the electoral process are twofold: first of all, the electoral coalitions have been broken down into various electoral arenas, frequently along the lines of the specific elective office at stake. In this way the American political system has witnessed the rise of a type of personalized politics that creates incentives for the individual candidates, as well as the political leaders and representatives, to build their own, personal, electoral support coalitions, with the mentioned effects on voter turnout. Second, the decline of the notion of collective belonging, encouraged by the emergence of personalized politics, had not been distributed uniformly across the electorate. On the contrary, diminishing electoral participation (which is the visible expression of declining sentiments of collective belonging) has manifested itself differentially, with the effect of penalizing the political left more than the right. Although electoral abstention does constitute a general phenomenon that affects different classes and social groups, nevertheless (as Burnham has shown) its extent correlates with divisions of social class and income. Hence, electoral demobilization is at the same time general and selective, in the sense that it weakens the political system but disproportionately so in the left camp (i.e. the Democratic Party). This differentiation, Burnham argues, helps to explain a peculiar trait of the American political system, namely the existence of a genuine political right combined with a rather less genuine political left. This is why, even in the absence of the electoral hurdles put in place at the end of the nineteenth century and maintained erect for the following century, political competition by now has assumed such characteristics so as to leave little hope for an electoral remobilization.

It is therefore this competition that one has to look at, if the aim is to understand the reasons for the low level of electoral participation that so spectacularly characterizes American politics. The disintegration of party bonds in the permanent electoral campaign, which envelopes the working of a large part of the political system, is the cause of the deteriorating relations between institutions and citizens, symbolized by growing feelings of political and electoral alienation in significant, and selected, parts of the electorate. In the view of these scholars, American politics seems to have moved closer to that "state of nature" the architects of the parties had sought to overcome from the outset of the new republic. The original state of the American republic could barely be called democratic, considering the strata (not only African Americans or women, but also the poor and the illiterate) excluded from effective participation in the decision-making process. With the emergence and subsequent development of political parties, this political and social disequilibrium was (at least partially) redressed, precisely because the parties soon came to function as the vehicles for a broader participation of the citizens in public affairs, and of an equally encompassing endeavor of civic and political education. A return to the republic's original state, instead, is bound to promote a renewed imbalance of electoral competition (politically to the benefit of the right, and socially to the benefit of the rich), which in the past had been mitigated by the political parties.

3.4.4 Comparing interpretations of non-voting

In conclusion, the three approaches discussed here present different diagnoses of, and cures for, the low level of electoral participation characteristic of American politics. Yet, they all provide us with important clues. Although the decision whether to vote is not beyond utilitarian considerations, nevertheless the rules that have governed the functioning of the electoral system for almost a century have created a trajectory of low voter turnout which subsequently became institutionalized. With the elections of 1896, voting became an opportunity instead of a duty as the decision to register was no longer mandatory but discretionary. Those elections marked the definitive defeat of the progressive populism and the rise of the conservative wing of the Republican Party; the majority party of that time.

As a result of the 1896 elections a process of electoral reform was initiated which led to the weakening of the local parties and to the de facto disenfranchisement of significant sectors of the electorate (in particular, minorities, poor white voters, parts of the working class). For a long time, such legal and administrative devices have constrained electoral participation, institutionalizing a predisposition toward the interests and culture of the middle class. In combination with the constraints of the separation of powers, such devices have turned the parties into particularly weak organizations. Weak parties, in turn, were unable to transform the pressures for their democratization into an opportunity to strengthen their position by redefining themselves.

Thus, with the introduction of the primaries, electoral politics has come to focus ever more strongly on the individual candidates. This personalization of politics has further diminished the identification of the voters with the parties. Step by step, both candidate-centered politics and low electoral participation came to be institutionalized, mutually reinforcing each other. Once this trajectory was institutionalized, it has proven difficult to change its course by the adoption of legislation and other measures (from the Voting Rights Act of 1965 to the Motor-Voter Act of 1993) that have lowered the administrative and juridical hurdles. Contemporary political competition continues to display such characteristics as to prevent a renewed mobilization of the electorate. With the decline of the parties amongst the electorate, American politics has become a gigantic and individualized electoral market, and therefore an inhospitable environment for a type of political competition able to mobilize voters on the basis of its programmatic contents and long-term perspective.

3.5   Political Parties from Decline to Transformation?

We know that in Philadelphia a separated government was created which, because of the principle of checks and balances, could only function by means of the collaboration of the three main branches of government (the House of Representatives, the Senate, and the president). Organized on the basis of different constituencies, differentiated terms of office, and constitutionally delineated prerogatives, the institutions of separated government gave rise to a Madisonian governmental system, based on the principle that the federal government should indeed be able to take the necessary decisions, but only by means of consensual deliberation between representatives of different constituencies and with distinct temporal horizons.

The ink on the approval of the new federal Constitution had not yet dried when the Madisonian system revealed its weakness exactly on the level of governmental decision-making. Already with Jefferson's first presidency (1801–4, with a subsequent second four-year term), an unexpected operationalization of the Constitution emerged, based on the use of the political party in order to connect the separated institutions. Thus, a Jeffersonian practice was inserted in the Madisonian model of government:[41] which is to say that electoral politics had managed to insert itself into the Constitution.[42] Without a political party able to link the majority of Congress with the president, separated government did not seem able to function appropriately. Jefferson's intuition was clearly borne out by the emergence and development of a mature party democracy since the 1830s. After male suffrage was introduced, only the political parties could integrate the new voters without simultaneously provoking a paralysis of the government.

Although it is true that political parties operating in a system of separated government do not have an easy life, the long-lasting pre-eminence of the legislature in national politics did, however, substantially mitigate the hardships of their existence. Having traditionally been coalitions of state and local political groups, the pre-eminence of Congress, given that it is structured to represent territorially defined interests, had helped to protect the organizational coherence of the national political parties. But, naturally, the progressive governmental ascendancy of the president, together with the nationalization of congressional electoral politics, were bound to make the institutional habitat within which the political parties operated more inhospitable. With the 1930s, the party system, which was already fragmented in the individual states, also fragments vertically in the single institutions of government. Nationally, the two-party system survived, but it did so in the form of several sub-systems at the level of the presidency, the House, and the Senate. Under these conditions, national political parties could recognize themselves as such only once every four years on the occasion of the national convention that selected the candidate for the presidency. Once the lights were turned off and the convention was over, each institutional sub-segment of the party regained its autonomy. Nevertheless, at the federal level, these sub-segments would enter into coalitions, thus providing the president with a stable link with the leader of his party in Congress.

Only parties weak in terms of organizational and ideological cohesion would accept conditions that would further undermine their position. This is exactly what happened with the reform of the system for selecting the presidential candidates initiated by the Democratic Party in 1972. The diffusion of primaries, implied by that reform, delivered the final blow to the party's capacity to preserve a collective identity. Since the 1970s, electoral politics has come to acquire a candidate-centered nature. Obviously, candidate-centered politics has had systemic consequences for electoral democracy. The candidates have progressively come to build their own personal parties, composed of professional and issue-oriented supporters. The national party structures have progressively been transformed into service organizations for the candidate that emerges victoriously from the internal competition: providing tremendous technical, but no political, support for the candidate.[43] In this new electoral context only those candidates would succeed who could dispose of huge financial resources to promote their own candidacy, or of mobilizing ideological resources to impose their candidacy on their own party; as was the case with the neoconservative Republicans of Newt Gingrich during the 1990s. The point is that candidate-centered politics has been problematic for electoral democracy because the voters are no longer able to bring about de-alignments and thus re-alignments without political parties that aggregate their interests.

Indeed, American politics has been traditionally interpreted in terms of the analytical concepts of de-alignment and re-alignment.[44] The first concept aims to clarify the characteristics of the process of undermining or erosion of an existing party alignment. The concept of re-alignment instead seeks to describe the emergence and consolidation of new loyalties centered on a rival party. Analytically, there is not necessarily a relation of causality between a process of de-alignment and the successive re-alignment. A re-alignment, to be considered such, should imply the launch of at least three dynamics: (a) an enduring shift in voting behavior and above all party loyalties able to last for a generation; (b) a shift in the institutional balance of power between the two parties, able to secure for the new majority party the control, for a reasonable number of years, of the branches of government (the presidency and the two chambers of Congress); (c) a shift in the balance of power between the main interest groups (and thus also in the intellectual climate that surrounds the discussion of public affairs), of such an extent as to stabilize the new power relations between the parties.

For these reasons, true re-alignments have occurred on only a few occasions (1852–6, 1896, and 1932–6) in the nonetheless long democratic history of the country.[45] After 1956 (but especially after 1968) this process was interrupted. The New Deal coalition, which asserts itself with the realignment of 1932–6, came to be considerably weakened in the 1970s and a new conservative coalition progressively rose to dominance in the following decade. Some social and ethnic groups (like the younger generation, the white voters of the south, the northern working class), and some territorial interests (of the south-western states) distanced themselves from the Democratic Party, to transfer their loyalties to the Republican Party. However, the disintegration of the New Deal coalition did not bring a Republican re-alignment. From the 1970s to the 1990s the federal government remained divided and so too the electorate. The unified party government of the period 2003–6 owes more to the shock of September 11, 2001 then to a re-alignment of the electorate around neoconservative policies and the leaders of the Republican Party. Indeed, not only did the presidential elections of 2004 make evident that the electorate was evenly divided between the Republican and the Democratic candidate, but the mid-term elections of 2006 yielded a new divided government. Weak political parties could not assist in promoting new re-alignments, although such an outcome seemed to have been precluded by a continuous deep division within the general electorate.

In fact, certainly from the 1970s to 1990s, Jefferson detached himself from Madison, in the sense that electoral politics slipped out of the Constitution. In those decades, America seemed to have become what it was at the beginning of its republican experience: a separated government without parties. It was as if, at the end of the twentieth century, the Constitution designed at the end of the eighteenth century were truly realized. According to the Constitution, the task of the governed is not to elect the government, but to select the governors entrusted with the task to deliberate on the basis of reciprocal checks. The candidate-centered politics, which has fragmented the electoral competition, offered few incentives for electoral mobilization around issues of general interest. However, a counter-trend came into existence with the 1990s as an effect of the ascendancy of the neoconservative coalition. Already with the mid-term elections of 1994, a party-building process had started again, especially on the Republican side. Nevertheless, this did not suffice to promote a new electoral and political re-alignment. It is hard to establish the relation of cause and effect between party transformation and electoral decline. It is a fact, however, that voter turnout has diminished even further in the presidential and congressional elections since the 1970s. It should not come as a surprise that, under these conditions, there is a growing percentage of voters who deliberately split their ballot, supporting the candidate of one party for the presidency and the candidate of the rival party for Congress. Simultaneously, as was predictable, the percentage of voters who identify with a party has decreased significantly (declining from three out of four voters in the 1950s to three out of five in the 1990s), while the percentage of independent voters has grown considerably with respect to both parties (having tripled since the 1950s to reach one third of the electorate in the 1990s).

Whereas electoral democracy requires the construction of social and ethnic coalitions, post-electoral democracy, in contrast, implies the formation of institutional and para-institutional coalitions. In a post-electoral democracy, the actors that count are the institutions of government as such, allied with the media or the courts, whereas in an electoral democracy the actors that count are the parties, the movements and the voting citizens. Thus, candidate-centered politics, associated with a regime of divided government, has ended up substituting the elected for the voters as the source of public policy. Without Jefferson, the Madisonian system, applied to a mass society, has ended up fueling a permanent institutional conflict: the battle between the political parties has progressively been transformed into a clash between the institutions of government.

During the last two centuries, the secret of success to American democracy consisted of the de facto constitutionalization of the parties, albeit in the context of a Constitution that did not envisage them in principle. By means of Jefferson, Madison was able to reach the twentieth century. The success of this secret has since been significantly reduced. In the presence of fragile electoral bases, the Madisonian system has ended up fueling a form of politics marked by a high degree of institutional conflict, although one might certainly argue that inter-institutional conflict is intrinsic to the system of separated government. However, without mobilizing new voters through effective party organizations, America risks returning to Philadelphia and the idea of a "republic without parties" that the founding fathers had entertained.[46] This is an idea, it must be added, they were forced to abandon early on in order to meet the demands of a democratizing society. In the fully democratized society of the twenty-first century, can America rely on candidate-centered parties for connecting voters with institutions? Madison may continue to rest in peace. Can one say the same for America?

3.6 Conclusion

It is hard to claim that America is a democracy without the people, i.e. a democratic dynasty. America continues to be one of the world's most remarkable and creative laboratories of electoral democracy.

Few other democracies can boast of more than half a million elective public offices. No other democracy has a similar combination of general elections and primaries, and in no other democracy are the elections for the House of Representatives and for one third of the Senate held every two years. If one takes into account the state and county governments, the offices of councilor of various municipalities, the position of judge or county sheriff, each year thousands of elections are held in America in which millions of voters take part. Also taking into account the petitions, the referenda, the recalls, and proposed constitutional amendments at the state or federal level, one may say that America is engaged in a permanent electoral campaign.

Accordingly, it is no surprise that voters are asked to take dozens of decisions simultaneously in the polling booth. The American permanent electoral campaign has no equivalent in any European national democracy. In those countries, the members of parliament remain in office for at least twice a long as their counterparts beyond the Atlantic; the holders of all the administrative and judicial offices are selected by public hiring and not through elections, and the powers of legislative initiative of the citizens are limited or non-existent. The Canadian-English political scientist Anthony King is right when he argues that "the American people are, and have been for a very long time, the western world's 'hyperdemocrats.' They are keener on democracy than almost anyone else and are more determined that democratic norms and practices should pervade any aspect of national life."[47]

But even if America is not a democracy without the people, its people, however, count for less than they should do. Voter turnout continues to be low and, above all, political competition appears to be asymmetrical (i.e. much more favorable to the right than the left, and to the upper-middle than the lower-middle strata). The voters may be asked to take dozens of decision in the polling booth, but too few voters actually take those decisions. The existence of a wide area of non-vote represents a significant burden on the functioning of the democratic system. In fact, the more the ranks of the non-voters swell, the more the power of the economic and social elites in national politics grows. Certainly, it does not make much sense to compare electoral participation in America to that of the European nation states. America is a continent of 300 million inhabitants; the destination of continuous waves of immigrants whose primary concern is not to participate in public life but to rise above the misery from which they came; a country marked by a high

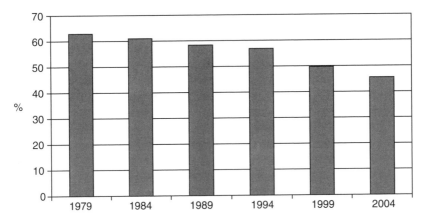

Figure 3.2 Participation in the elections for the European Parliament, 1979–2004. Average EU
Source: www.elections2004.eu.int

territorial mobility that makes it difficult to build the common identity necessary to support civic life (each year between 1980 and 2001, on average 16 percent of the population changed homes[48]). Its dimensions, its complexity and the differentiation of the American democracy significantly hinder the process of identification between individual citizens and the federal institutions. After all, this is an experience that Europe too is beginning to undergo. Although voter turnout in the member states of the European Union is higher than in America, the same does not hold true for the elections to the European Parliament.

A glance at figure 3.2 is sufficient to realize that voter turnout in the elections to the European Parliament is even lower than the figures recorded for the American presidential elections (in the elections of June 2004 the average turnout was 45.5 percent). In sum, America has cultivated important virtues but has also acquired a fair share of vices. America holds many elections, but few vote.

4

A Democracy for the Rich?

4.1 Introduction

One of the most common criticisms of America concerns its social egoism. America is depicted as the reign of the most unbridled individualism, its society as a jungle where only the fittest survive, its mass culture as a form of primitive consumerism. As Marco Tarchi has argued,

> the individualism, the narcissistic cult of the self and the promotion of social egoism, translated into the imperative of success measurable in dollars (a person is what he has) and in the assimilation of social relations to a menacing jungle of exasperated and ubiquitous competition, are only some of the more conspicuous and superficial aspects of the "typical" behavioral pattern implicit in the American model.[1]

The German Thomas Assheuer wrote in *Die Zeit* that "despite the 'golden 1990s' there is more poverty in the United States than in any other large industrial country."[2] Similarly, the American economist Jeremy Rifkin argued, "if we compare the health care for the ordinary people, then Europe wins (if compared with the US)."[3] Others have even claimed that America is a sort of totalitarian factory where, "because of the traditional and ever growing weakness of the trade unions, those who hold a, usually precarious, manual job, are, to all extents and purposes, totally at the mercy of their 'bosses.'"[4] In short, America, if it is a democracy at all, is a democracy for the rich.

There is no doubt that this criticism points to an existing feature of American society, namely that it is one of the most inegalitarian societies of all the advanced democracies. According to World Bank figures, at the end of the 1990s the richest quintile of the American population earned 11 times more than the poorest quintile, whereas in Japan the richest quintile earned 4.3 times more, in Belgium 4.6 times more, in Germany 5.8 times more, in Canada and France 7.1 times more, and in the United Kingdom 9.6 times more.[5] Moreover, according to the figures of the Congressional Budget Office, the richest 1 percent of the American population has witnessed an inexorable growth of the share of national wealth it controls. From the beginning of the 1980s to the end of the 1990s, this share went from 9.3 percent to 15.8 percent.[6] Looking at more sophisticated indicators, like the Gini index (see table 4.1), one can see that there is not only considerable income inequality in America but that it has been increasing systematically since the late 1960s. At present America records the highest level of inequality amongst the OECD countries, excluding Eastern Europe and Mexico.[7]

In sum, it is true that there are profound social disparities at the basis of American democracy. It is a democracy where the rich are many and their wealth is incomparably greater than the disposable income of the average American family. Whereas in 1999 the average wealth of an American family amounted to $60,000 dollars, the richest person in the country, Bill Gates, had amassed a fortune of $85 billion. Furthermore, the relation between the largest fortune of the country and the average wealth of an American family has gone from 4,000:1 (in 1790) to 1,416,000:1 (in 1999). However, such criticisms tell us little about the reasons for this inequality and the broader context into which it is inserted. In fact, American democracy, more so than a democracy for the rich, is a market democracy.

In America, the market constitutes a source of legitimacy for democracy, rather than the opposite (as is the case in all European countries). The market continues to enjoy such legitimacy because of its dynamism, or rather because of its proven ability to integrate groups and individuals (in particular continuous waves of poor immigrants from all over the world) into American society. Thus, this social inequality is accepted because its composition is ever-changing. In addition, these and other similar criticisms fail to recognize the importance of the specific political processes, which, since the 1980s, have contributed to exacerbating social inequality. In fact, this social inequality is not only the expression of a dynamic

Table 4.1   Gini index of income inequality in America, 1967–2001

Year	Gini index	Year	Gini index
1967	0.399	1985	0.419
1968	0.388	1986	0.425
1969	0.391	1987	0.426
1970	0.394	1988	0.427
1971	0.396	1989	0.431
1972	0.401	1990	0.428
1973	0.397	1991	0.428
1974	0.395	1992	0.434
1975	0.397	1993	0.454
1976	0.398	1994	0.456
1977	0.402	1995	0.450
1978	0.402	1996	0.455
1979	0.404	1997	0.459
1980	0.403	1998	0.456
1981	0.406	1999	0.457
1982	0.412	2000	0.460
1983	0.414	2001	0.466
1984	0.415		

The Gini index measures the income distribution in a country (and thus the degree of inequality). The index can take values between 0 and 1, where a value 0 corresponds to perfect equality, and a value of 1 corresponds to perfect inequality. Looking at the historical development of the Gini index in the USA one sees a constant increase in income inequality since 1968. In the 40 years prior to 1968, inequality was more moderate. Income inequality has risen from 40% in 1967 to 47% in 2001. See A. S. Alderson and F. Nielsen, "Globalization and the great U-turn: Income inequality trends in 16 OECD countries," *American Journal of Sociology*, 107 (2001).
Source: US Census Bureau, at www.census.gov/

market society, but also the effect of a successful political revolution, namely the neoconservative revolution, initiated by President Reagan in the 1980s, radicalized by the Speaker of the House Newt Gingrich in the 1990s, and subsequently embraced by President George W. Bush in the 2000s. This neoconservative revolution has radically called into question the redistributive policies of the federal state that were launched between the 1930s and the 1960s, delegitimizing them culturally and hollowing them out fiscally. Thus, even if it is true that the American democracy is socially inegalitarian, it is also true that its disparities are the outcome of structural (the role of the market) and political (the victory of the neoconservatives) factors.

This chapter is structured as follows. First, I will describe the historical evolution of the relation between market and democracy in America, as well as the implications of this relation for the social responsibilities of the state, as they have come to be defined between the 1930s and the 1960s. The next section is devoted to an analysis of the neoconservative revolution against the New Deal order. Here, I am not concerned with social policies, or with the welfare state model that has come to be institutionalized in America. Rather, what interests me is to outline the political logic of the American market democracy, in order to show that it is different from a democracy for the rich.

4.2 The American Commercial Republic

4.2.1 The decentralized formation of the American market

The evolution of American market democracy has followed a trajectory radically different from that of the European market democracies. At the roots of this divergence lies a different historical relationship between the state and the market; a difference not only of degree, but of kind. America and the countries of Western Europe have constructed different types of public authority because they have experienced diverse (historical and cultural) circumstances in the latter's formation. Since market society preceded the formation of a modern bureaucratic federal state in America, public authority has predominantly come to regulate social relations. In the countries of Western Europe, where the formation of a bureaucratic territorial state preceded the birth of a market society, public authority instead has arrived to define the very nature of social relations.[8] That is, whereas in Europe the state has sought to constitute civil society as such (with its educational, cultural, and more generally social policies), in America public authority has limited itself to regulating the development of civil society, given that the latter had formed prior to and independently of it.

Given this relation between society and state, a contractualist vision has progressively asserted itself during the nineteenth century in America. Democracy has come to be interpreted as the outcome of a contract between individuals and social groups (territorially organized), concluded in order to better promote their specific interests.[9] The European nation states' experience couldn't be more different. Here democracy was only able to assert itself definitively in the second half of the twentieth century, after a dramatic sequence of conflicts between ascending social classes and bureaucratic interests in defense of their privileges (and in particular of their control of the state). Whereas, therefore, in America democracy preceded the state, in Europe democracy had to assert itself against the state.[10]

In America, democracy did not have to struggle with an absolutist state in order to gain constitutional recognition, nor did it have to develop in a social and economic context of scarce resources to be divided amongst a growing population, as was the case in the European countries (especially the continental ones). In America economic freedom (or more precisely the freedom of enterprise), even if shaped since the colonial era by religious and communitarian constraints, predates the birth of political freedom and thereby has guaranteed the latter's development. In European countries instead, (and in France and Germany in particular) it was the conquest of political freedom that created the conditions for the full development of economic freedom.[11]

Based on this different sequence of the formation of the state, it is frequently pointed out that in America, contrary to European countries, a modern market economy was able to develop in a stateless context.[12] These differences in timing have also impinged upon the ideological predispositions toward the market economy, in addition to the concrete structures of market relations themselves. Having formed prior to the state, the market was able to enjoy a far superior legitimacy in America as compared to Europe, where instead the development of the market was the outcome of public policy. As Elkin has pointed out, from the outset of the new republic the entire political elite shared the idea that "the commerce was to be the engine for the prosperity . . . valuable in itself and necessary for the stability of the new republic."[13] Ever since the foundation of the new American republic, the market and freedom of commerce have enjoyed a degree of social legitimacy without equivalent in Europe; so much so that the new republic for a long time was defined as a "commercial republic."

In America, the market has somehow promoted the formation of a modern civil society, to the extent that the latter has come to identify with the former. Of course, in both America and Europe economic freedoms, once established, needed to be protected by the public authorities in order to develop. Also in America the market economy has required specific political intervention in order to become institutionalized. Without the public protection of property rights and without the public recognition of the economic interests and the proper spheres of economic activity it would not have been possible to create the preconditions that underpin any market. As Polanyi showed a long time ago, markets are political constructions and not natural phenomena, and American history does not furnish counterarguments.[14]

Yet, although Polanyi was correct in recognizing that the existence of a legal order is (and was) an indispensable condition for market activity, and although he stressed the role public authorities played for building the infrastructure supporting market activity, however "he did not specify the particular instruments that the state might use in pursuing that goal."[15] And it is in this respect that the way in which the American market was constructed reveals its peculiarity in comparison with Europe. Prior to the Civil War of 1861–5 the promotion of economic activity primarily was a matter for the states. As McDonald argued, through state and local governments enormous resources were transferred from public to private uses.[16] One has only to think of "the distribution of public lands, the granting of legal privileges and immunities, direct capital investment in some projects – especially railroads – and the provision of a wide variety of police, education and social welfare services." Bryce himself in his famous book on America (perhaps the most important study of America in the second half of the nineteenth century) showed how, for the whole period prior to the Civil War, the federated states had come to play a fundamental role in the promotion of economic activity, and how they had jealously guarded their territories from any possible outside attempts to gain control.[17]

This decentralized support for the market was made possible by a crucial factor, namely the states' control over tax revenues. Only with constitutional amendment XVI of 1913 did the federal Congress acquire the "power to lay and collect taxes on incomes, from whatever source derived, without apportionment among the several States, and without regard to any census or enumeration." As several studies have shown, for all of the nineteenth century, with the partial exception of the Civil War period, federal public expenditures as a share of gross national product reached only one fifth or one sixth of the level recorded in the countries of Western Europe during the same period.[18] Thus, for over a century since its inception, the new American republic depended on the fiscal resources of the federated states rather than of the federal state. Congressional government enabled the federated states to put up effective resistance to every attempt to centralize the fiscal power at the federal level. Hence, the different structural and institutional context of America and the individual European countries has generated two opposite paths of constructing a market economy. In the era of congressional government, the decentralized states took charge of constructing the legal and institutional preconditions of the market, whereas in the centralized European states this task fell exclusively to the central authority.

4.2.2 *Judicial power and market building*

The segmentation of the market along the lines of the federated states has proven very early on to be a constraint on America's economic development. The favorable conditions for economic development led to growing pressures for the expansion of the sphere of business to the entire territory of the country. Yet, the restrictions imposed by the states formed a significant obstacle in this respect. And those restrictions were also supported by Congress, which was largely controlled by local and state interests. Hence, the new ascending groups of the American economy, i.e. those economic actors who were eager to expand the sphere of their activities, in the last quarter of the nineteenth century ended up turning to the courts[19] because Congress had proven impermeable to their requests, the president did not yet exert sufficient influence, and the courts disposed of a policy-making role.

But, as the state courts defended the states' interests in preserving their tariffs and customs duties, the task of promoting a free market economy at the federal level fell to the federal Supreme Court. On the basis of decisions of historic importance, like *Gibbon v. Ogden* (1824) and *Brown v. Maryland* (1827), and subsequently on the basis of the so-called Commerce Clause of article I section 8.3, of the Constitution (according to which Congress has the power "to regulate Commerce with foreign nations, and among the several States, and with the Indian tribes"), the Supreme Court gradually started to dismantle the trade barriers introduced by the states and to facilitate the adoption of federal laws in support of the creation of a continent-wide market.

In America, since 1803, the judicial power had succeeded in imposing its right of judicial review of all laws, and this right encouraged the courts to take on a policy-making role instead of merely applying the law. In fact, with the power of judicial review, the judiciary had become a genuine actor in the legislative process, as it could suspend a law deemed unconstitutional. Obviously, the courts' ability to subject all passed legislation to judicial review was bound to influence Congress in its legislative activity. Moreover, because the power of judicial review fell to the entire judicial system, and not just of its Supreme Court, its exercise has turned out to be rather unpredictable. Since the beginning of the nineteenth century, any American judge of any county and any state can suspend the application of a federal law if its unconstitutionality can be demonstrated. Such rulings, of course, can be appealed and submitted to the judgment of the next higher judicial level all the way up to the federal Supreme Court, whose decisions are final. The federal Supreme Court, like the state supreme courts, stands at the apex of the judiciary, and thus rules both on (extraordinary) matters of constitutional importance as on matters of ordinary legislation.

The power of judicial review should not be confused with the constitutional review of approved or proposed legislation in the countries of Western Europe, in particular after the Second World War. In the European countries, the task of adjudicating on the constitutionality of approved laws is entrusted to a specific body, the Constitutional Court, with a mixed composition (of representatives of the judiciary and of the political authorities) and institutionally located outside of the judicial system. Thus the countries of Western Europe have continued to preserve the principle of supremacy of parliament, whereas America, from the start, has gone in the direction of the supremacy of the Constitution.

The virtues of the national market also brought out its correlated vices. In particular, the nationwide market led to the formation of industrial and financial corporations that had proven able to distort the logic of free competition in order to attain monopoly positions. The new barons of steel, oil, finance, and the railroads had accumulated such resources as to be able to control the entire national economy. And because of their economic power, they were also able to exert influence on the working of the system of government. Popular and institutional reactions against these concentrations of economic might were not slow in coming. Populist movements and political leaders mobilized in order to neutralize the power of the new economic oligarchies, and they did so in the name of economic and political freedom threatened by the gigantic accumulations of wealth that had sprung up in the country. This mobilization led to the introduction of a strategy of market regulation.

The task to safeguard the "public interest" of free competition in the regulated sectors was delegated by the political authorities to specific and independent ad hoc agencies who were authorized to exercise simultaneously executive, legislative, and judicial functions. The president and Congress both had a say in the appointment of their personnel, but only the latter could authorize the funds necessary to run these agencies. These agencies have thus been the instrument with which the federal state has sought to maintain the competitive nature of the market, to promote fair competition between the economic actors, and to neutralize monopolies or oligopolies sufficiently powerful to negatively impact on the public interest in continuous economic growth. However, this regulatory strategy has not been without its failures. The powerful private interests quickly adjusted to the new game, devising efficient strategies to bend the new policies to their own purposes. More than a few of these regulatory agencies were "captured" by the interests they were supposed to regulate, with the effect of emasculating the anti-trust policy they were called on to implement. Certainly, the capture of some agencies subsequently prompted the mobilization of the excluded interests, which in turn pressured the Congress to better define the statutes of independent agencies in order to maintain their independence from the regulated interests.

These contradictions notwithstanding, America is the first country in the world to have adopted anti-trust legislation with the Sherman Antitrust Act of 1890, which confronted the challenges of the large corporations that had sprung up as a result of the formation of a nationwide market. Since then, the American market is amongst the most regulated markets in the world. Market regulation continues to be informed by liberal principles of free competition. Such a strategy revolves around regulating the market from the point of view of the consumer rather than the worker. One might criticize the effectiveness of such a strategy in protecting the weaker groups in the market, or one might question the underlying philosophy of the regulatory policies. However, one cannot plausibly maintain that the American market is a jungle where only the strongest survive.

It is worth noting that the strategy of market regulation, as opposed to direct state control in the form of nationalization of strategic sectors, as has occurred in European countries, was imposed by the specific institutional and cultural conditions of the country. The institutional dispersion of national sovereignty (inherent in the American compound republic) and the existence of a widespread culture valuing economic freedom, made it rather unlikely that the federal state would pursue a strategy aiming to supplant private initiative with public intervention in order to guarantee the public use of strategic resources. Hence, the industrial America that emerged after the Civil War pursued a policy of market regulation precisely because such policies could be implemented even in the absence of a centralized public authority.

The European story is rather different, not only because nowhere in Europe has the judiciary been able to play an autonomous role in policy-making, but also because Europe is marked by political and not judicial intervention in the market. Ever since the Colbertist experience of absolutist France, the creation of a thriving economy has been considered a public and not a private priority in Europe; or rather, a necessary condition to guarantee the military prowess of the individual countries engaged in territorial conflicts and power games with other countries. Thus in Europe it was the mercantilist ideology, based on direct state ownership of strategic resources, rather than the regulatory perspective, that has accompanied the development of nationwide European markets. In Europe, mercantilism was a necessity for territorial states involved in continuous wars of expansion or survival. In situations of uncertainty, the development of a strong national economy could not be left to the vagaries of the "animal instincts" of private entrepreneurs. In turn, as Calleo argued, mercantilism has thus encouraged imperialism as a public strategy for accumulating more resources.[20] This is why in Europe the development of a nationwide market coincided with the colonial expansion of the states, whereas this was not so in America where the drive for territorial expansion was primarily directed toward the western hemisphere.

Faced with the tremendous challenges of war and the competition for the control of the economic resources needed to fight it, the states of Western Europe could not limit themselves to introducing a reliable system of property rights, an efficient tax collection system, or a stable system of trade regulation. Rather, the state had to identify and control the sectors considered crucial for its economic and military growth, taking direct responsibility for their development and stimulating from above the conclusion of corporatist agreements between the representatives of the main economic resources (capital and labor) so as to guarantee the social stability of economic development. It is not surprising that, in the face of the dramatic economic crisis of the 1930s and the epochal transformations induced by the Second World War, Europe reacted with a strategy of nationalization of crisis sectors which has resulted in the state (in many cases) directly controlling a considerable part of the country's economic activity.

Although it experienced similar circumstances in the 1930s and 1940s, America confirmed its regulatory strategy, thus preserving the private nature of the market. In Europe, the civil servants have taken the place of private entrepreneurs, whereas in America the latter have directed the public agencies charged with solving the problems of economic crisis and the subsequent mobilization of resources for war. In Europe, therefore, economic mercantilism was replaced during the twentieth century by the strategy of nationalization, made possible by the centralized control of fiscal resources. The state has become an economic actor per se, rather than the promoter of the institutional preconditions of a market economy. In America, on the contrary, the federal state has continued to preserve the private nature of the market, supporting it by legal rather than political intervention. Even when the federal state started to intervene noticeably in society and economy with the New Deal policies prompted by the Great Depression of the 1930s, it has systematically taken care not to replace market forces.

In sum, whereas in America the market economy has benefited from a widespread consensus, the same does not hold true in Europe. In the countries of Western Europe, the market was accepted only to the extent that it was transformed in a social market economy or a controlled economy. This explains why the European market has always combined private ownership with public ownership, and above all why the constitutions adopted after the Second World War considered the pursuit of private interests legitimate only when consistent with the public interest, as was defined by the state through its sovereign parliament (or by its high-level functionaries). Thus there have been two different paths for the construction of a market democracy, the regulatory (market-supporting) American path and the mercantilist (market-replacing) European one. The American path suited the system of separated government characterized by weak and incoherent federal public authorities. The European road instead was better adapted to centralized systems of government with strong and coherent national public authorities.

What appears interesting though is that the post-Second World War process of European integration has taken the American path.[21] The formation and development of the European common market, in fact, owes more to the judiciary than to the political authorities. The trade restrictions between the member states of the European Union (EU) have been largely dismantled by crucial decisions of the European Court of Justice, prompting the separated Community institutions to promote legislation for the creation of a single European market. Thus, the EU has come to be governed with judges as has been the case in America from the beginning.[22] Moreover, EU legislation has been of an exclusively regulatory nature, just as in America. The EU, like America, is a decentralized system with a weak central authority, with separated supranational institutions sharing decision-making powers, and with a rather limited budget. Governmental systems of this type cannot pursue mercantilist strategies of controlling the market, even if they wanted to.

4.2.3 The social responsibility of the state

Given the characteristics of the American market democracy, it was rather improbable that it would embark on the creation of a universalistic welfare system like the countries of Western Europe after the Second World War. The different historical trajectory traveled by the process of construction of American democracy inevitably contributed to produce different outcomes on the two shores of the Atlantic. Whereas in Europe democracy has had a strong statist character, one cannot claim the same for America. The historical trajectory of the European countries rested on the congruence between the state and the public interest; but in America, the public interest rather coincided with the satisfaction of the highest number of private interests.

For this reason, in America a "civil society democracy" has developed, whereas Europe is characterized by a "statist democracy."[23] Once having been consolidated, historical trajectories cannot easily be neutralized. Although the systemic pressures for the expansion of the social responsibilities of the state have been similar in America and Europe since the 1930s, they nevertheless have produced different institutional outcomes, i.e. different models of state–economy relations.[24] Although both in America and Western Europe the original civil and political citizenship rights were subsequently enlarged with social and economic rights, nevertheless such an expansion has assumed rather different characteristics and institutional forms on the two sides of the Atlantic.[25]

Of course, both in America and European countries the borders between state and society have become more fluid. The adoption of

a growing number of public policies of social and economic import
has activated informal arenas of communication and negotiation
between the representatives of functional interests, those in charge
of specific administrative agencies, and the heads of ministries or
presidential departments. Both in America and in Europe, the
growth of social and economic state intervention has served to
strengthen the executive at the expense of the legislature (in the
former, the presidency at the expense of Congress). Yet, whereas
Europe reacted to the social crisis induced by the collapse of the
market and the mobilization for war with the construction of an
universalistic and redistributive social state (starting with the British
Labour government of 1945), America has responded to the same
crisis by creating a residual and industry-based social state.[26]

Hence, whereas Keynesian Europe set itself the goal of reducing
social disparities by means of redistributive policies and the provision of universalistic social services, Keynesian America set itself
the goal of protecting specific groups, namely those excluded or
penalized by the market, but without changing the ownership
structure of the latter. Certainly, those two different outcomes are
related to the different strengths of the trade union movements, and
their allied parties, in America and in Europe.[27] But the different
strength of trade union and worker movements in America and
Europe, in turn, is the outcome of a different historical trajectory
of the construction of the market and democracy on both shores of
the Atlantic. In particular, the fact that American democracy was
established earlier than in Europe, led the American workers to
keep separated their political participation from their workplace
mobilization.[28]

Moreover, in America, as we have seen, social expenditure historically has been largely controlled by the states, which, in turn,
has hindered the emergence of a national labor movement. As
Theda Skocpol has shown in a path-breaking study, America had
disposed of a proto-welfare state by the second half of the nineteenth century, but its social programs were expressly designed to
respond to the needs of specific groups, like Civil War veterans,
their families, their wives, and their children.[29] Those programs,
obviously, were organized and implemented on the local and state
level. In America, the granting of universal male suffrage at the
beginning of the nineteenth century and the ethnic divisions within
the working class have been a considerable obstacle to the formation of a collective identity. In addition, the system of separation of

powers certainly did not facilitate the emergence of national parties representing class interests, i.e. programmatically and organization-ally cohesive parties of a social-democratic nature like the European parties that have emerged during the twentieth century.

The system of separation of powers was conducive instead to the class conflict being fought out in the courts. When a conflict is expressed by judicial means, it tends to impinge in a particularistic sense on the interests involved. In fact, given the ease of access to the courts and the latter's power of judicial review, the trade unions have ended up contesting unwelcome laws by going to court rather than by trying to gain the support of the legislators. But this, of course, has further segmented the social demands for better protec-tion. In Europe, by contrast, economic mobilization has enabled the workers to also conquer political rights. Thus, they came to democ-racy as working class and not as factions or individual workers. In addition, the relative cultural homogeneity, at the national level, of the industrial workers has favored the development of a class-iden-tity not burdened by diverse ethnic, linguistic, and religious belong-ings. Thus, in European countries the conquest of a parliamentary majority has been a necessary precondition for obtaining social protection and, in turn, better social protection has strengthened the political struggle of the workers and their parties. In European countries, the mobilization of inclusive and hierarchically struc-tured trade unions, with organic links to allied parties, has been crucial for obtaining legislation beneficial to an entire social class. In America, on the contrary, the structure of policy-making has retained its pluralistic nature, with the result of producing specific legislation for specific interest groups or specific industrial sectors.

In addition to being without the support of working class move-ments, proposals for social protection of a universalistic kind (in particular the establishment of a national health system) have found considerable obstacles in their way, above all of a cultural and insti-tutional nature. In America the universalism of social and health-care policies has had to come to terms with the racial question, or rather with the opposition (from southern states in particular) to awarding full citizenship to African-American citizens. Moreover, Congress has consistently rejected proposals for a national health system. The reason for this lies in the early mobilization of the medical class (due to the early development of modern schools of medicine) and of private insurance companies (like Blue Cross and

Blue Shield), i.e. in their ability to exert tremendous pressure on the members of Congress by means of their huge financial and electoral resources. Resistance to health-care reform in particular had become evident already during the 1930s, even if it did not manage to prevent the introduction in 1935 (because of the dramatic social climate of those years of unemployment) of two universalistic programs, namely Social Security and Old Age Survivors and Disability Insurance, the latter improving the conditions of a large part of the agricultural population, including African Americans.

Still, at the turn of the twenty-first century, America lacks a national health system and this continues to set it apart from European countries in a significant way. However, one should also keep in mind that European welfare states, in the crucial phase of the institutionalization of its universalistic programs (like national health-care systems), did not have to contend with the problems deriving from a racially divided society and a well-orchestrated mobilization of powerful interest groups. In short, in the years immediately following the Second World War, the racial homogeneity of the beneficiaries of welfare programs and the weakness of the medical schools (which had not yet seen mass enrollment) have created favorable conditions in Europe for the advocates of universalistic programs. In addition, one should also keep in mind that in America a system of public education developed more than three generations earlier than in Europe, although it segregated African Americans up until the 1960s. This system constituted a sort of functional equivalent of the European welfare states, as it aimed to enable the younger generations (in particular the children of new immigrants) to improve (though individually) their social conditions.[30]

Of course, America has long been able to cultivate its predisposition toward the market due to the exceptionally favorable circumstances in which it could develop, such as the vastness of the available territory, the abundance of resources, the absence of serious internal threats, its geo-territorial isolation, and British naval protection. Yet, as soon as this context changed, in particular during the twentieth century, it was no longer sufficient to guarantee equal opportunities to the individual without regard for the social outcomes. As Hirschman has argued, the notion of a societal interest asserts itself where and when those that lose out in individual competition do not have an exit option toward more favorable conditions.[31] At this point, they have no option but to resort to "voice," i.e. to protest, to request some form of public intervention that will rebalance what individual competition had unbalanced. The disappearance of the frontier, the development of corporate capitalism and massive industrialization ended up altering the individualistic logic of the market, which was no longer able to regulate itself (assuming it ever did). An institution external to the market had to be entrusted with the regulatory task of ensuring fair competition. The emergence of the federal and regulatory state at the end of the nineteenth century and its evolution into the New Deal state of the 1930s provided the reaction to the conflict between individual liberty and the well-being of society. Subsequently, the Second World War, with the sacrifices it claimed from the weakest strata and the minorities, steered this state in the direction of a modern welfare state.

It was the 1960s, however, that would prove to be a true turning point in the history of the American federal state. With the "war against poverty" programs advocated by Democratic President Johnson, the federal state strengthened the already existing national and universal social programs, like Medicare and Social Security, while launching specific programs tailored to the needs of specific groups, like Medicaid and Aid to Families with Dependent Children (AFDC). These programs were part of a broader politics of promoting and protecting civil rights (symbolized by the Civil Rights Act of 1965, which gave African-Americans back their dignity as citizens). Moreover, war created the conditions for an expansion of the role of the state. In fact, the war in Vietnam could not continue without broadening domestic support, in particular amongst those groups (minorities, the poor, and the younger generations) who were disproportionately paying its price in terms of human lives. Thus, during the 1960s America became more similar to Europe, even if differences remained between them.

However, the discontinuity introduced in the federal state policies was bound to activate its anti-bodies. In reaction to the fiscal problems created by the military defeat in Vietnam and the dramatic rise in oil prices caused by President Nixon's declaration of the inconvertibility of the dollar into gold, conditions were created for a tremendous mobilization of sectors of the middle classes and groups of a conservative persuasion for whom the social legislation of the previous decade had been an affront to the American tradition of the commercial republic and self-sufficiency. This social discontent, concentrated in particular in the southern and western states, was soon exploited by the religious and populist right wing of the Republican Party.

4.3   The Neoconservative Revolution

4.3.1   The populism of the middle classes

Even if the underdevelopment of the American welfare state is attributable to historical and structural causes, its post-1960s weakening is due to specific political factors, i.e. to the success of neoconservatism. In fact, since the 1970s, America has been the location of a tremendous and successful political and ideological experimentation that has given rise to what may best be defined as neoconservatism.[32] It is better to define such experimentation as neoconservative instead of conservative, because of its peculiar features. Neoconservatism managed to successfully marry two historically distinct, if not conflicting, political currents in the history of the country, namely populism and elitism. This was an extraordinarily skilful political operation, carried out by a new group of leaders and activists that started to coalesce during the presidential campaigns of the southern right-wing and four-time Alabama governor George Wallace in 1964 and 1968.

The success of Richard Nixon in 1968 and 1972 and Ronald Reagan's failed challenge to the candidacy of Gerald Ford at the Republican Convention of 1976, confirmed the pre-eminence of the traditional East Coast wing of the Republican Party, although they could not hide the growth of a more radical Republican electorate in the southern states. Indeed, a new Republican majority was emerging in reaction to the welfare (and in particular racial integration) policies introduced in the 1960s by Democratic presidents and Congresses (in continuity with the New Deal policies supported also by the Republican President Dwight Eisenhower in the 1950s).[33]

Ronald Reagan deserves credit for the idea, until then considered unnatural, to channel the new popular discontent of the south-west into the river bed of the traditional conservative elitism of the east. This was an idea that had already started to circulate in Europe, in particular with Margaret Thatcher, who became prime minister of Great Britain in 1979 (and remained so for 11 consecutive years). But it was mainly the first presidency of Ronald Reagan (1981–4), and in particular his first two years in office when he enjoyed a "honeymoon" with the still Democratic House and newly elected Republican Senate, that transformed this idea into an engaging national policy. Starting with these two years, neoconservative politics has demonstrated its ability to call into question the fundamental assumptions of the New Deal liberalism on which the postwar federal state was constructed. Neoconservatives were able to transform the two major critical interpretations of New Deal liberalism into political tools.[34]

The first interpretation ran as follows: the post-Second World War American democracy entered into crisis because it was over-burdened by demands from myriads of interest groups, themselves motivated by liberal policies, to the point that the state was reduced to an arena for bargaining and negotiating between organized inter-ests. This interpretation, as is well known, had achieved a certain international notoriety in the 1970s, as the core idea of Samuel Huntington's presentation on the "State of the United States democ-racy" to the assembly of the Trilateral Commission in 1976.[35] But although the Harvard political scientist was soon to become the advisor of Democratic President Jimmy Carter, his interpretation of the particularistic limits of liberalism would become a tremendous instrument of popular mobilization, in the hands of the new conservatives.

Historically, populism has been characterized by its hostility toward the establishment, understood in terms of narrow elitist groups concentrated in the commanding heights of the economy.[36] Due to the above interpretation, the new populism's hostility toward the establishment was instead aimed at the new public elites, under-stood as the ensemble of civil servants, representatives of functional interests and legislators responsible for the social policies of the federal state, and no longer as the traditional social and economic elites. This was no mean change because the new populist current called into question a system of public policy, rather than the eco-nomic power positions of the socially privileged, as had been the case in the past.

Hence, since the 1970s, and propelled by the outbreak of a novel and serious stagflationary crisis, this new establishment of orga-nized interests and public officials, constituting the New Deal regime, has come to be held responsible for the paralysis of national politics. Indeed, since the 1930s, American liberalism had sought to provide each interest group with the ability to organize in the public arena, in order to counterbalance the unequal distribution of resources between them in the private arena.[37] This applied in par-ticular to the interests liberalism represented, i.e. those groups with a traditionally weak position in the market, such as salaried employ-ees and the various racial and social minorities. From Franklin D. Roosevelt to Lyndon B. Johnson, the Democratic presidencies had persistently pursued the goal of stimulating and supporting the organization of disadvantaged social groups by means of federal intervention that provided financial resources, legal recognition and administrative protection. Once fully organized, it was hoped that these groups would be a counterweight to the traditionally influential groups in the system of organized interests. "Organize!" was the imperative of the post-Second World War liberalism.

By means of the organization of interests, American liberalism thus sought to construct an inclusive and effective public sphere. Public policy was conceived as a parallelogram of various forces, kept in equilibrium by opposing and counterbalancing pressures. Such a notion is anything but alien to the American political tradition according to which democracy coincides with the pluralism of organized groups.[38] Madison himself had outlined the preconditions of modern pluralism, when he argued that in a compound democracy one ambition would be counterbalanced by another ambition, or rather that an interest group would mobilize to counterbalance the requests or demands of another one. With the New Deal liberalism of the 1930s and the Great Society program of the 1960s, one might say, Madison's wish had been fulfilled. Thanks to the policies of the fight against poverty and of specific federal agencies, even the most marginalized and weakest groups had started to organize, thus putting themselves in a position to exert an influence on the decision-making process (concerning, for example, the distribution of federal resources in the large inner-cities). In short, the minorities, the poor, colored women, and the underclass of the urban ghettos had become the bearers of interests now recognized as legitimate. Their acquired organizational capacity had allowed them to obtain social programs tailored to their specific needs (such as the Aid to Families with Dependent Children).

However, interest group liberalism ended up producing a paradoxical effect. The ad hoc programs that were introduced, not having a universalistic nature (as the European welfare programs), backfired. The neoconservative critique depicted the newly included interests as those of the new insiders, i.e. as the interests of groups who enjoyed a privileged position due to their inclusion in the dominant governmental coalition. Thus the minorities and the poor, i.e. the outsiders by definition, once organized by federal functionaries or empowered by congressional committees and agencies of the presidency, came to be depicted as parasitic groups profiting from other people's work (because of the assistance they received).

This is no mean paradox, if one remembers that at the beginning of the twentieth century those same interests had formed the social basis of urban populism, which had first supported the attack of the Progressive Era on the corrupt machines of the party bosses and, subsequently, Roosevelt's attack on the institutional machines of the Republican bosses.[39] The arguments they had developed in more than half a century of struggle and mobilization were turned against them, and what's more by social strata that had traditionally proven to be impermeable to those arguments, and that, in any case, continued to benefit from public expenditures as (or more than) the groups they denounced.[40]

Being an outsider is a relational position: one does not feel an outsider in the abstract, but only in relation to someone else who is perceived to be an insider.[41] The (white) middle class had felt excluded from the Great Society programs, or rather provoked by those policies especially designed to accelerate racial integration. The fiscal crisis of the 1970s transformed such sentiments into mass-based social discontent. Yet, such discontent would have remained without political consequences had it not been mobilized by able political entrepreneurs who supplied it with a means of expression and a populist outlook, combining, particularly in the southern and western states, the aversion to taxation with a religious revival. In fact, the new populism of the middle classes, as has been argued,[42] was able to consolidate when taxes and the bible met: i.e. when the dissatisfaction with a tax burden[43] further increased by inflation and the biblical reference to a city free of parasitic bureaucrats and politicians came together in an anti-political cocktail.[44] This mixture could not but identify the Democratic Party as its main adversary, not only because it had been identified with the government since the presidential elections of 1930s, but also, and above all, because it was perceived as being the party that used the taxes levied on the middle classes to support exactly those groups (the minorities and the poor) that the new middle classes most disliked.

The new Republican majority, which had already manifested itself in the presidential elections of 1968 and 1972, definitively asserted itself in the double victory of Ronald Reagan in 1980 and 1984. The new Republican majority found its institutional stronghold in the presidency. This time, but from the opposite side of the political spectrum compared to the progressive populism of the 1910s and 1930s,[45] the president figured as the spokesperson of the outsiders. Yet Congress was perceived as the institution representing the special interests of consolidated groups of insiders. That the minorities and poor only made up a small part of the interests that "were in," was not important. Neoconservative populism had managed to turn them into the symbol of the overload from which democracy suffered and which the middle classes were forced to support through their tax liabilities.

4.3.2   The updated elitism of the neoconservatives

The second critical interpretation of liberalism used by neoconservatism was the following: due to this overload, the American postwar democracy had engendered such a diffusion of responsibility as to give rise to a full-blown crisis of public authority. Of course, the neoconservative critics were not the only ones to note that America was undergoing a crisis of authority. Already in the 1960s liberal scholars had located the causes of this crisis in the particularistic nature of Democratic politics.[46] But this critique went largely unheeded, in particular by the Democratic Party.

Neoconservatism was responsible for turning the crisis of public authority into a political issue, even though one of its leaders (Richard Nixon in 1974) was forced to abdicate from the presidency, for abuse of power, when faced with the near certainty of his impeachment by Congress. Neoconservatism succeeded in doing so by imprinting on the public discourse the equation between crisis of authority and expansion of the federal state. This was an equation of strategic relevance, because by imposing the view that the expansion of the federal state had to be considered the cause of the country's problems, neoconservatism became able to marry populism with elitism. American populism, ever since the episodes of Jackson and Bryant in the 1830s and 1890s respectively, was marked by its opposition to the strengthening of the federal state.[47] The territorial origins of populism were rural, its social basis lay in smallholdings and its ideology was characterized by Jeffersonian anti-statism with a strong anti-federalist icing. All these factors combined to make populism politically predisposed to obstruct any accumulation of power at the center because this would have engendered the development of an "oppressive bureaucracy" and increased the fiscal burden, both essential concerns for smallholders or artisans.

On the other hand, anti-statism had constituted the cultural breeding ground of traditional conservatism (with the exception of Hamilton), whose social roots lay in the business elites of the country. For these elites, state intervention inevitably represented a threat, because it primarily aimed to regulate relations between producers and consumers, on the basis of an anti-monopolistic culture whose legal foundations had been constructed already in the 1890s.[48] Big business had not easily accepted such federal intervention in the "natural" functioning of the market. Yet, this allegedly "natural" order by now was called into question by a large section of public opinion, mobilized by influential social movements. Having lost the battle for the defense of their monopoly positions, the business elites usefully retreated to a strategy of capturing the federal agencies charged with preventing the formation of undue concentrations of economic power. Yet, the success of this strategy did not mitigate their animosity toward the federal state, which was still considered their enemy.[49]

As the modern federal state could be seen as a full-blown creation of the Democratic Party, and since its public policies had ended up benefiting those social groups traditionally opposed to business, the revival of anti-statist sentiments allowed conservatism to remain faithful to its historical identity while, simultaneously, overcoming its minority status by means of an alliance with those sectors of the middle class that formed the backbone of the new populism. It is difficult to overlook a stunning paradox: elitism, which traditionally had figured as the unyielding enemy of populism, in the end was relegitimized thanks to its alliance with the latter. The economic and social elites, presenting themselves as the advocates of a general interest debased by the particularistic nature of the welfare policies, were able to become the representatives of a discontent that had been directed against them in the past. Thus, the state had become the problem and not the solution. Whereas at the beginning of the twentieth century, populism had given strength to a campaign against business corrupting politics, at the end of the twentieth century it was employed in a campaign against politics corrupting business.

On this ideological foundation neoconservatism succeeded in becoming the predominant national political movement of the 1990s. The conquest of Congress by a Republican majority in the mid-term elections of 1994 provides the evidence of its institutional and political predominance. For the first time since the end of the Second World War, the Republican Party, led by the neoconservative Newt Gingrich, came to control both chambers of the legislature. Republican predominance expressed a conservative majority equipped with a program and a coherent public philosophy. Power relations within the Republican Party came to be redefined. Newt

Gingrich represented the direct heirs of Reaganism, in an open polemic with the old Republican establishment.[50]

Under George H. W. Bush's presidency (1989–92), the elitist component of the Republican Party sought to distance itself from the populist section of the party by embracing a traditional moderately conservative model led by the enlightened and paternalistic social elites of the north-east. Bush's defeat in the 1992 presidential elections also meant the defeat of those elites and their political culture. The success of Gingrich therefore represented a victory over the traditional Republican Toryism, championed at that time by Senate majority leader Robert Dole. In short, Gingrich had managed to show that the Republican Party could only win when entering into an alliance with the white middle-class populism of the southwest, already mobilized by religious movements. Only that populism was able to provide a mass-basis for the traditional Republican elitism, albeit at the price of radicalizing the latter to the point of eliminating its traditionally moderate outlook.

The "Contract with America," i.e. the political-programmatic manifesto signed by more than 300 Republican candidates for the House of Representatives while standing on the steps of Capitol Hill on September 27, 1994, marked the transformation of the Republican Party, both on the programmatic and organizational level.[51] On the programmatic level, the "Contract with America" summarized the principles and goals that had accompanied the rise of neoconservatism. The principles were those, upheld repeatedly by Reagan, of accountability, responsibility, and opportunity. These goals in turn pointed straight to the heart of the liberal state, by proposing to drastically limit its capabilities by means of a substantial reduction of the fiscal burden and a significant downsizing of social welfare to effectively contain the role of the state within the confines of balanced budgets.

On the organizational level the "Contract" signaled the final transformation of the Republican Party into a structure connecting crucial constituencies through the use of new sophisticated electoral technologies. Its political effectiveness derived from the centralization of its congressional caucus, which linked it directly with the galaxy of religious movements (of the Christian right in particular), interest groups (like the National Rifle Association), civic associations and political action committees that had sprung up since the 1980s.[52] In the following years the party has become an extremely efficient structure for helping candidates to spread their political message and to raise funds.

Already under Reagan's leadership, the Republican Party had started to march in the direction of a cadre party, well organized, well financed, and well connected with a network of ideological, religious, and social groups. Having actively contributed to the electoral campaigns of the ex-governor of California, Newt Gingrich was both heir to and protagonist of Reaganism. It was that experience which guided him in the process of party-building, although within the constraints of American candidate-centered politics. The result was that during the 1990s, in Congress and in the House of Representatives in particular, the Democratic President Clinton was confronted with a sort of party government, supported by a congressional Republican caucus provocatively defined as "Leninist," both because of the discipline of its members and because of the vertical decision-making processes that characterized it.[53]

4.4   The Weakness of the Democrats: The Two Clinton Presidencies

The twin victory of Democratic Bill Clinton in the presidential elections of 1992 and 1996 did not threaten the neoconservative hold over the institutions of government and the country. First, the victory of 1992 owed more to the limited credibility of the incumbent president (George H. W. Bush), and the providential presence of a rather competitive third candidate (Ross Perot) who managed to split the conservative vote, than to the appeal of Democratic policies. One should not forget that Clinton won those elections with a little less than 43 percent of the popular votes. Second, the victory of 1996 owed much to an economic cycle enormously favorable to the president (and to which his policies of budget austerity certainly had contributed). Unemployment had systematically declined (from 7.1 percent in 1993 to 5.6 percent in 2000), while more than 8 million new jobs were created between 1992 and 1996. Inflation had been kept under control and disposable income had grown. The budget deficit had been eliminated. It was not surprising that Clinton's approval ratings were at very high levels (on average around 60 percent) in 1996 and remained so in the subsequent four years.

Yet, Clinton could not manage to capitalize politically on his economic successes. Indeed, he gradually came to adopt many of the neoconservative perspectives of his adversaries. Perhaps it could not have been otherwise, given that he had to confront a Republican Party that was systematically engaged in an effort to question his personal integrity. And perhaps it could not have been otherwise, after the failure of his ambitious project to establish a national health system, despite the fact that Congress had a democratic majority in 1993 and 1994 when this policy was pursued. The bankruptcy of the president's initiative to establish a national health system had (yet again) demonstrated the strength of the institutional opposition mounted by the main interest groups linked to the private health system (above all the American Medical Association [AMA], but also the private health insurance interest groups). According to figures published annually by Congress, the AMA in particular continues to be the interest group that donates most (or nearly most) to the electoral campaigns of congressional candidates. In fact, thanks to their enormous contributions to the electoral campaigns of candidates of both parties and especially those who already have or are likely to gain a seat on the congressional committees with responsibility for social policies, these groups have proven to be extraordinarily influential when it comes to blocking any reform in the direction of a universal public health-care system. This is another example of the "tyranny of the minorities," if one takes into consideration that surveys continue to show a majority of Americans is in favor of such a reform.[54]

Clinton did come to adhere to the new dominant ideology of replacing welfare with workfare, thus also stimulating a conceptual redefinition of social policies. The symbol of this redefinition was the abolition of the Aid to Families with Dependent Children (AFDC), a program with a rather limited budget specifically tailored to single mothers with children. In any case, the entire philosophy of public welfare was overhauled, in the light of the principle of individual responsibility rather than public assistance.[55] Thus having found refuge from neoconservative criticism, Clinton subsequently moved skillfully to get the Republican Congress to approve some important elements of his electoral program, such as the increase in assistance to poor children; the increase of the minimum wage; the increase of the food stamp program; increased funding for Medicaid; the introduction of the family leave program that allows parents to dedicate their time to the family for a certain period without losing their job; the approval of the Head Start bill which doubled the funding for promoting scholastic excellence in disadvantaged urban areas; the introduction of a bill that required

V-chips to be installed in new television sets thus enabling parents to control what programs can be watched by their own children; and, finally, the introduction of a bill that made possible the hiring of 100,000 new public school teachers, in addition to thousands of new police officers to be employed in the fight against urban crime.

In short, the figures show that overall social expenditure did not decline during the 1990s, even if a significant number of competences in the field of social policy were transferred from the federal government to the states (some of which, by the way, use a more universalistic system than the federal one, e.g. Wisconsin's Budget Care). In fact, in the Clinton era (1993–2000), federal expenditure on social security has oscillated between 12.2 and 12.4 percent of GDP, whereas state and local expenditures on welfare oscillated between 8.4 and 8.6 percent of GDP.[56]Considering overall social expenditure, the view of some observers that neoconservative America continues to provide a more robust social safety net than some southern European countries would not seem unfounded.

Rather, the neoconservative revolution has served to delegitimize especially those federal welfare policies aiming to alleviate poverty and reduce marginalization. Certainly, the 1990s witnessed a significant reduction of poverty. The percentage of the population living in poverty decreased from 15.1 to 11.3 percent between 1993 and 2000. But this decrease was not due to the policy of substituting welfare with workfare, but to the favorable economic conditions of that decade (which in turn were certainly related to the balanced budget policies of the Clinton presidencies). And yet, many of the newly created jobs were not able to free the previous welfare recipients from the threat of poverty. According to several estimates, in 2000 14 million Americans earned less than 50 percent of the poverty line, whereas 24 million earned less than 150 percent of the poverty line.[57] With the economic downturn during the following presidencies of George W. Bush (due also to his policies of radical tax cuts and increased expenditure), poverty has again started to grow dramatically (notwithstanding the workfare programs launched in the previous decade).

In fact, according to data from the US Census Bureau, the percentage of the population living in poverty went from 11.7 percent of the population in 2001 to 12.5 percent in 2003 (corresponding to 35.9 million citizens), 12.6 percent in 2005, and 12.3 percent the following year.[58] This corresponds to 36.5 million citizens living in poverty (5 million more than six years before, when the first neo-conservative presidency of George W. Bush was inaugurated), of which 13 million are children and youth below 18 years of age. Accordingly more than 17 percent of children live in poverty. More-over, the number of uninsured children under 18 (which dropped steadily from 1999 to 2004 thanks to an expansion in coverage of low-income children under two programs operated jointly by the federal and state governments, Medicaid and the State Children's Health Insurance Program) has started to increase again in 2005 and 2006, to reach 8.6 million in the latter year. A bipartisan bill approved by Congress in 2007, to authorize and expand the expiring State Children's Health Insurance Program, was vetoed by George W. Bush in October of the same year because, as the House Republican leader John Boehner stated, "it envisions a government-run health care system."

It needs to be said that none of the social policy measures adopted during the 1990s made any inroads on one of the most disturbing aspects of the American social security system. In 2000, 43.6 million citizens were without access to health care, notwithstanding the economic growth of the 1990s. During the presidencies of George W. Bush the number of citizens without medical insurance has increased. According to the data of the US Census Bureau , between 2001 and 2003 over 1.4 million citizens joined the ranks of those without medical insurance (a total of 45 million, equal to 15.6 percent of the population), even if 1 million joined the ranks of insured citizens (bringing them to the record number of 243.3 million individuals).[59] In 2006, the number of uninsured Americans increased by 2.2 million, arriving at 47 million from the 45 million of 2003 (and 44.8 million of 2005). It is worth noticing that the citizens without medical insurance are not always the same individuals, but are frequently those who have been made redundant and are looking for work in that period, making it difficult to mobilize them electorally or politically because their composition is continually changing.

In sum, there is no doubt that America, at least since the 1980s, has come under a neoconservative hegemony, needless to say the victory of neoconservatism has also been due to the Democrats' difficulty in proposing a feasible alternative. For all of this period, Democratic politics has not been able to go beyond the perspective of interest group liberalism. It is a fact, though, that neoconserva-tism has managed to make the criticism of the federal government coincide with the criticism of Democratic politicians (and bureau-crats), thus pointing the new populism toward anti-politics.

4.5   The Anti-politics of the Elites: Term Limits and Recall

The most characteristic objectives of the anti-politics of neoconservatism were those of congressional term limits and recall, both developed to constrain or dismiss incumbent politicians. Already in the making in neoconservative circles during the 1980s, term limits became a central issue in the following decade; so much so that in the "Contract with America" the Republican candidates committed to transforming this proposal into a constitutional amendment. Term limits have become a highly popular proposal with a pronounced capacity for mobilization. The support mobilized in favor of term limits was subsequently transferred to rather less popular proposals, though ones which still displayed a clear anti-political content. The political success of the neoconservatives has been due especially to their capacity to promote the symbolic intersection of the issues they raised.

The movement for the introduction of term limits manifested itself for the first time in 1990:[60] Primarily in Colorado where a referendum approved the introduction of term limits in both the federal and state legislature; and subsequently in California and Oklahoma where, again in popular referenda, two resolutions were passed that limited the number of terms a candidate could serve in the legislatures of the respective states. In 1992 California, this time in contrast to Oklahoma, also extended the term limits to the federal legislature, and in this it was joined by an additional 13 states that approved similar limits. With the exception of North Dakota, these states also simultaneously approved term limits for the respective state legislatures.

The proposals to limit the number of legislative terms have had two specific characteristics. First, none of them was retroactive, so that the only legislators affected were those elected after the passing of the constitutional amendment or the regular bill. Second, in most cases the constraint on the number of terms was soft and to be understood in relation to a certain number of years (e.g. six out of eight years), so as to permit a second candidacy after a withdrawal period, generally a full term, from the institution to which the candidate subsequently aimed to return.

Inevitably, such proposals solicited a reaction from the courts. Both the state supreme courts as well as the federal Supreme Court have had to intervene. The latter did so with the decision in the *US*

Term Limits Inc. v. Thornton case of 1995, in which it ruled unconstitutional, i.e. void, federal term limits introduced by state legislation. Only Congress, the Supreme Court maintained, may pass legislation concerning its own internal functioning. In addition, the constitutionality of legislative term limits has been the subject of a heated legal and political debate. According to some, term limits may be introduced by means of regular legislation, whereas others (the majority) hold that this can be done only by means of a constitutional amendment. The decisions of the supreme courts of Massachusetts, Oregon, and Washington, concerning state-level term limits, have swung the balance toward the latter. Those courts, in fact, established that state-level term limits were a constitutional matter and thus could not be introduced by state legislatures. As a result, the legislatures of Idaho and Utah voluntarily repealed, in 2002 and 2003 respectively, a bill on term limits that they had previously passed, in the face of the threat of annulment by the respective state supreme courts. In any case, the outcome is that, in 2006 (see table 4.2), no less than 15 states (14 by means of constitutional amendments and one by regular bills) provide for one form or another of legislative term limits.

During the 1990s, the movement that has supported the introduction of legislative term limits also took up the issue of the recall of incumbent elected representatives before the expiration of their mandate, should they no longer enjoy the support that had allowed them be elected. The most spectacular case has been the recall of the incumbent governor of California in 2004. Dissatisfied with his budget policies, the voters had collected a sufficient number of signatures to call a new election, even though the governor had only served half of his term. The governor was defeated, in good measure because of the particularly punishing procedure adopted. In fact, the incumbent governor could neutralize the recall only with an absolute majority of the ballots cast, whereas (as was the case) his opponent could be elected with a simple majority or plurality. Even if some states, like North Dakota and Oregon, explicitly stipulate that the recall may not be applied to members of the federal Congress, this obviously holds true also for the recall legislation adopted by the other states (see table 4.3), for the reasons that the federal Supreme Court has set out in its decision of 1995, namely that the states may not legislate on the functioning of the federal Congress.

With the introduction of term limits and recall the policies of the incumbent politicians have come to be tightly controlled by the

Table 4.2 Legislative term limits, February 2006

State	House (years)	Senate (years)	As of
Arizona (C)	8/10	8/10	1.1.1993
Arkansas (C)	6	8	1.1.1993
California (C)	6	8	
Colorado (C)	8/10	8/12	1.3.1991
Florida (C)	8/12	8/12	11.3.1992
Louisiana (C)	12/16	12/16	11.23.1995
Maine (S)	8/10	8/10	1.1.1995
Michigan (C)	6	8	12.19.1992
Missouri (C)	8	8	1.1.1993
Montana (C)	8	8	1.1.1993
Nebraska (C)	8/12	8/12	
Nevada (C)	12	12	1995
Ohio (C)	8/10	8/12	1.1.1993
Oklahoma (C)	12	12	1.1.1991
South Dakota (C)	8/10	8/10	1.1.1993

A single figure indicates the temporal limit: a person cannot hold a legislative mandate for a number of years in excess of the one indicated. Two figures (e.g. 6/8) indicate that a person cannot hold a legislative mandate for more than six years during a period of eight years; thus if the duration of a mandate is two years then that person cannot serve more than three consecutive terms. (C) or (S) indicates whether the term limit was introduced by means of an amendment to the state Constitution (C) or by Statute (S).
Source: National Conference of State Legislatures, at www.ncsl.org

voters, or rather by those groups most able to mobilize for the purpose of influencing public decisions. Anti-politics has turned into the suspension of politics, due to an inability to take decisions for the longer term and, even more so, to take unpopular decisions (concerning taxation in particular). At the same time, anti-politics has also revealed its ambiguity. In fact, in the states that have passed such bills or constitutional amendments, incumbent congressmen have continued to be confirmed in office with very high percentages. Thus, anti-politics was mobilized by some groups only when politics heeded the interests of other groups.

Certainly, both the term limits and the recall have been presented as proposals designed to open the representative institutions to the people. After all, it was argued, if the representatives and senators can serve for only a limited number of years, then an increased competition for the seats will result (in addition to a reduction of

Table 4.3 State recall provisions for statewide and legislative officers, March 2006

State	Who can be recalled
Alaska	All but judicial officers
Arizona	All
California	All
Colorado	All
Georgia	All
Idaho	All but judicial officers
Kansas	All but judicial officers
Louisiana	All but judicial officers
Michigan	All but judicial officers
Minnesota	State executive officers, legislators, judicial officers
Montana	All
Nevada	All
New Jersey	All
North Dakota	All but US Congress
Oregon	All but US Congress
Rhode Island	Governor, Lt Governor, Secretary of State, Treasurer, Attorney General
Washington	All but judicial officers
Wisconsin	All

The District of Columbia also provides for recalls. Virginia is not listed amongst the recall states because it permits a recall only by means of trial rather than by a new election. In 36 states recall elections may only be held in local jurisdictions.

Source: Adapted from National Conference of State Legislatures, March 21, 2006, at www.ncsl.org/programs/legman/elect/recallprovision.htm

the privileged status these members have enjoyed hitherto). A more competitive Congress or state legislature, in turn, has an incentive to be more responsive to the needs of the citizens. On the other hand, during the twentieth century, the dissatisfaction of the citizens with politics had always targeted the legislature.

At the federal level, Congress had become, almost by definition, the scapegoat for bad policies. The presidency, thanks to the process of democratization of both the system for the selection of the presidential candidates as well as the elections for the Electoral College of the various states, had appeared more easily accessible to the voters (and thus more easily influenced by them). It is no coincidence that the movements that demanded a change in public policy had turned to the president. Congress, instead, because of the rigid institutionalization it had witnessed during the same period, appeared more impenetrable to changes in public opinion.[61] On the other hand, there is not a single opinion poll that does not reveal, or did not do so in the past, a permanent distrust by the voters of the members of the legislature, and Congress in particular[62] (see table 4.4).

Yet, as had already happened in the case of early twentieth-century populism, this time a movement for democratization has turned into its opposite.[63] After all, the term limits proposal was based on the conviction that incumbency was the reflection of a low responsiveness of the members of (state and federal) legislatures with respect to their voters, whereas in reality exactly the opposite was true. One might argue that legislative elections have become less closely fought in the last 30 years, not because legislators lack responsiveness, but quite the opposite: the members of the legislatures have been confirmed (in Washington DC as well as in the state capitals) with very high percentages precisely because of their individual responsiveness to the requests made by the voters of their

Table 4.4   Confidence in institutions, as at June 2006

Institutions	A great deal	Quite a lot
Military	41	32
Police	25	33
Church or organized religion	28	24
Banks	18	31
US Supreme Court	14	26
Medical system	14	24
Public schools	15	22
The presidency	15	18
Television news	12	19
Newspapers	12	18
Criminal justice system	9	16
Organized labor	9	15
Congress	5	14
Big business	6	12
Health maintenance organizations	6	9

Source: Gallup Poll, June 2006, at www.galluppoll.com/content/default. aspx?ci=1597

constituency, so much so that each representative or senator has become a sort of *ombudsman*, i.e. a public servant charged with addressing the complaints of individual citizens with respect to the gigantic federal or state bureaucracy.

As such, the members of Congress, notwithstanding the neoconservative revolution, have continued to practice constituency services, that is they have continued to focus on their capacity to provide help to the individual voters in their dealing with public bureaucracies. One might say that incumbency is the outcome of very responsive legislators but a not very responsible legislature; a legislature that is able to solve the problems of the single voters or communities of interest, but frequently unable to provide an answer to the general problems of the country. This is one of the reasons why the voters despise legislative institutions (starting with Congress), but appreciate their members as their individual representatives. Given that the introduction of term limits and recall did not affect incumbency, the result of the populism of the late twentieth century has been a delegitimization of politics, rather than the opposite.

In sum, in America, cyclical populist movements of social discontent have traditionally targeted positions of economic power, thereby weakening the exclusive structure of the dominant elites by prompting a turnover of individuals and a social broadening of their membership. Since the 1980s this discontent targeted the holders of public office, politicians and bureaucrats, leaving unaltered the remainder of the exclusive structure of the dominant economic elites. The tax revolt has turned out to be a tremendous opportunity to bolster the economic positions of the wealthy and wealthiest strata and has accordingly weakened the poorest.

According to data published by the Congressional Budget Office, between 1979 and 2004 the average after-tax income of the richest quintile of the population went from 42.4 to 50 percent of the overall income of the country, whereas for the poorest quintile it went from 6.8 to 4.9 percent.[64] The corresponding figures for the intermediate quintile are 16.5 (in 1979) and 15 percent (in 2004). Moreover, the richest 1 percent of the country went from earning 7.5 percent of overall income in 1979 to earning 14 percent in 2004. Although this anti-egalitarian tendency in income distribution started at the beginning of the 1980s, the data also show that it was further strengthened by the tax cuts introduced (through EGTRRA, JCWA and JGTRRA fiscal laws[65]) by the presidency of George W. Bush and the Republican Congress between 2001 and 2004.[66] One might argue that, in reality, the revolt of the white middle classes,[67] by delegitimizing politics, has ended up turning against them. The absolute beneficiaries of that revolt have been the wealthiest people of the country who increasingly pay less tax whereas the middle classes continue to pay more.

4.6 The Social Implications of American Liberalism

There is no doubt that America is an inegalitarian democracy. It certainly has provided a particularly hospitable environment for the wealthy, yet America is something else than a mere democracy for the rich. America is a market democracy, rather than a social democracy, as the majority of Western European countries are. Of course, these democracies are also embedded in a market economy, but in none of them does the logic of competition inform the functioning of the entire social system as in America. Hence, these American disparities should be acknowledged, but to be understood they must be placed in the structural and cultural context that characterizes the country.

The cultural context of American inequality is unequivocal. Historically, America is concerned with the liberal citizen, or rather with equality of the points of departure, rather than with the social citizen and the equality of outcomes. Furthermore, America was the first country in the world to have institutionalized liberal citizenship. Liberal, in this context, means that the form of citizenship is based on the recognition of civil and political rights, before (if not, instead of) social or economic rights. This liberal citizenship was not extended universally. Rather, from the outset the new republic was burdened by two vices, namely the exclusion of African-Americans from citizenship and the subjection of women. Whereas African-Americans were not allowed to become citizens because they were considered inferior to white men,[68] women for a long time were not able to enjoy citizenship because they were seen to be better suited to performing private rather than public duties.

Nevertheless, even with these limitations, at the end of the eighteenth century, America inaugurated the era of individual liberty, understood as a precondition of social cohesion. Whereas the Europe of the *ancien régime* maintained that social cohesion was the outcome of coercion, of authority imposed from above, and of the traditional social hierarchies, the new republic in America instead practiced the idea that social cohesion resulted from the choice of individuals, or rather from the covenant between them (and the states in which they operated). The "We the People" with which the Preamble to the Constitution of 1787 opens, and with which the citizens of the various states conclude the fundamental pact which gave birth to the new republic is a plural (We) and not a singular (as in the European tradition, where *popolo, peuple,* or *volk* are always reified as a single and unitary subject).

In the absence of the state, it fell to the individual citizens to promote and support government, understood as self-government, on the various societal levels. This is one of the reasons why American individualism has generally been a social individualism,[69] on which the liberalism of that country was able to build its progressive narrative.[70] This, instead, did not come to pass in Europe, where individualism, when it asserted itself, acquired an anti-statist and anti-social connotation (and thus tendentially anti-progressive). Whereas in Europe individuals were able to assert themselves only in opposition to the state, in America there was no central authority to oppose and individuals were able to assert themselves by building the states (and thus the federal state). Liberal America finds its foremost expression in the first ten amendments to the Constitution (the Bill of Rights). Indeed, they embody the liberal mission of the country. With the Bill of Rights, civil liberties, for the first time in history, acquired constitutional dignity.

By awarding these rights constitutional rank the individual citizens have found refuge from arbitrariness and coercion, or rather have gained a tool for resisting coercion and arbitrariness. By means of those ten amendments, America has become the land of individual liberty, the reference point (and not only in abstract terms) for all those in the world who suffer because of the absence of liberty. America has become the republic of the sovereignty of the individual; a republic watchfully presided over by the Supreme Court. Yet, although these individual rights are a necessary bulwark against each attempt to curtail liberty, nevertheless their juridical formulation in the ten amendments has constrained the provision of public goods (for example, the second amendment to the Constitution hinders the prohibition of the use of private firearms). Alternatively, by turning them into an ideology they have come to hinder a more equal distribution of wealth. In short, the meaning of social individualism changes with the historical context.

Also the structural context of American inequality is unequivocal. The American market is not unregulated, but exactly the opposite. However, it is regulated for a purpose different from that adopted by Western European countries. Historically, America has regulated the market in order to protect the consumer instead of the worker. And the consumer has been protected by means of competition. Here, a sort of institutional symbiosis between the market and democracy emerged, as both are guided by the principle of competition; between the institutions of government or private companies respectively. The American market democracy sets itself the goal of preventing monopoly positions, in the economic and the political sphere, a goal pursued by means of creating obstacles to the concentration of power.

Such a strategy inevitably had to produce disparities but those were considered acceptable because they were the outcome of a process of free and fair competition. The neoconservative revolution has managed very successfully to focus this goal exclusively on the political sphere, and no longer also on the economy as was the case in the past. This has made it possible to dismantle many of the social policies introduced by the Democrats between the 1930s and 1960s, by reducing the fiscal revenues at the disposal of the federal state and by calling into question their social legitimacy.

Thus, a market democracy, which had already acquired the vice of inequality, has become even more insensitive on this issue with the victory of neoconservatism, to the extent of significantly reducing the integrative capacity of the country's market democracy. As has been written, at present "mobility is declining in American society (fewer individuals manage to improve their own economic position over time, irrespective of the economic cycle); the economic position of the children is more than ever highly correlated with that of the parents . . . the apple does not fall far from the tree even in the country of opportunity."[71] This is a momentous change in a country that has always justified its disparities with reference to its dynamism and the fluid nature of its societal hierarchies, as well as with its capacity to integrate countless generations of immigrants from all over the world, providing them with an opportunity for economic advancement as no other country has ever done. Between 1991 and 2005 more than 13,983 million legal immigrants (plus a considerable number of illegal ones) entered America, implying an average annual rate of immigration of 3.4 per 1,000 inhabitants.[72] Recent social developments, however, would seem to challenge the integrative capacity of the American market democracy. How will America react to this challenge?

4.7 Conclusion

For the moment, I will limit myself to pointing out that, although America, for cultural and structural reasons, did not resolve to create a universalistic welfare state, it should not be mistaken for a Darwinian society in which only the fittest survive. For all its social individualism, America is also the country of the mobilization and organization of civil society. American civil society has been and continues to be rather more diversified and engaged than any other western civil society. Even though the number of those who go "bowling alone"[73] has increased, the number of national associations with civic and social purposes has also increased. As the data show, the total number of national non-profit associations has increased from 6,000 in 1960 to 22,449 in 2001.[74] This means that millions and millions of people are engaged in activities of social assistance that in European countries are generally administered by civil servants and official welfare agencies.

No other democratic country has a comparable associational culture to the American one. The void between the state and the market that frequently can (or could) be found in European countries is non-existent in America. Many social, educational, and medical services are directly run by groups of citizens, like immigrant associations, religious movements, cooperatives, or mutual aid societies. The widespread associational culture continues to form one of the backbones of democratic American self-government. It still holds true today what Bryce wrote at the end of the nineteenth century (taking up de Tocqueville's reflections of the 1830s), namely that in America "associations are created, extended, and worked ... more quickly and affectively than in any other country."[75] In short, although American liberalism has acquired the vice of inequality, it has still maintained the virtue of self-government.

5

An Imperial Democracy?

5.1 Introduction

Foreign policy continues to be the main target of criticism of (not only) the European observers of America. Whereas that criticism had died down immediately after 9/11, with the attack on Afghanistan in 2002 and the occupation of Iraq in 2003 it has resumed with an unprecedented vigor (at least since the Vietnam War of the 1960s). On the other hand, the unilateral decision of President George W. Bush to invade Iraq without the authorization of the Security Council of the United Nations provoked a forceful resumption of European distrust of America and hostility toward the latter's use (or abuse) of its military might.

For some observers, "the war unleashed after 9/11 against the Afghan government has . . . sanctioned the unquestionable right of the planetary policeman to punish those guilty of hostile and unwelcome attitudes,"[1] or: "the attack on Iraq is an operation of imperial imprint."[2] This opinion is shared by many other observers, who have argued with respect to the war on Iraq, that "what we are confronted with is an implicit but substantial declaration of war on the whole world, and of which the whole world is invited to take note."[3] This act of war allegedly aims to build a particular global empire. In fact, it is argued, "the empire the Americans have in mind should have a clearly 'totalitarian' character. It should not limit itself to political control from above . . . but rather be based on the uniformity of economic and social views."[4]

In sum, America wants to "create an empire which – sustained by their overwhelming military superiority – extends to the entire international society, and from which no one can even hope to escape."[5] According to the former French President of the EU Commission, Jacques Delors, "The US tries to transform the world into a spitting image of itself, the Bible in one hand and the revolver in the other." The German leader of the conservative CDU/CSU Wolfgang Schaeuble warned "against a dominance of the US in international politics."[6] Peter Gauweiler of the Bavarian CSU declared that "we must make it clear to the Americans . . . that they cannot exterminate other cultural aspirations on this planet . . . as they did with Apaches and Sioux."[7] A whole issue of *Der Spiegel*[8] was dedicated to the question: "Will America become democratic again?" As the German philosopher Peter Sloterdijk argued, at the beginning of the twenty-first century, there are "two rogue states . . . the US and Israel, which refuse any type of alignment with the international community due to their self-conception."[9] In other words, "the whole world must fear a superpower/empire with a missionary drive."[10] It is necessary, therefore, that "this US neo-imperialism should be countered by . . . a European neo-neutralism."[11]

Is this European criticism addressed mainly to the unilateral foreign policy of the George W. Bush presidency? It does not seem so. As it was argued in *Die Zeit*, the George W. Bush presidency is in continuity with American post-Second World War foreign policy: "those who are not for us are against us, used to say the Cold Warrior John Foster Dulles, and G. W. Bush is saying the same thing today."[12] For the European critics, continuity exists between the post-9/11 unilateralism and the strategies pursued previously by America. Some even hold that unilateralism is the result of the American isolationist tradition, in the sense that "isolationism has proven to contain, as its essential core, unilateralism, at its turn based on 'exceptionalism.' "[13] Or better, "at the centre of American international behaviour stands the conviction that the country, being altogether different from the other countries in this world, has the right, or even the duty, to act only in accordance with its 'vocation.' " Thus, with the presidencies of George W. Bush (2001–8), isolationism has shown its militarist and interventionist face, but this face has been a part of America's view of the world ever since the nineteenth century. The presidencies of George W. Bush, so to speak, have represented the autobiography of a nation, making clear what America has been all along.

One may say that there are two constants in the criticisms from all the European political quarters. The first concerns the interpretation of America as an imperial power by design. American imperialism is considered the thread that runs through the entire history of the country; it is the ultimate expression of its inherent need for superiority over other countries. The second constant concerns the interpretation of the post-9/11 unilateralism, which follows the tradition of the imperialist nature of the country. Is this really so? Here, I will proceed as follows. First, I will review the relationship between foreign and domestic policy in the American democracy. Second, I will discuss the foreign policy America has pursued after 1945 in the bipolar international context of the Cold War. Third, I will analyze the post-Cold War transition, i.e. the foreign policy of the 1990s. Finally, I will consider the implications of the terrorist attacks of September 11, 2001 and the "Bush doctrine" that was designed to address these changes.

5.2 Foreign and Domestic Policy in America

More than in other democracies, in America there is a very close relationship between foreign policy and domestic politics. It is not very plausible to maintain that foreign policy is a mere reflection of domestic politics. Yet, it is equally implausible to claim the opposite. America in particular has witnessed a constant tension between both sides, which at times has given rise to reciprocal support and at times to dramatic crises.[14] Even though it developed in especially favorable geographical and environmental conditions, American democracy has never managed to escape the imperatives of foreign policy.[15] From the start, the young republic had to confront the problem of how to protect its domestic development from the external pressures of the major European powers. America was born in a liberation struggle against the major European power of the eighteenth century, Great Britain; a colonial power which, although defeated, continued to harbor considerable territorial interests on the North American continent, just as the other big European powers, foremost France and Spain, continued to entertain expansive ambitions in the same region. In such a context, America had to pursue a foreign policy able to exploit the rivalries between the European powers to safeguard the possibilities of its own economic and territorial growth.

The so-called isolationism of the nineteenth century corresponded to a systemic requirement, namely to give priority to the accumulation and growth of domestic resources, in the case of a country whose territory was continuously expanding. In fact, America's desire to distance itself from the power struggle between the European powers went hand in hand with a strongly expansionist approach in the western hemisphere. The country engaged in a permanent war against the Indian tribes to evict them from their territories; a war that led to genocide in some cases. Above all, America adopted the so-called "Monroe doctrine," expounded by President James Monroe in 1823, which stipulated not only the need to free the western hemisphere from the presence of European powers, but also the right of America to control the political developments in both the north and the south of the American continent. This "doctrine" has served to justify recurrent American military interventions on the continent, including the war against Mexico of 1845–8 in which America acquired vast territories at the border with this country.

Yet the industrial development of post-Civil War capitalism served to push America beyond the borders of its continent. Since the end of the nineteenth century, American troops have been deployed much further from home. They defeated the Spaniards in Cuba and the Philippines, and were deployed in the Pacific Ocean in order to enforce the "open door policy," i.e. the opening up of Asian markets to American products. However, the American continent (and in particular Central and South America) remained the strategic region of interventionism. Not even the intervention in the First World War brought about a change of perspective. Congress' rejection of President Woodrow Wilson's proposal to join the League of Nations took the country back to its America-centered perspective, if only for a brief period. In actual fact, this perspective would change radically with the intervention in the Second World War, and with the legacy of that war: the formation of a bipolar international system based on the confrontation between the American and Soviet nuclear superpowers.

Although isolationism should not be confused with the absence of foreign interventions, it can hardly be interpreted as a form of unilateralism *avant la lettre*. America was rather concerned with the protection of its internal development and with expanding its sphere of economic influence, without changing the decentralized structure of its own institutional system.[16] It continued to be governed by Congress and its committees, for all of the nineteenth century. As the representative of state and local interests, Congress eyed the creation of a federal military apparatus with extreme suspicion, for fear of excessive taxation among other reasons. As a result, this apparatus remained rather feeble for all of the century, being composed for the most part of voluntary militias and the reserve, i.e. persons destined to return to civilian life after demobilization. The federal Congress was so concerned with retaining control of defense policy that it even claimed the right to appoint high-ranking officers of the armed forces during the Civil War, notwithstanding that it had to face the leadership of a president like Abraham Lincoln. One needs to await the Second World War to witness the formation of a permanent military establishment, directed by the president (in his capacity of commander in chief), yet still under the control of the powerful congressional committees on armed services and foreign affairs.[17]

Hence, "politically the first 140 years or so of American independence were not a quiet time in American foreign relations. Virtually every presidential administration from Washington's to Wilson's sent American forces abroad or faced one or more war crises with a great European power . . . American fighting forces were found in every ocean and on every continent during this time of isolation and innocence."[18] Nevertheless, such wars fitted in the traditional mold of conflicts, procured or not, by a young power anxious to protect its own growth from the more consolidated European powers. In any case, during this period America never managed to call into question the strategic (naval) supremacy of Great Britain, but rather benefited from British maritime protection to promote its own seaborne trade. For all of the nineteenth century, therefore, the fundamental relations between domestic politics and foreign policy remained much the same as they had been since the foundation of the republic. America, as the result of a particular geographic location, had chosen to develop a modern civil society without the support of a modern federal state. Even if the constitutional design of the founding fathers had repeatedly been challenged, in the area of foreign policy, by incumbent presidents (from Washington onward) who had sought to expand the limits of their constitutional prerogatives, these challenges had encountered an insurmountable hurdle in the peripheral location America had chosen for itself in the system of international relations. Not even the First World War managed to take that hurdle even though it had revealed the economic strength and international influence the country could have.

In the end, the crisis of the 1930s and the Second World War, with its outcome of an armed peace between the two major allies of the anti-Nazi coalition, were responsible for radically changing the relationship between domestic and foreign policy. The dual emergency of the economic crisis and the war ushered in a nationalization of American politics i.e. an expansion of the federal government and in particular of the presidency.[19] Immediately after this, the military confrontation with the Soviet Union (symbolized by the Korean War) had provided an additional impetus for a strengthening of the decision-making powers of the president in the field of foreign policy. "Presidential imperialism" in foreign policy was the outcome of that strengthening, to the extent that it constitutes an institutional development brought about by external factors, which the various presidents promoted irrespective of their party affiliation, their leadership style, or their ideological leanings. In short, this institutional development was the result of the political elite's decision to equip the country with the decision-making resources necessary in order to play the role of a major actor on the international system (a view outlined in the well-known report, *National Security Council 68*, written during the first months of 1950).

From the Second World War until the military defeat in Vietnam at the beginning of the 1970s, the internationalism of American foreign policy went hand in hand with a redefinition of the institutional equilibria of the system of government. The elements of this redefinition were spelled out by Wildavsky.[20] The new internationalism of the country gave rise to the institutionalization of two different decision-making regimes (or two informal "Pillars," to use EU's language) within the system of government; one regime related to foreign policy and another one for domestic policies. One might say that postwar America witnessed the existence of two presidencies: each regime being distinctive in terms of the characteristics of the political arena in which its actors operated, the configuration of political forces, and the means through which presidential supremacy was asserted. Why did this happen?

For two main reasons, according to Wildavsky: first of all, because of the geo-political competition with the Soviet Union, which had caused a dramatic expansion of the international responsibilities of the country, to the extent that foreign policy concerns had come to dominate the presidential agenda. Thus in little over ten years, the institutions of foreign policy (from the armed forces to the diplomatic corps, international alliance systems, and intelligence services) were established that would strengthen the decision-making capacity of the presidency (and in particular of the "personal president"), with respect to Congress, in this policy field.[21] Second, because of the bipartisan character that foreign policy had come to acquire with the presidencies of Truman and Eisenhower, which in turn was due to the solid internationalist consensus existing within the political (and economic) elites of the country. This consensus was reflected in a relation of trust between Congress and the president. Moreover, the relatively centralized organization of the legislature permitted the president (and his staff) to keep it constantly informed by involving its leaders in strategic presidential decisions. Yet, this twin decision-making regime did not alter the constitutional structure that continued to create incentives for the president and Congress to struggle for the control of foreign policy.[22]

With the model of the two presidencies Wildavsky pointed to the existence of a double cleavage in national politics that did not coincide with the division between the two main political parties: to the division between liberals and conservatives in domestic politics corresponded a spurious trans-party division between (a large majority of) internationalists and (a small minority of) isolationists in foreign policy. This double and non-coinciding division had produced different ways in which the presidential supremacy was asserted: more contested in domestic policy than in foreign policy. In a 1989 article with Oldfield, Wildavsky himself subjects this model to criticism. Its main defect was held to be to have mistaken a contingent pattern for a constant of policy-making.[23] Indeed, in the latter days of the Lyndon B. Johnson presidency (1965–8),[24] both the elite consensus and the strength of the internationalist coalition visibly started to crack. Indeed, it subsequently collapsed under the blows of the military defeat in Vietnam. The breakdown of consensus would provoke a renewed salience of Congress on matters of foreign policy, also by means of integrating into the latter policy-making process groups hitherto found on its margins.[25] The effect was to make the assertion of presidential supremacy in foreign policy less straightforward.[26]

Nevertheless, the first argument made by Wildavsky has proven to be of continued validity. Certainly, after Vietnam and until the end of the Cold War, no president was able to claim foreign policy as an arena for technical problem-solving, unlike Truman, Eisenhower, Kennedy, and Johnson who had used it to shield themselves from the pressures of the pluralistic process. But, of course, the end of bipartisanship in foreign policy in the two decades of political discontent following 1968 and the subsequent emergence of a partisan cleavage corresponding to the division in domestic politics did not amount to the end of the presidential supremacy in international affairs. In sum, the equalization of the foreign policy conditions to those of domestic public policies has not prevented the post-Vietnam presidents from asserting decision-making supremacy, albeit in a different way (e.g. by seeking more frequently the rhetorical support of public opinion, rather than the consensual support of the establishment) than their postwar predecessors. However, there can be no doubt that the 1970s witnessed a vertical crisis of the so-called "imperial presidency," i.e. of the specific decision-making regime that had come to be institutionalized in the field of foreign policy after the Second World War.[27] Is it plausible to argue that the "imperial presidency" (imperial in its relations with Congress and the other institutions of separated government) corresponded with "an imperial foreign policy"? What foreign policy strategy did America pursue during the long period of the Cold War?

5.3   Hegemonic America and the Cold War

Even though the Second World War ended without a proper peace treaty, no other war has given rise to such an institutionalized international system; a system which becomes even more institutionalized with the outbreak of the Cold War in 1947, and in the wake of the confrontation in Korea between the two main victors of the war against Nazism. America, in particular, has promoted one of the most radical transformations of the international order ever recorded in history. In fact, it helped to bring into existence a dual international order, a highly militarized order (concerning the relations between the two super powers), and a highly institutionalized order (concerning the relations between the western nations, including Japan).

As Ikenberry has convincingly argued, those two aspects of the international order were strongly interrelated.[28] The more the military standoff between America and the Soviet Union intensified, the more the process of the institutionalization of the alliance between the western countries plus Japan deepened. Whereas the highly militarized international order had been justified by the theory of containment of the power of the Soviet Union (as was set out in the "long telegram" cabled by George Kennan from Moscow in 1946),[29] the highly institutionalized international order was justified with reference to the theory of multilateral cooperation with the industrial democracies of the West and Japan (a theory with a clear Wilsonian imprint). One might say that the confrontation with the Soviet Union was a traditional confrontation between superpowers engaged in preserving their respective spheres of influence and preventing the expansion of the sphere of influence of their adversary. On the contrary, the multilateral cooperation between the western countries and Japan represented a true novelty in the international system.

The confrontation with the Soviet Union was traditional in the sense that it was based on an updated vision of the balance of power. The crucial difference, with respect to previous confrontations between great powers, lay in the resources (of power and legitimacy) employed in support of the reciprocal competition, namely the recourse to the nuclear threat and the use of political ideology. America and the Soviet Union confronted each other as advocates of alternative models of society, i.e. in the name of the universalistic and thus mutually incompatible democratic and communist ideologies. Those ideologies would likely have ushered in a "hot" war had they not been constrained by the reciprocal nuclear threat. The balance of nuclear terror thus promoted the relative stability of the international bipolar system. This international order, in short, was made possible by scientists, was guaranteed by soldiers and was legitimated by ideology. It is the other international order, instead, that reveals the radical innovation introduced by America in the system of relations between the states of (mainly) the western area. This new international order was made possible by the political and economic elites that had been formed under Franklin D. Roosevelt's New Deal and emerged during the post-Second World War debate.

There are no historical precedents for the winning side in a war deciding not to humiliate (economically and politically) the defeated powers. And yet this is what America did between 1944 and 1951. Within the framework of the United Nations (UN), founded in 1945, America moved, first of all, to create international institutions designed to promote economic stability and trade, as well as to regulate financial and monetary transactions. The Bretton Woods Conference of 1944 already outlined the main institutions that were to promote and manage the new international economic order, such as: the International Monetary Fund (IMF), founded in 1945 and operative since 1947, with the task of stabilizing interest rates and promoting the structural adjustment of the economies; the World Bank (WB), operative since 1946, with the task of financing the economic development projects of its member countries; GATT (General Agreement on Tariffs and Trade), operative since 1948, with the task of abolishing and reducing tariffs and import and excise duties between its member states, so as to promote non-discriminatory trade. GATT was intended to be a temporary organizational solution, until such time as a broader organization of world trade would have been created, which, however, happened only in 1995 with the birth of the World Trade Organization (WTO). Both the World Bank and GATT were affiliated with the UN, and became the economic instruments to promote the new political order. In addition, the dollar established itself as *the* international currency, because it was the only currency able to guarantee its convertibility into gold (the gold-standard).

The political basis of this international order had already been outlined in the Atlantic Charter of 1941, largely inspired by Roosevelt and his internationalist advisors. The Charter, in fact, talks of the necessity to establish multilateral institutions for the shared management of common problems. Hence, more so than its internationalism, post-Second World War America is characterized exactly by this multilateral vision of international institutions, i.e. by the idea that such institutions will be more stable and legitimate the more their management provides for the involvement of the member countries in decision-making. It was during the war that America defined its vision of an open international order managed by multilateral institutions. Naturally, such a vision had to come into conflict after the war with the British system of imperial preferences and with all projects for the reconstruction of the old colonial systems.[30] Out of interest or vision, post-Second World War America became the protagonist of a radical critique of the European vision of an international economic and political order organized and segmented along the lines of the former colonial structures. This radically different outlook between America and its main European allies (Great Britain and France, in particular) was bound to create more than a few tensions between them, culminating (and being resolved definitively in favor of America) during the so-called Suez Crisis of 1956, when America decided not to support the Franco-British claim for control over the canal (thus legitimizing the decision of the new nationalist Egyptian government).

Although the system of the UN was intended as an universalistic system, the Cold War had drastically reduced its scope. Soon America set to work within the western bloc to create institutions of military and political security. In Western Europe, these institutions became all the more vital with the outbreak of the Berlin crisis of 1948, which lead to the division of that city. Notwithstanding some initial doubts (George Kennan, for example, argued that a bipolar world would have altered the equilibrium between democracy and power in America, in favor of the latter), the American elite thus came to pursue with determination the strategy of the dual international order. America decided not to humiliate Germany, Japan, or Italy but rather sought to promote their economic recovery with the Marshall Plan of 1948. Likewise America committed to reintegrating these countries into a wider system of economic and military alliances. Yet, it did so to support its long-term interests, investing them with the necessary international legitimacy. The point is that those interests were pursued by means of a benign hegemony that took into consideration the interests of its partners as well.

The American strategy, therefore, was extraordinarily far-sighted, aiming to lay the foundations of support for the international power of the country. This strategy was based on a quid pro quo: America's partners recognize its leadership (and its strategic interests) and America will take into consideration their requests. A reciprocal recognition was thus institutionalized into a system managed in a multilateral way. Moreover, this system was more vital to Europe than to America. For at least the first postwar decade, in fact, the European political leaders feared being abandoned rather than dominated by America. This explains their speedy approval of the NATO Treaty (North Atlantic Treaty Organization) in 1949 and the gradual integration of West Germany into the alliance (of which it formally became a member in 1955). According to Lord Ismay's famous words, "NATO was created to 'keep the Russians out, the Germans down, and the Americans in.'"[31] Once having guaranteed military security, America moved to promote the economic security of Western Europe, facilitating the formation of both the European Coal and Steel Community (ECSC) in 1951 and the European Economic Community (EEC) in 1957. Both institutions were aimed at integrating Germany into a wider European framework.

In fact, without America it would have been more difficult for the former European enemies to cooperate (in particular, the French and the Germans). The presence of America as an external power with strength superior to all the other European countries combined, provided guarantees to all of them. America was the "third" power able to mediate between the various national interests in Europe because it deployed the strength necessary to perform such a function of mediation and persuasion. The evident and large asymmetry of power between America and its European allies was not a source of tension for the latter because the former exercised its leadership in an open and institutionalized way. The constellation in Asia was similar. And in both Europe and Asia, America guaranteed the preservation of the alliance's internal equilibrium exactly because it was a geographically distant power. Even though these alliance systems had turned America into a European and Asian power, this role was accepted by its allies because America remained an extra-European and extra-Asiatic power. America emerged from the war as a power in the ascendant whereas the European countries now were declining powers. Nevertheless the institutionalization of their cooperative relations had allowed for such asymmetries to be absorbed by the common project of an anti-Soviet alliance. Naturally, these asymmetries of power were bound to create occasional tensions between America and its allies, as in 1965 when France took the polemical decision to exit from NATO's military command, although remaining a member of its political organization. Its internal tensions notwithstanding, the system of alliances constructed immediately after 1945 endured for the whole of the Cold War period.

And so in Europe, as in Asia, America pursued a strategy that differed from the traditional balance of power. The American strategy was to replace the balance of power with an international order based on binding international institutions, governed by means of multilateral agreements between the member countries. This is why America must be considered a hegemonic, rather than an imperial, power. This international order has been the result of a particular interpretation, on the part of the pre- and post-Second World War American political elites, of the causes of the war and the preceding economic crisis. The war was interpreted as the result of a closed international system, segmented into trade blocs that were in permanent tension with each other, subjected to continuous pressures from emerging countries in search of resources (raw materials, in particular) with which to fuel their economic growth and their political ambitions.

This interpretation stands at the root of the Atlantic Charter, or rather of America's commitment to guarantee a world open to trade and respect for human rights. Of course, those principles were not only the outcome of the Wilsonian vision of a world made safe for democracy. They also reflected the economic interests of the large American corporations that needed free trade in order to conquer foreign markets, or rather of those Hamiltonian elites who were primarily concerned with a world made safe for the market.[32] These elites needed to alter the structure of the previous colonial empires, including the one of their close friend, Great Britain, in order to maximize the opportunities for the expansion of American capitalism.[33]

Naturally, the compound nature of the American democracy, with its decision-making processes open to the influence of a plurality of groups and individuals, also constituted a guarantee for the Europeans that American power would not be managed in an arbitrary and arcane way. Rather, the allied countries were able to intervene in this decision-making process in a variety of ways (engaging in lobbying activities, activating the links with the respective immigrant communities inside the country, mobilizing cognitive and intellectual resources), almost on a par with domestic actors. But above all, the reluctant nature of American hegemony was a guarantee for the Europeans. American reluctance had its roots in the long period of isolationism and in its deep-seated suspicion of the colonial vision of the European elites. Precisely to underline the discontinuity with such a vision, American internationalists immediately confronted the problem of the legitimacy of international power by working effectively to create the UN. These two aspects of American hegemony, institutional and cultural, made it permeable to external influences and therefore less threatening. American hegemony allowed for reciprocity between the hegemon and the countries in its sphere of influence, a reciprocity guaranteed by the constitutionalization of this relation. For this reason, Ikenberry characterizes the postwar international order of the West not only as *hegemonic*, but also as *liberal*, as it was legitimized by institutionalized negotiations between America and its allies.[34]

Hence, from the end of the Second World War to the end of the Cold War, America acted to create a bipolar international system organized according to different logics: a highly militarized logic, as in its confrontation with the Soviet Union, and a highly institutionalized logic, as in its alliance with the western countries and Japan. It is needless to point out that nothing similar was created by the Soviet Union in its sphere of influence; its relations with the other communist countries were characterized by the principle of military dominance and not by institutionalized hegemony. In short, the western order was organized in multiple layers of economic, political, and security institutions, around which intergovernmental and transnational relations between America and its allies developed. By institutionalizing the American hegemony, this order legitimized but also limited its exercise. While having been strengthened by the Cold War, it was designed and launched well before its outbreak. By means of the system of the UN the two logics have sought an equilibrium, albeit a precarious and contradictory one.

For the first time in history, this system sought to establish a quasi-constitutional international order, i.e. an order aiming to limit or influence the exertion of state power. These limitations on the exertion of power have affected America more than the Soviet Union, as the latter did not dispose of a domestic public opinion that might have protested against the infractions of international law by the leadership of the country. This is the reason for the particular tensions that have developed between America and the United Nations and that further intensified with the end of the Cold War.

5.4   The End of the Cold War and the First Gulf War

The end of the Cold War between 1989 (fall of the Berlin Wall) and 1991 (disintegration of the Soviet Union) inevitably called into question the postwar international order, starting with the highly militarized order that had pitted America against the Soviet Union. But even though America emerged victorious from the Cold War, it had paid a very high price. Already in the 1970s the policy of containment of the Soviet Union had had dramatic implications, with the ending of the gold convertibility of the dollar by President Nixon in 1971. The war in Vietnam especially had contributed to the calling into question of two preconditions of American hegemony: its economic strength and its liberal identity. Power and consent had greatly diminished, even if the imperatives of the Cold War did not permit an open contestation of the asymmetries within the western bloc. Moreover, between the 1970s and 1980s, the Cold War had dramatically intensified on the Soviet side with the hope of further weakening the giant wounded in Vietnam, and on the American side because of the need to demonstrate the determination of the country to contain communism wherever it emerged.[35]

After Vietnam, America did not hesitate to intervene alongside local dictators in developing countries to obstruct any process of democratization that might provide opportunities for communist or radical movements to exert political influence. With the brief and hapless parenthesis of the democratic presidency of Carter (1977–80), whose foreign policy was guided by the missionary vision of defending and promoting human rights on a global scale, the foreign policy of the Republican presidencies of Nixon (1969–74) and Ford (1974–6) and subsequently of the two Reagan presidencies (1981–8) were marked by a strong anti-communist commitment. Whereas the Republican presidencies of the 1970s had operated within the furrow of traditional realism, the two Reagan presidencies introduced a marked discontinuity in America's international stance. Reagan adopted the themes and the style of Jacksonian foreign policy, i.e. of a foreign policy that married power with American political values, and thus did not limit itself to containing the adversary but actively sought to pursue a strategy of confrontation. Such an aggressive and unscrupulous foreign policy had turned Reagan and the neoconservatives around him into the new ascendant political group in national politics; a rise dampened by the Republican presidency of George H. W. Bush (1989–92).

However, the crisis of the Soviet Union inevitably left a big void in the international system, radically changing the consolidated parameters of American foreign policy. At this juncture the (first) Gulf War broke out. It represented the true beginning of the post-Cold War era, bringing to the fore the dilemmas of a transition period, of an era, that is, in which the previous order has collapsed and the new order is not yet born. Therefore it is necessary to dwell on this war, and on the history that surrounds it between August 2, 1990 (Iraqi invasion of Kuwait) and February 17, 1991 (George H. W. Bush's proclamation that Kuwait had been liberated), to understand the first consequences related to the collapse of the geo-political equilibrium of the Cold War.

As Wittkopf emphasized, the Gulf War was "the first post-Cold War crisis" and a "defining moment" of the new post-Cold War order, "symbolizing the dramatic changes that have taken place in the world in recent years."[36] The presidency of George H. W. Bush encountered great difficulties in justifying the American military intervention. After having considered Iraq an ally during the Cold War (and after having supported it in the war against Iran in the 1980s) and having assisted this country in various ways, the presidency found itself unprepared at the moment of the Iraqi invasion of Kuwait.[37] How to face the first international crisis that did not fit the mold of the communist peril? The reply of George H. W. Bush was in continuity (on the level of foreign policy) with the internationalist and multilateral postwar tradition, but represented a break (concerning the domestic institutional implications) with the practice that had become pre-eminent after the imperial presidency's military defeat in Vietnam.

Let's examine this in more detail, starting with foreign policy. The presidency of George H. W. Bush understood that America, although putting itself forward as the country that would underwrite the international order, would have to play its role of global superpower within significant economic and ideological constraints. Certainly, Bush was able to launch his spectacular diplomacy, which permitted him to swiftly assemble an anti-Iraqi coalition hitherto considered impossible, on the basis of the strong American military presence in the Persian Gulf, deployed in the first days of November 1990 (with an operation named "November Surprise"[38]). It was this extraordinary demonstration of military mobilization that helped America to have the UN approval of the fundamental resolutions that would put Iraq with its back against the wall. Nevertheless, the episode of the Gulf War also constitutes evidence of the American awareness that the country did not dispose of the economic and ideological resources to act on its own as the international policeman. Furthermore, during this period, the Soviet Union, even though going through a dramatic domestic crisis, still maintained its superpower status (and the veto power in the UN Security Council), with all the consequences this implied. Accordingly, the creation of the international coalition in which America was the dominant power also required the consent of the dying Soviet Union.

Despite the pressures of the neoconservatives in the Pentagon to shed the shackles of multilateralism, George H. W. Bush preferred to follow the established path of international collaboration, if only to spread the financial burden of the military intervention, and also at the cost of seeming to confirm the existence of an inverted colonial relation between America and its allies, with the former in control of the arms and the latter controlling the purse strings of the alliance. With George H. W. Bush the old Republicans of the realist school had returned to the White House, many of whom had been educated in the presidencies of Nixon and Ford, rather than under Reagan. This explains why the military intervention was designed to liberate Kuwait, but not to topple the political regime in Iraq. Although defeated militarily, Saddam Hussein was left in command, albeit his regime was subjected to a strict UN embargo and even more stringent inspections by the armed forces of the victorious multinational coalition. For the realists at the White House, the dethronement of Saddam Hussein would have opened up an extremely dangerous power void in Iraq and the surrounding region.

Even if George H. W. Bush recognized the existence of a new system of constraints on the external level, on the domestic level his decisions aimed to reduce not only the system of checks and balances proper to separated government but also the new congressional activism in foreign policy triggered by the crisis of the imperial presidency. From this point of view, the 1991 Gulf War acquired all the characteristics of a true "presidential war," as Bush turned the Gulf crisis into a formidable occasion for reasserting the exclusive control over foreign policy by the president. Referring to Truman's experience of 1950 (when America embarked on an undeclared war against North Korea, on the basis of a UN resolution calling for the intervention of the "free world"), Bush used another UN resolution to mobilize half a million American soldiers, without asking for the authorization of Congress. What's more, in 1950 there was no War Powers Act, which required presidents to notify Congress of the deployment of substantial national military forces abroad, and to withdraw them within 60 days should Congress not approve their use (with the possibility of an additional 30 days in particular cases). Referring to the UN, Bush confronted Congress with a fait accompli.[39] The debate on the reasons for going to war that took place in Congress in the first days of January 1991, was shaped by the situation that had developed on the ground. Few doubted what would have happened on January 15, at the expiration of the UN ultimatum, if Iraq had decided not to withdraw from Kuwait.

Thus one can understand the unease of many observers when they heard Bush say: "It was argued I can't go to war without the Congress. And I was saying, I have the authority to do this."[40] In these two propositions, not only the entire American Constitution (with its distinction between declaring war and making war)[41] was turned on its head; but so was the presidential policy of consistently seeking the consent of Congress, despite presidential claims to pre-eminence in foreign policy. In short, Bush re-imposed the supremacy of the executive in a context of dissent instead of consent on international strategies. This is the novelty which caused Draper to comment disconcertedly that no previous president had ever claimed to have a monopoly on the power to go to war.[42] As Hendrickson wrote, the 1991 Gulf War shows that "the great issue we face is not between isolationism and internationalism, but the way in which we conceive our international responsibilities and the methods to carry them out."[43] In sum, it is true that in the Gulf War America displayed decisive power, although this decisive power was put not only to the service of designing a new international order, but also to designing a new domestic order.

The importance of the Gulf War lies in the contradictions it brought to light. On the one hand, it showed that America did not dispose of the necessary economic and ideological resources to pursue unilateral strategies. On the other hand, it brought to the fore the tendency of the president to impose a renewed decision-making "imperialism" in the field of foreign policy, kindling the fear, already awakened by the institutional choices of the Reagan presidencies, that the Constitution was in danger. The Gulf War gave new prominence to the decision-making role of the presidency, a role which had been considerably weakened in the wake of the defeat in Vietnam and the threat of a presidential impeachment in 1974. Certainly, the presidency recovered under Reagan, but the Iran-Contra Affair, made public in 1987, ended up further undermining its role.[44] Of course, this renewed activism represented a challenge to the constitutional equilibria, which had already been subjected to severe strains during the Cold War to the point that Foreign Affairs, in its lead article of the issue immediately following the election of Clinton to the presidency, wrote that "the new President will need to restore constitutional checks and balances after decades of Cold War erosion that culminated in the Iran-contra and Iraqgate scandals."[45]

5.5   The 1990s and the Schizophrenic Power

5.5.1   The unilateralist perspective

The Gulf War of 1991 thus brought to the fore the characteristics of the transition from the certainty of (bipolar) international order to a new but uncertain (unipolar) order. At the beginning of the 1990s, global politics no longer was divided into two opposing camps, each one controlled by a superpower. The collapse of the Soviet Union left the world with only one superpower,[46] or rather with a hyperpower, to use the definition proposed by the French foreign minister in a conference held at the Institut Français des Relations Internationales on June 12, 1995. A hyperpower, according to Calleo, is a power "whose supremacy extended to every aspect of the world's economy, technology, language, and culture."[47] The United States now saw itself as the victor of history, chosen to propagate democracy everywhere. Not surprisingly, the rest of the world might see this as a pretention to global hegemony. America has been a hegemonic power since the Second World War but until the 1980s its hegemony had been exerted within its sphere of influence. With the collapse of communism, America instead could assert its hegemony on a global level. One might say that a hyperpower distinguishes itself from a superpower by the fact that its hegemony does not know geo-political, economic, or cultural constraints.

Yet the new international system had opened a deep rift in the political elite between the Democrats, who (with Clinton) gained control of the presidency in the elections of 1992 and 1996, and the neoconservatives (led by Newt Gingrich), who took control of Congress in 1994 (and dominated until 2006). This rift would become so acute as to mark all of the 1990s. This confrontation did not pit isolationists against interventionists. Rather, the dividing line ran between two radically different interventionist options. Both were based on the common observation that the post-Cold War world had acquired an unipolar structure that obliged America to play, for one generation at least, the role of the world's only superpower: the only power able to promote and underwrite a new international order. On the other hand, neither the European Union (EU) nor Japan could play a leadership role in the international system, given that they remained political and military dwarfs even if they had become economic giants. This common observation gave rise to different strategies because the same international power structure allows different ways of exercising leadership.

One perspective on foreign policy that emerged in that decade was the unilateralist view, embraced and pursued by the neoconservative majority of Congress, in particular under the leadership of the Speaker of the House of Representatives Newt Gingrich. Many of the advocates of unilateralism had worked for the Reagan presidencies, although they received the cold shoulder from the George H. W. Bush presidency. Elaborated in various cultural foundations and discussed in numerous political journals, the unilateralist strategy put forward a well-defined interpretation of the post-Cold War international system.[48] According to this interpretation, the post-Cold War world was anything but pacified. Rather, a new and serious threat had already become apparent: namely the proliferation of "rogue states," i.e. small but aggressive states equipped with weapons of mass destruction. In this respect, Saddam's Iraq constituted a textbook example of a rogue state, an example of a state in possession of a developed military apparatus, thanks to the enormous financial resources deriving from the production and sale of oil, organized in a hierarchical manner, and motivated by a strong anti-Western grudge, such as to provide the necessary ideological and emotional thrust to sustain an authoritarian control of society.

For the unilateralists, a world able to look after itself is nothing but a pipe dream. International stability can only be the outcome of an appropriate military strategy by the big powers, and by America first of all. There is no doubt that such an interpretation did have a certain consistency. In a period in which many expected a return to the foreign policy of normal times, the neoconservatives insisted that America continued to live in abnormal times, as the new threat represented by the small to medium rogue states (actively engaged in opposing western influence, particularly in regions with vast oil reserves) would doubtless soon materialize. Employing a clearly Jacksonian language, the unilateralists maintained that America's national interest in safeguarding its security and the supply of strategic economic resources should enjoy priority over any other consideration. That meant also that the country should no longer allow itself to be kept in check by multilateral institutions: "America first." This is why the unilateralists, who had only played a marginal role in the presidency of George H. W. Bush, vigorously defended the latter's decision to go to war with one of the most dangerous rogue states.

The domestic implications of the unilateralist perspective, however, have been paradoxical. In fact, it required the pre-eminence of the presidency in the management of foreign policy because, it was argued, the unpredictable threat of rogue states (contrary to the predictable one of the rival superpower in the Cold War order) can only be handled by a national security apparatus able to act with swiftness and readiness, meaning an apparatus freed even more of the constitutional constraints of separated government. Yet, for all of the 1990s, the presidency continued to be controlled by the adversaries of unilateralism, something neoconservatives never recognized as legitimate. Accordingly, the Republican Congress continued to attack the presidency, together with the courts and the states, leading Calleo to observe that "despite the President's continuing popularity with the electorate and his impressive achievements in the economic field, [the Clinton] presidency has been subjected to the most savage constitutional attack since Nixon's time."[49]

As the editor of *Foreign Affairs* wrote, the neoconservatives saw the Gulf War as the first example of a presidential war because it demonstrated that "only the United States could have organized the coalition and prosecuted the war."[50] In short, in the unilateralist view, with the end of the Cold War, the American capability to exert its power within the anti-Soviet Union block should be transformed into a capability to play a security role on a global scale. After all, as Joffe pointed out "there is also pleasure in being Number One. To exert power is better than suffering it; to be at the helm is better than hunkering down in the hold."[51]

5.5.2 The multilateralist perspective

The Clinton presidencies (1993–2000), instead, pursued a multilateral strategy. According to the advocates of this strategy, the end of the Cold War had diminished the importance of geo-military strategies and had led to a diffusion of international power.[52] This was in the interest of America which had paid a very high economic price to safeguard its leadership of the western bloc in the previous international order. Naturally, the end of the Cold War did not mean the end of all international threats, and the country, therefore, still had an important role to play (on the political and military levels) to guarantee the birth of a new international order. But, it was argued, those threats no longer have an exclusively geo-military significance and thus can be confronted through multiple strategies, including economic and trade strategies. In fact, under Clinton, America placed all its bets on economic globalization, of whose acceleration it certainly was the engine. For this reason, the Clinton presidencies worked to revitalize the international multilateral institutions (starting with the UN), in order to promote a responsible redistribution of military responsibilities and the respective economic costs, as well as to expand the number of countries (starting with China) involved in an internationally regulated trade. This was not a scenario for a pacified world, but rather of a world that did not envisage America playing the role of global policeman.

It is no surprise that, in the multilateral perspective, the 1991 Gulf War represented a positive example of a conflict of the post-bipolar era, to the extent that it had demonstrated that America did not dispose of the economic resources and the international legitimacy to go it alone. To cite the then editor of *Foreign Affairs* again, the Gulf War had led the multilateralists to draw the opposite conclusion from their adversaries, namely "that the United States could organize the coalition only through the cooperation of a diverse collection of powers."[53] Hence the 1991 Gulf War made clear to multilateralists that American international initiatives required the support, economic support first of all, of allied countries. America continued to be exposed to a gap not unlike the one conceptualized by Lippmann in 1945, i.e. too many international responsibilities in relation to the limited domestic resources.[54] Accordingly, America needed to reduce its military "overstretch"[55] that had resulted from the confrontation with the Soviet Union, by means of greater collaboration, both with America's traditional allies as well as its new friends emerged from the collapse of communism. For the multilateralists, this did not exclude that America would continue to safeguard its international leadership by means of global, though selective, interventions.[56] Yet, America would have to recognize that the structure of international power had become rather more diversified than in the past. As Nye wrote,

> the distribution of power in world politics has become like a layer cake. The top military layer is largely unipolar, for there is no other military power comparable to the United States. The economic middle layer is tripolar and has been for two decades. The bottom layer of transnational interdependence shows a diffusion of power.[57]

Even though "the victory over Iraq . . . seemed to set the stage for a resumption of the U.S. world policeman role in disrepute domestically since Vietnam,"[58] President Clinton immediately sought to reduce that role by declaring himself willing to entrust the institutions of international cooperation with tasks of a military nature. Some even talked of a superpower without a sword.[59] On the domestic level, the multilateral perspective entailed the vision of a strengthened collaboration between the two main institutions of government, not least because Clinton did not have an alternative, given that he was faced with a Congress tightly controlled by his neoconservative adversaries since 1995. Yet, this vision had few possibilities of being realized. Actually, between the multilateralists of the presidency and the unilateralists of Congress a rather tough struggle broke out immediately over the control of the country's foreign policy. The outcome was a sort of foreign policy schizophrenia throughout the 1990s.

On the one hand, Congress claimed (and obtained) an ever more assertive role in foreign policy but, given its internal structure, this implied a growing influence of interest groups, private lobbies, large corporations, highly politicized PACs, and district and state constituencies interested in specific problems. As Calleo argued, the unilateral Congress of the 1990s pursued a foreign policy constituted by a "highly incoherent aggregate of private agendas."[60] On the other hand, President Clinton, particularly after 1996, sought to oppose a multilateral strategy based on the twin principles of promotion of democracy and expansion of the market to the mounting unilateralist initiatives of Congress. In other words, he sought to promote the idea that America's task should be "to enlarge the number of democracies, since 'democracies don't fight one another,' and expand the number of market economies and global prosperity, since prospering nations do not have time to fight one another."[61] The enlargement perspective represented the functional equivalent of containment in a world without the threat of the Soviet Union. In this sense, Clinton harked back to the Wilsonian tradition, or at least its rhetoric. But his Wilsonian approach (i.e. the international promotion of democracy through multilateral institutions) was openly contested by Congress.

In fact, from 1995 onwards, Congress systematically challenged the president's position in the area of security and defense. Congress opposed the extension of the Nuclear Non-Proliferation Treaty, blocked the approval of the Chemical Weapons Convention, prevented the ratification of the Convention on the Rights of the Child, rejected the crucial Comprehensive Test-Ban Treaty (in 1999 the Senate voted 48 in favor and 51 against on this treaty, i.e. 19 votes short of what would have been necessary for approval with a qualified two-thirds majority), constrained the president to renegotiate the ABM treaty, and suspended the payment of the American contribution to the UN.

The president tried to put up resistance to these congressional positions, threatening to use his veto from time to time or making some concessions, but the neoconservative wind blows with such a force in Washington, DC that he frequently ended up adjusting to the views of the leaders of the legislature. For example, in 1999 he signed the National Missile Defense Act, which he had previously criticized vehemently. In the previous year (1998), Clinton was also constrained to sign the veto-proof Iraq Liberation Act which made "regime change" the official policy of the US. Admittedly, on other occasions, Clinton did manage to promote his own agenda, but this only occurred when he was supported by a cross-party coalition in Congress. Concerning the expansion of the market, his most important achievement was the approval of the NAFTA (North American Free Trade Agreement) in 1993. Yet, a few years later, in 1997,

Congress, notwithstanding the president's request, refused to renew the so-called Fast Track clause, which gave the president the authority to negotiate trade agreements with other countries (with Congress, however, retaining the right to approve or reject the reached agreement in its entirety).

As far as the promotion of democracy is concerned, the most important achievements were the congressional support, both for the Dayton Accords of November 21, 1995 (with which America laid the foundations for the pacification of Bosnia) and for the military intervention in Kosovo in the spring of 1999 (with which America, at the helm of NATO, managed to interrupt the ethnic cleansing of the Muslim population). Yet, those presidential achievements were the exception and not the rule. Congress continued to obstruct many humanitarian or peacekeeping initiatives proposed by the president, in particular those in which American troops would have had to operate with the authorization or under the direction of the UN. As has been argued, "Congress and the president were frequently at loggerheads over funding for the non-military aspects of America's foreign policy institutions. Between 1991 and 1998 there was a 25 percent decline in the international affairs budget (State department and related agencies)."[62] In short, one might get the impression that the 1990s confirmed the age-old adage of American politics, namely that the president proposes but the Congress disposes. Certainly, that decade demonstrated how a separated government works when the presidency and Congress are controlled by radically different political majorities.

This is why America, in the 1990s, has behaved as a schizophrenic hyperpower, rather than an imperial power, regardless of whether it did so out of conviction or reluctantly. This schizophrenia certainly was (also) due to the nature of the governmental decision-making process. As Joseph Nye Jr has remarked, "American foreign policy-making is a messy process for reasons deeply rooted in our political culture and institutions. . . . In foreign policy, the Constitution has always invited the president and Congress to struggle for control. That struggle is complicated when the Congress and presidency are controlled by different political parties."[63] In the 1990s, these domestic structures, combined with the absence of an apparent enemy, made the identification of a national interest altogether implausible. Rather, with the rise of Congress, American foreign policy has become privatized, given the enormous influence exerted by specific private groups over its strategic sectors, like the mid-western exporters of agricultural products and steel. As Jervis has argued, at the end of the 1990s important sectors of American foreign policy were "captured" by interested groups as had already long happened in many regulatory policies.[64] In sum, "if there is one country in which one cannot understand foreign policy without linking it to domestic politics, it is the United States."[65]

It goes without saying that this schizophrenia did create more than a few problems, in particular for America's allies. As an example, one may recall the American request for the European countries to adhere to the decisions of Congress concerning the embargoes against Cuba and Libya, as if those decisions had a universal importance or had been taken by a supranational legislature. Thus, in the 1990s, America found itself as a hyperpower without rivals in the outside world, corresponding, on the domestic side, to an unprecedented division of the political elite, in addition to a fragmented decision-making process. In the past, the threat of communism, on the external side, and presidential leadership, on the internal side, provided the necessary justifications and resources to discipline the political and social actors involved in foreign policy. However, the disintegration of communism and the crisis of presidential government left America with an extremely conflict-ridden decision-making process on foreign policy.

5.6 George W. Bush's America and the Second Gulf War

With the victory of the Republican candidate George W. Bush in the contested presidential elections of November 2000, and the confirmation of the Republican majority in the House of Representatives (in the Senate the decision of a Republican to leave the party caucus handed the Democrats a wafer-thin majority of one seat), conditions were ripe to overcome the divided government of the 1969–2000 era. With George W. Bush's shift toward neoconservative positions, after having won the elections on a platform of compassionate conservatism (in domestic policies) and selective intervention (in foreign policy), the preconditions were in place for a reduction of the previous schizophrenia. Within a short period of time, in fact, the president adopted the unilateralist agenda pursued by Congress since the elections of 1994.

Thus, well before the terrorist attacks on New York and Washington, DC of September 11, 2001, American foreign policy had become more coherently unilateralist and therefore rather less schizophrenic. Already during the eight months between the presidential inauguration and the terrorist attacks American criticism of international agreements and institutions had grown ever more insistent. The attacks radicalized this approach to foreign policy, but did not determine it. Certainly, in order to carry out the intervention in Afghanistan, the president had embarked on a massive diplomatic campaign in order to build a solid international coalition, with the friends and the former enemies of America. Moreover, in order to lend the necessary international legitimacy to the intervention, the president persuaded Congress to honor its financial obligations toward the UN. This policy was so effective that some observers came to hold that 9/11 had produced a softening of unilateralism. However, as Hoffmann has pointed out, they declared its demise too soon.[66]

Notwithstanding such diplomatic overtures, the new elites that had first conquered Congress, and subsequently the presidency, were more than ever convinced that 9/11 confirmed what they had been saying ever since the 1991 Gulf War, namely that America was exposed to a new threat, which required the adoption of a new strategy.[67] In addition, they maintained that 9/11 had enabled a radical shift of the political center of gravity to the right, tilting the balance of power between neoconservatives and liberals in favor of the former. Exactly because the neoconservatives felt that they had a solution awaiting a problem in order to be implemented, whereas the Democrats saw themselves confronted with a problem lacking a solution, the neoconservative solution was turned into a precise international strategy, internally consistent and revolutionary in its implications: i.e. unilateralism as the new form of America's global rule and also as an opportunity for asserting presidential dominance of the separated government. In short, the neoconservatives were the only ones able to propose a matching reply to the challenge thrown down. And since the challenge had been so terrible, they could present their foreign policy revolution as the only feasible strategy.[68]

This strategy was rooted in the ideas developed in the 1990s and in the experience of the two Reagan presidencies of the 1980s. In the unipolar world, the threats to the international order are more dangerous still than in a bipolar world, because they originate from constellations of anti-western terrorist groups connected (or able to connect) with rogue states committed to challenge America and its allies. These new actors behave in novel and unpredictable ways; they do not respect any international rules and are endowed with enormous technological and financial resources. Thus, the analyses of the 1990s on rogue states were enriched with the new terrorist menace giving rise to what was subsequently named the axis of evil (i.e. the possible alliance between the former and the latter). Allegedly, this axis had singled out the dominant power in the new unipolar order as its main enemy. Because of this, it was argued, America must reassert the priority of its own security over other considerations related to the global order, thus acting, if necessary, also outside the constraints of the institutions and the body of international law that have structured the post-Second World War international system.[69]

Accordingly, America must take on the task of changing those political regimes whose existence constitutes a challenge to the international order over which it presides. The post-9/11 neoconservative strategy thus rearranged two fundamental threads of the Jacksonian foreign policy tradition, adapting them to the new conditions of the unipolar world. The first is the thread of assertive nationalism, which emerged during the 1990s and according to which foreign policy should have the objective to guarantee the principle of "America first." The second thread is the one of democratic imperialism, according to which foreign policy must seek to export (and impose) democracy throughout the world even through military means, because only its diffusion can warrant international stability.[70] Thus, the post-9/11 unilateralism has not only been nationalist, but has also acquired an imperialist overtone.

The end-result of this redefinition of the enemy and of international threats was a new foreign policy doctrine, the so-called "Bush doctrine." This doctrine was first announced by the president in his *The National Security Strategy of the United States* of September 20, 2002 and confirmed through 2006.[71] The ambitions of this doctrine are on a par with the doctrine of containment developed in the period immediately following the Second World War. What are its guiding principles? First, America must maintain its military superiority over the other powers in this world: "Today, the United States enjoys a position of unparalleled military strength and great economic and political influence. . . . We must build and maintain our defenses beyond challenge."[72] The international system is unipolar in military terms and must remain so for a long time to come. Second, America must liberate itself from the constraints of the multilateral institutions erected during the previous era because they hamper safeguarding its own security and the security of its allies and partners.

In the face of the new threat of global terrorism and rogue states, multilateral institutions not only obscure America's responsibilities but they also weigh down its ability to act, preventing it from moving with the autonomy and the swiftness required for an adequate reply to those threats. To quote the president again: "In exercising our leadership, we will respect the values, judgment, and interests of our friends and partners. Still, we will be prepared to act apart when our interests and unique responsibilities require."[73] But also in this case, the president makes explicit a practice already initiated by the neoconservatives in Congress. In fact, as the *Economist* observed, in its first two years the presidency of George W. Bush

> has shunned a new International Criminal Court, the treaty for which has been ratified by [as of 1 June 2008, 106] other countries . . . has pulled out of efforts to agree on a verification protocol for the Biological Weapons Convention. It also rejected the 1997 Kyoto Protocol on climate change . . . Perhaps most alarming, however, has been its recent disregard for the Geneva conventions on prisoners of war in determining the legal status of people it has captured in Afghanistan and taken to Guantanamo Bay for questioning.[74]

Third, America, in confronting the borderless challenges of international terrorism, claims the right to intervene anywhere in order to anticipate any possible future threat to its own security, and not just to respond to an attack. This view constitutes authentic subversion of the so-called Westphalian principles that have underpinned the international system for the last four centuries and which were adopted in 1945 by the UN. States can no longer be considered sovereign on their territory, if they pose a threat to America or the international order. Nor can postwar international law, which is based on the reciprocal recognition of national sovereignty, be considered an obstacle to a preemptive intervention, if the latter is motivated by the necessity to anticipate a future threat: "To forestall or prevent . . . hostile acts by our adversaries, the United States will, if necessary, act preemptively. . . . the United States cannot remain idle while dangers gather."[75]

Of course, it is up to America to determine whether a country poses an international threat or not or, in any case, a threat to its interests. And when America decides to act, it will do so with the support of the willing, and if necessary also without the legitimacy of the UN. As the former secretary of defense Donald Rumsfeld made clear: "It is the mission which determines the coalition, and not the other way around."[76] This means that America no longer considers collaboration with its traditional allies, starting with European countries, to enjoy priority, especially since Europe does not exist as such. To a journalist's question as to why the Europeans had not supported the American strategy against international terrorism, Rumsfeld replied: "Europeans do not exist. There are Germans, Britons, French but not Europeans. Those who criticize the United States do not have an idea of what they are talking about."[77]

Fourth, America must change the international status quo since it no longer provides protection against the apocalyptic violence that terrorists or rogue states may unleash. International stability, therefore, is no longer a collective good and a priority of American foreign policy. Here, more than elsewhere, is the revolutionary character of the neoconservative strategy; a strategy aimed at contrasting the idea of a decline of the West,[78] even if that means generating a sort of "permanent revolution" of the international system (to use the words of Leon Trotsky, who, by the way, inspired influential neoconservative thinkers in their youth). As the president argued: "In the new world we have entered, the only path to peace and security is the path of action."[79] In short, America should be much more militant and show much less respect for the global or regional equilibria, as several neoconservative pundits have argued for some time.[80] But the calling into question of the external equilibria obviously must and does imply an equivalent calling into question of the domestic equilibria. If indeed America is engaged in a permanent revolution abroad, then it cannot remain prisoner of its domestic constitutional constraints. If America is at war, it must also protect itself accordingly from the threats originating from within. Multilateralism is wrong abroad, as it is domestically. As the president asserted, "While we recognize that our best defense is a good offense, we are also strengthening America's homeland security to protect against and deter attack."[81]

Thus, in the name of a national emergency, the president and Congress have radically reformed the structure of the national security apparatus, integrating all competences within the new presidential department of Homeland Security (with the Homeland Security Act of November 2002), an unprecedented feat in American history. Most important perhaps, in tandem with Congress the president passed a bill, the Patriot Act of October 26, 2001, which drastically curtails the civil rights of individuals suspected of links with terrorist activities. Such an outright attack on individual rights had not been mounted since the McCarthyism of the 1950s. The Patriot Act, insisted on by the ultra neoconservative Attorney General John Ashcroft, invests the federal security agencies with unprecedented powers of gathering information, even at the cost of violating the privacy of suspected individuals, of detaining suspects without any legal protection, as well as subjecting them to interrogation hidden from appropriate public scrutiny.[82]

From this point of view, the domestic implications of the "war on terrorism" are rather more revolutionary than those of the Cold War. It is not only a matter of repositioning the presidency (finally liberated from its Democratic usurpers) at the center of the decision-making process on foreign policy, but also to establish it as the dominant institution in domestic policy.[83] The detention of "enemy combatants" (as they were defined) at Guantanamo Bay in violation of the Geneva Convention, the torture allowed in detention camps of suspected terrorists and the freedom of action granted to the federal security agencies constitute the several sides of a single coherent institutional project: namely to create an "emergency presidency" free from the constraints of domestic and international laws.[84]

These principles provide an exhaustive picture of the revolution introduced by the "Bush doctrine" in American foreign policy. They are able to account for the ideological determination with which the neoconservative elite in control of presidency and Congress embarked on the war against Iraq in the spring of 2003, without considering contrary opinions and concrete evidence casting doubt on that decision. The mid-term elections of November 2002 created the conditions to implement that decision. Those elections not only confirmed the Republican majority in the House but also handed back control of the Senate to the Republicans. Not surprisingly a few months later, in the spring of 2003, George W. Bush took the decision to invade Iraq knowing that he would not encounter significant congressional hurdles, even though having only little or no evidence of Iraq's capacity to acquire weapons of mass destruction, or concerning its involvement in the carnage of 9/11.

But even if the president did not encounter hurdles in the legislature (the so-called Joint Resolution to Authorize the Use of US Armed Forces Against Iraq passed the House by a vote of 296–133 and the Senate by a vote of 77–23 in October 2002), he found many in domestic and international public opinion,[85] as is shown by the annual *Transatlantic Trends* reports published since 2001.[86] Indeed, the decision to invade Iraq did not gain the support of the UN Security Council. That decision put into practice a design worked out in neoconservatives circles, namely to make Iraq the *test-case* of the new unipolar order.[87] Thus, with the Second Gulf War, neoconservatives have sought to bring the post-Cold War transition, initiated with the First Gulf War, to a conclusion. The test, however, failed dramatically.[88] America has demonstrated that it is able to win the war, but unable to bring peace. Indeed, after just one year of military occupation of Iraq, unilateralist America had to return to the UN to obtain the necessary legitimacy to try and stabilize the occupied country. Thus, very soon, the neoconservatives had to recognize that the UN (although it does not dispose of its own troops, its administration may be excessively expensive and its policy programs may not be impermeable to corruption) continues to be necessary in order to justify the most important international decisions. Just as Stalin's mockery of the Pope ("How many divisions does he have?") has been avenged by history, so the neoconservative mockery of the UN has met the same fate. This return to the UN represented a tremendous political and moral defeat for neoconservative America.

The success of the Democrats in the mid-term elections of 2006 formalized that defeat at the domestic level as well. That success was the expression of a public opinion scandalized by the abuses and mistakes the Presidency made without serious checks on the part of the Congress. Thus, step by step, the clear imperial impulses of the neoconservatives came to meet the constraints of the multilateral structure, internationally and domestically.[89] The supporters of America as a new Rome, as well as the supporters of the president as a new Emperor, that is as the undisputable commander-in-chief of the country, had to face the resistance of constitutional orders (at both domestic and international levels) that were created exactly for contrasting those unilateral aspirations. In sum, American unilateralism has proven to be incompatible with the structure of the multilateral institutions that continue to organize the international system, a system that does not allow for the formation of a rigid international hierarchy with America at its helm.[90] At the same time, presidential unilateralism has proven to be incompatible with the structure of multiple separation of powers which continues to characterize American compound democracy.[91]

5.7   Conclusion

Let us return to the two criticisms mentioned at the beginning of the chapter, starting with the first. Can one claim that America is or has been an imperial democracy? If we take empire to mean the *direct control* of a given territory with the purpose of creating economic relations that favor the center to the detriment of the periphery of the empire, then it should be obvious that America has never been an empire (with the brief parenthesis of the occupation of Cuba and the Philippines at the end of the nineteenth century and Iraq at the beginning of the twenty-first century).[92] Rather, in many ways, its economic relations with the countries in its sphere of influence were exactly the opposite. It was America that provided an outlet for their products, rather than the other way round (as shown by the persistent American trade balance deficit with developing countries). If, with Walzer, we take empire to mean "a system of political domination, not necessarily direct,"[93] through which a government gets what it wants from the other dominated governments, then it is difficult to claim that America is an imperial power also in this respect. Certainly, America exerts a substantial influence over its allies and adversaries, but does not succeed in obtaining from them whatever it wants.

To cite an example, the American decision to invade Iraq was contested by many of its allies. It should be sufficient to recall that even Belgium (and not only France and Germany) threatened to use its veto in NATO against involving the organization in the invasion of Iraq; or to recall Turkey, to cite another example, whose parliament refused to grant American troops access to Iraq via its southern border. In both cases, America has had to respect, albeit grudgingly, the position taken by those countries. Obviously, America has not given up promoting its economic interests worldwide, nor intervening directly in the political affairs of countries located in regions it considers of strategic importance for its own interests. For example, in countries like Iran in 1953, in Chile in 1971, and Grenada in 1983 its interventions were brutal and unscrupulous (and in violation of international law). In those and other cases America did not hesitate to ally itself with clearly anti-democratic political forces and with decidedly authoritarian political leaders, justifying all this with the need to contain the Soviet Union's expansion. In sum, within America there has been no lack of political forces and economic interest that have pushed for an imperial management of its international power.

However, this is only part of the story, because America has taken a rather different approach with western countries (but not with authoritarian Spain or Portugal, whose dictators were supported by America until the 1970s, or with Greece during the military regime of the 1960s). Already before the outbreak of the Cold War, America helped to build a complex system of multilateral institutions that have radically altered the conception of international order, even if this system has proven to be congenial to the country (in the sense that it contributed to increase its reputation) during Cold War confrontation with the Soviet Union. As no other power that emerged victorious from a war had ever done before, America first assisted the defeated countries economically and then inserted them into a system of political and military alliances. This multilateral system was certainly directed by America but not dominated by it as the Soviet Union did in its bloc. Hence, the American hegemony has been of a political and military nature, but it was not a form of imperial rule because it was based on consensus and reciprocity. America could request its allies to support its strategic interests precisely because it was willing to take into consideration their specific interests. Post-Second World War America has created a western (multilateral) liberal order consistent with its domestic (multilateral) liberal order. Of course, just as the domestic order was challenged by internal forces (think of the various attempts to create an "imperial presidency"), so the international order has witnessed similar episodes (think of unscrupulous interferences in the internal affairs of several countries, even allied, for pursuing "imperial impulses").

Hence, after 1945 a hegemonic international order emerged, but not an imperial one, even if American hegemony was exercised in different ways in the western bloc and in developing countries (and within the same western bloc). Accordingly, the argument that America is imperialist by design does not seem supported by the facts. Whenever America has sought to turn toward empire (or direct rule), forces have mobilized in the country forcing a retreat. America, obviously, is also a big power, the expression of powerful economic and cultural forces, whose interests (necessarily) imply a continuous expansion of the country on the international level. For this reason its foreign policy continues to express the inevitable contradiction (and unprecedented in such proportions) between internal democracy and external power. To quote Calleo, the country must live with "the profound tension between the US as a national democracy and the US as a global hegemon," a tension which is not easily manageable.[94] This is why those critics of America err when they see only the latter part of the tension, as do those apologists of America who confine themselves to seeing only the former.

This being so, the second criticism (i.e. that unilateralism constitutes a coherent development of American foreign policy) does not seem very convincing either. If we take unilateralism to mean the exercise of force outside the constraints of international institutions, the unilateralist America that invaded Iraq in 2003 does not follow at all in the footsteps of the foreign policy tradition of the country. Rather, the strategy pursued after 9/11 constitutes a true break with the foreign policy elaborated and implemented after the Second World War, i.e. when America established itself as a global power or superpower. Whereas post-1945 multilateral America sought to resolve the contradiction between democracy and power by becoming (globally) hegemonic, post-9/11 unilateral America has sought to transform this hegemony into global domination. However, to quote Walzer again, "unilateralism is not the normal way to exercise American power,"[95] exactly because America was instrumental in building the multilateral institutions that have characterized the post-Second World War international order. Indeed, the will to go it alone in Iraq represented a break with that tradition, an attempt to take America beyond the constraints of liberal hegemony.[96]

This attempt, however, has doubtless been unsuccessful. America does not dispose of the economic resources and the political legitimacy to pursue a unilateral strategy.[97] But also on the domestic level, the constitutional structure and the cultural system are of no help to an imperial vision of America. This is so not only "because Americans have not the stomach for imperialism,"[98] but also because America does not have the necessary decision-making structures for supporting imperial ambitions. The compound republic facilitates access to the decision-making process of political and social forces of different hues, and any push in the direction of empire is bound to provoke a push in the opposite direction. The pluralist nature of American politics turns the formation of a stable domestic consensus, of whatever nature, into a fragile undertaking. Even though the media have undergone a process of ownership restructuring during the last twenty years, thus reducing the margins for critical public discussion, they nevertheless continue to provide an arena for public debate that is not very congenial to the exigencies of imperial consensus. American public culture, although internally divided into different currents and traditions, remains firmly anchored in the commitment to democracy, a commitment hardly compatible with denying political sovereignty to other peoples or countries. After all, the American republic was born in the first anti-colonial revolution of the modern era.

In sum, America has neither the necessary mentality nor the internal structures to become an imperial power. As Hurrell argued, it is destined to play the role of a hegemon whose power is necessary but not sufficient to govern the world.[99] Of course, America is not an angel descended from the heavens to save humanity. Although it is not an imperial power, it is a power concerned with promoting or protecting its own interests and decisions abroad. This action might conflict with the multilateral institutions constructed after 1945, but it cannot be maintained in permanent tension with those institutions. As the experience of the failed invasion of Iraq shows, America has no chance but to work within the constraints of the multilateral system and the president within those of the separated government. However, although a world led only by America is not entirely secure, a world bereft of American leadership would be far less so.

6

America as Method

6.1 Introduction

If the argument so far is plausible, then it is difficult to see America as a "model." Of course, I am aware that it has been (and continues to be) considered a model, and not only in Europe.[1] Yet, the idea of America as a democratic model derives from an exceptionalist interpretation of the country, which is as suggestive as it is unsatisfactory. Yet, this theory still seems to organize the thoughts of the critics and supporters of America and keeps turning them into an ideology. In reality American democracy is a contradictory democracy and not a coherent democratic model. What distinguishes it from other democracies (in particular European ones) is the method employed to resolve its contradictions and not the harmony of its (alleged) democratic model.[2] Here I will proceed as follows. First, I will try to free America from the theory of exceptionalism to reinstate the centrality of its contradictions. Second, I will analyze these contradictions, or rather the antinomies that have progressively shaped the structure of American politics. Third, I will analyze the evolution of those antinomies in the light of the history of American democracy. Finally, I will present my interpretation of America as a democracy that has employed the competitive method for keeping its internal tensions under control.

6.2 American Exceptionalism

The term American exceptionalism became widely popular at the turn of the nineteenth century, when, in particular in Europe, the problem arose of understanding the reasons for the organizational and political weakness of the labor movement in America. America was the only industrialized country without a significant laborite or socialist party. The problem, of course, had not gone unnoticed by the founders of the international socialist movement, Karl Marx and Friedrich Engels; nor did it escape the attention of Vladimir Lenin and Leon Trotsky, the founders of the international communist movement. The American case seemed to challenge one of the most poignant theoretical conclusions reached by Marx in his magnum opus *Capital*, namely that the economically most advanced country would present the less advanced countries with the image of their future, a conclusion that led many socialists to maintain that the most advanced capitalist economy would be the first to usher in socialism. However, although being amongst the most advanced economies, America appeared to be the country least hospitable to socialist ideas.

The most significant answers to the problem came from two scholars with socialist sympathies. In 1906, Werner Sombart published in his native Germany, *Warum Gibt es in den Vereinigten Staaten keinen Sozialismus?* and in the same year the Englishman H. G. Wells published *The Future of America*. Both authors advanced the idea that America was exceptional due to a combination of economic and sociocultural factors. It was the only country in which general suffrage (for white males) was introduced before the full development of an industrial economy. Americans had been able to identify as citizens before identifying as members of a social group and so political citizenship was perceived as an individual prerogative, and not, as was the case in Europe, as the result of collective action and thus as a social, if not class prerogative. This combination of political events, in a country rich in resources, geographically open, and characterized by the anti-deferential culture typical of religious dissent, conspired to undermine the historical preconditions of socialist politics.[3]

Soon though, with the development of the social and historical sciences, exceptionalism, born from an internal issue of the international socialist movement, became the popular cultural key for the definition of the national identity of America as distinct from other countries. As those sciences had developed in Western Europe and in America, it was inevitable that this exceptionalism came to be conceptualized as an American deformity of what was considered to be a normal (i.e. European) model of historical development. Thus, for the better part of the twentieth century, the debate about exceptionalism furnished the background for the elaboration of a veritable national ideology, subsequently defined as "Americanism." The studies of Seymor Martin Lipset, and in particular his path-breaking book of 1963, subsequently provided a systematic analysis of this concept.[4] Americanism refers to a combination of egalitarianism and populism, voluntarism and anti-statism, individualism and moralism, a mixture that (at least in these proportions) was said to have no equivalent in any other advanced country. This combination, it was argued, not only helped to explain why there was no socialism in America (because America, in some sense, had been socialist from the outset). But above all, it helped explain why America was so unlike the other advanced European countries. These beliefs are said to have accompanied the development of the country, bending the model in a peculiar direction. The origins of this peculiarity have been traced, by Daniel Bell in particular, to the experience of democratic development in absence of the state.[5]

American exceptionalism resides in the fact that, for the better part of its history, this country has been the archetype of a self-governing civil society, whence the importance of Americanism as an ideology. America has engendered those attitudes, widespread amongst the elites as well as the masses, which have protected the country from the anti-liberal threats of statism. These attitudes have subsequently shaped the rise of the federal state, in particular in the wake of the economic crisis of the 1930s and the international crisis of the Second World War. After this dual economic and military crisis, America necessarily had to take a more statist and centralized direction, but this occurred within institutional and behavioral constraints that limited the impact.

The interpretation of America as an exceptional democracy was subjected to severe criticism during the 1980s and 1990s.[6] A first challenge derived from research in the field of political economy that demonstrated the inadequacy of analyzing the development of a country on the basis of domestic considerations alone. In reality, especially after the Second World War, the industrial democracies have been subjected to similar pressures originating from the international economic and political system.[7] The domestic structure of the relation between politics and market has acquired comparable characteristics in developed countries, as it is shaped by the imperatives of the process of industrialization and post-industrialization.

With particular reference to the two shores of the Atlantic, it has been shown how a certain "Europeanization" of America (due to the growth of its federal state) came to correspond to an equally relevant "Americanization" of Europe (due to the strengthening of its market sector). In effect, while America in the 1960s and 1970s moved in the direction of Europe by introducing more extensive social security programs, in the 1980s and 1990s the countries of Western Europe moved in the direction of America, downsizing the welfare state and extending the private sector. In short, as Wilson remarked at the end of the 1990s, "American politics has more in common with the politics of several other advanced industrialized democracies today than with American politics in the past."[8]

A second challenge derived from public policy studies, which, through the analysis of specific public policies, were able to demonstrate the existence of several models or patterns of public intervention in America. In some, but not all, policy areas America clearly differs from other advanced countries.[9] Richard Rose even holds that, when analyzing American public policies in aggregate terms one may note that they are anything but peculiar, forming part of a American-Pacific model that characterizes a set of countries of (very) recent industrialization around the Pacific rim.[10] Thus, these studies of a strongly comparative nature provide us with a rather more multi-faceted and less ideological image of America.[11]

One cannot deny that the theory of exceptionalism has produced some of the most interesting analyses of American democracy, and has played an important role of scientific provocation, which has obliged European scholars to come to terms with American developments.[12] Nevertheless, the theory of exceptionalism did not pass the comparative test, not only because it was formulated prior to the full development of transnational research, but also because of its conceptual limitations.[13] In fact, the theory of exceptionalism was based on the idea of a priori or standard pattern of development, from which America diverged. Yet, transnational research shows that neither normal nor dominant models of development exist, even if the evolution of the individual countries may display common characteristics.[14] Thus, once the concept of a standard model of development was rejected, the theory of exceptionalism lost its scientific appeal. Obviously, the calling into question of this theory does not imply the need to abandon research on the distinctive elements of the American path of political development.

Here, I will argue that what distinguishes America is the method with which its contradictions, or better its *antinomies*, have been confronted in the course of its democratic development. The American democracy (which emerged from the revolution against Great Britain of 1776; the Philadelphia constitutional convention of 1787; and the first ten amendments of 1789, which were consolidated during the nineteenth century with reconstruction after the Civil War of 1861–5) is a democracy marked by four constituent antinomies: two of an institutional nature and two of a societal nature. These antinomies have been the subject of this book and by analyzing them here I will try to draw together the threads of my argument.

6.3   The Societal and Institutional Antinomies

The first pair of antinomies concerns the social nature of American democracy, which I define as follows: (i) *the maximum of market and the minimum of state*, (ii) *a society of groups and a nation of individuals*. I will start by considering the first antinomy.

Despite the neo-feudal model established in the south by fugitive English aristocrats (fleeing the parliamentary revolution of 1688 known as the Glorious Revolution), America has been marked much more sharply by the culture of those anti-aristocratic English fugitives who landed around 70 years earlier on the East Coast. It was this culture that made its mark on the subsequent socioeconomic evolution of the colonies (first) and of the confederation and federation (later).[15] This culture was defined as "naturally" Lockean,[16] in the sense that it was able to assert a contractualist view of American democracy.[17] It was able to do so because neither group of fugitives was confronted with an absolute state to constitutionalize, nor did they have to set up a social system with few resources to distribute to an exponentially growing population, both political and social circumstances that have significantly and negatively conditioned the development of the European nation states.

In America, as we have seen, the market arose before the state and, although economic freedom (of enterprise) was restricted by communitarian-religious constraints, it preceded the birth, and therefore guaranteed the growth, of political freedom (of speech and action). The market was thus the first institution able to impose order on social relations, or at any rate to rationalize its development in an expanding polity.[18] Of course, the concrete construction of the market, and therefore its development in the course of the first half of the nineteenth century (in the north especially), required constant intervention by the states, who were the driving force behind the construction of the necessary legal and material infrastructures of American democracy.[19] Nevertheless, the market was able to preserve the social recognition of being the source of individual freedom. Whereas in Europe the market has found justification as (mainly) an institution of efficiency, in America it has been perceived as (mainly) an institution of freedom.

I now turn to the second societal antinomy. When Jefferson managed to convince the political elite of his country to sweep the dust of religious conflict under the carpet, by means of that astute declaration of freedom of conscience that celebrated the rigid separation of state and church, at that moment, whether or not he was aware of it, he laid the basis for a modern pluralist society. For it was from the (recognized) pluralism of religious sects that the pluralism of social interests derived. America invented pluralism out of necessity because only recognition of the plurality of religious preferences in the country could save it from confessional disintegration. Once religious pluralism was ratified, recognition of the pluralism of social, economic, and cultural interests inevitably followed.[20]

It is indubitable that this religious origin of pluralism is a curious phenomenon indeed when set in the context of contemporary democracies. And yet no other democracy originated as a country of emigrants prompted to leave their homelands for religious reasons as well as socioeconomic necessity,[21] the only major exception being African Americans, who were brought to America against their will.[22] The pluralism of groups that emerged from this historical circumstance, and which was given theoretical formalization in Madison's *Federalist* no. 10, would have an unusually (for the period) dynamic character. These groups displayed transitory forms of social identification and political organization, not the permanent ones that came about when they expressed membership of broad economic categories or inclusive social classes.

Without a past, America was more aware than other countries of the need to invent a present.[23] Without a state, America was more aware than other countries of the need to invent a nation.[24] It is difficult to establish with precision the degree of cultural awareness possessed by the founding fathers (and I do not only refer to those who gathered in Philadelphia in the summer of 1787), yet one is obliged to stress the novelty of their undertaking: to create a nation based on a constitutional pact between distinct states and their citizens and not already justified by the existence of a territorial state.[25]

A nation, that is, which recognized itself as such on the basis of a pact among individuals (although organized within distinct states) rather than on the basis of an accord or a compromise among rival social powers (as happened in the Europe of the nineteenth century, with the compromise between the aristocracy and the rising commercial class). Thus in America, from the very beginning of the new republican experience, a sort of Janus-faced society was created which elsewhere would have been the outcome of a laborious process. On the one hand there was the society of individuals, without which it would have been impossible to conceive the idea of the constitutional pact. On the other hand there was the society of groups given the task of guaranteeing the equilibrium on which the constitutional pact rested; individuals and groups, it should be stressed, that were territorially organized.

The second pair of antinomies concerns the institutional nature of American democracy, which I define as follows: (i) *separated institutions and democratic government*, and (ii) *compound republic and democratic empire*. I shall begin with the former. With its preoccupation to separate governmental institutions, the American Constitution continues to be the only eighteenth-century liberal constitution among the established democracies. The practical liberalism of the new Constitution (an expression of the need to unite distinct and independent states) was combined with the theoretical liberalism of its inspirers (Locke and Montesquieu in particular), and a robust dose of Republicanism (derived from Machiavelli). These cultural currents were combined in order to answer a specific need: i.e. how to relate the fear of power to the necessity of its use.[26] America inaugurated a system of government which, though influenced by Tudor England, proved to be very distinct from the system that was institutionalized in Europe (in post-Tudor England in particular). While Europe was laboriously seeking to bring the king into parliament, in the same period America decided to exclude its king (the president) from parliament (the Congress).[27] Whereas the former strove to appease, the latter strove to divide.

However, this operational separation of powers (operational, that is, by virtue of the principle of checks and balances introduced by Madison) from the outset had to come to terms with a historical experience that ill-fitted the reasons adduced to justify it. Constitutional liberalism found itself forced to adapt to electoral democracy. The Constitution had no time to settle down before the wind of the electorate blew in through its windows. Indeed, liberal America, which had established itself on the principle of the fear of power (also, and perhaps principally, power sustained by the majority) could not gainsay itself by evading the necessity for its democratic (or better, popular) legitimization. Thus America was the first country to introduce universal suffrage (i.e. male and white) and therefore the first to create a modern party system as the indispensable means to substantiate those recognized electoral rights. Hence on the one hand the insistent endeavor to set operational limits on powers, and on the other the equally insistent pressure toward the latter's electoral legitimization.[28]

I now turn to the second institutional antinomy. In America, federalism was born from a rooted anti-majoritarian and anti-centralist prejudice. The enduring ambiguity that characterized the (confederalist) theory of the pre-eminence of the rights of states over the rights of the state can only be explained in the light of the deep-seated (federalist) theory of the diffusion of state power. From its beginnings, however, the federal republic had to reckon with the logic of a state of large territorial size (or better, a state not prevented from becoming such). Indeed, following Madison's *Federalist* no.10,[29] it was thought that the large size was the antidote to the illness (despotism) typical of the small size, and that federalism in turn was the antidote to the illness (the expansionist instinct or spirit of power) suffered by states of large territorial dimensions (and a fortiori those of continental extension). America expanded territorially for more than a century and yet remained compound. In fact, for a large part of the nineteenth century, the pressure for increasing the role of the federal center brought about by the geographical expansion of the polity was effectively checked by the decentralizing tendencies of a democracy structured around a multitude of states and localities.

Certainly, the equilibrium between the latter America and the America of the empire was very fragile, nevertheless it proved to be surprisingly stable for a good part of the nineteenth century. This was due to the capacity of the federal institutions (and Congress in particular) to represent and balance the social and cultural forces associated with them. When the logic of the great continental state came to predominate, any minor mishap was enough to galvanize the forces of anti-colonial if not isolationist America. In the same way, when the logic of the states and local democracy seemingly triumphed, its institutions and economy soon spawned the interests and cultures of an anti-isolationist America concerned with making the world safe, if not for democracy, then certainly for the market.[30]

6.4   Political Change and American Antinomies

If these may be considered as the antinomic foundations of American democracy as it became established up to and through the Civil War, then it is worth investigating how those antinomies reacted to the changes that subsequently came about. I begin with the first social antinomy, the one relative to the relationship between state and market. With the formation of the great corporations in the second half of the nineteenth century, the market lost its role as the natural arena of societal interchange. The place of Jefferson's yeomen was taken by the great capitalists – great because they proved themselves able to gain a monopoly in crucial production sectors. The challenge raised by the monopolistic reorganization of the market could not be countered by the minimal state. And yet it was a challenge that had to be neutralized if the market was to be preserved as the source of social mobility via economic competition. As we know, this engendered the birth in the 1880s, and its uninterrupted expansion thereafter, of a federal state endowed both with increasingly broad regulatory powers and an increasingly tight administrative organization. Although the market did not easily accept such intervention by the federal state, it nevertheless ended up adapting to it.

Let me consider the second social antinomy, that between groups and individuals. Partly as a result of the federal centralization of the twentieth century, but mainly as the outcome of the functional complexity of industrial society, the pluralism of groups has also come to assume – especially since the New Deal years – an oligopolistic configuration. Public policies have been increasingly conditioned by great organized interests, in accordance with the pattern that Lowi has called the "liberalism of interest groups."[31] In short, the individualistic basis of liberalism has been progressively eroded, with repercussions on the cultural identity of the country itself. Individual interests have been able to achieve recognition for themselves only by becoming an organized group, for only by organizing themselves have they been able to participate on a stable basis in the formation of national public policies. Nonetheless, this organization has never acquired the neo-corporatist features that one can see in Europe, where, moreover, corporatism was able to exploit its previous legitimization in the interwar period, in both its authoritarian and Fabian versions.[32]

Once the identity of the functional group lost its temporary and instrumental character (in pursuit of a specific public policy objective) and acquired a permanent one, the conditions were created for the transformation of the identity of the cultural group itself, in the sense that the "melting pot" was gradually superseded by the "salad bowl" (in a melting pot the ingredients are blended; in a salad bowl they retain their original features); the single-colored nation was gradually replaced by the rainbow-hued nation.[33] This led to the ineluctable erosion of the constitutional bases of American identity. Indeed, at the beginning of the twenty-first century, the America of the hyphen (which subordinated the original national identity to the subsequently acquired American identity) for the first time seemed less attractive than the America without the hyphen, the America of distinct and separate identities.

Moreover the first institutional antinomy concerning the relationship between separated institutions and electoral democracy has undergone significant changes. Under the pressure exerted by the external exposure of the country, as well as by the processes of democratization and nationalization, separated government was transformed in order to accommodate presidential government. While congressional government of the previous era looked with favor on the growth of modern party organizations, this has not been the case of presidential government in the post-Second World War period. When there is no institutional incentive for the fusion of powers, it is unlikely that institutionally cohesive parties will form, because the parties adapt to the features of the institutional system and not vice versa. Certainly, the weakening of the parties had more to do with their electoral and organizational levels than their institutional level. The party-in-the-electorate has weakened in terms of decreasing partisan identification on the part of the voters and the party-as-organization has weakened in terms of reduced capacity to organize electoral and political mobilization. However, with the quasi-institutionalization of a regime of "divided government" between 1969 and 2000, parties have increased their coordination capacities within the separated institutions.

I turn finally to the changes that have occurred in the second institutional antinomy, the one relative to the relationships between (federated) states and the (federal) state. First rapid industrial growth, and then America's international ascendancy, subjected the institutional structure of the compound republic to powerful pressures. While the New Deal had begun the nationalization process of American politics, the Cold War accelerated its internationalization. Power was increasingly transferred from the states to the state, but without this transfer finding justification in a coherent culture of the state.[34] Thus the America of the large federal state was forced to coexist with the America of the single states and localities, the America of imperial power with the America of the small county. It is not easy for America to be a global power because of the countervailing forces keeping the pressure on the decision-making powers at a state or a local level. In sum, the relationship between states and the state has continued to describe a seesaw motion: the ascent of the federal state has never been definitive; indeed, due to ascendancy of the neoconservative coalition at the turn of the twentieth century, the federated states have regained their influence in important policy fields.

6.5 America: A Model or a Method?

Granted that an "American model" exists, it nevertheless is a model founded on unequivocal antinomies.[35] If one bears in mind this antinomic nature of the American model, it also becomes easier to understand why it has, in most cases, dramatically failed when exported. In any case, it is useful to better understand the American *method* for dealing with those antinomies, because similar antinomies are structuring the functioning of the EU compound polity.[36]

The American method has relied mainly on the competitive principle for ordering the antinomies of the compound democracy. In fact, as regards the antinomy between state and market, America's history displays a predominantly *competitive approach*. America has never undertaken the statization of the market, although frequent attempts have been made to marketize the state. The American approach, inaugurated in the 1890s and then confirmed by subsequent developments, has been to transform the state into the regulator of the market, not its replacement. A regulation justified by pragmatic reasons, i.e. to keep the market competitive, since, if left to itself, it tends to generate oligopolies.[37] Also regarding the antinomy between groups and individuals, American history shows the pursuit of a competitive approach seeking to counterbalance the power of certain groups with the empowerment of disorganized individuals through legislative action. The same competitive approach has characterized the American method to deal with the institutional antinomies. As regards the contrast between the president and Congress, America has been mainly preoccupied to guarantee competition between them, more than to aggregate their views into a coherent party majority.[38] Indeed, when America was able to do that after September 11, 2001 it discovered that separation of powers is not easy to reconcile with centralized presidential predominance. Also in the case of the antinomy between states and the state, America has fostered competition between them for the control of sensitive public policies.[39]

Thus, the American method for dealing with both societal and institutional antinomies has been based mainly on a competitive principle. This competitive principle has produced, on the social level, a dynamic economy and a vital civil society and, on the institutional level, a stable and balanced political system. However, competition has also had its drawbacks, both at the societal and institutional levels. At the *societal* level, the competitive approach has generated evident inegalitarian effects. Certainly, the relation between market and democracy displays a contradictory nature everywhere. Indeed, Dahl and Lindblom have argued since the 1950s that markets, although necessary for supporting democracies, nonetheless prevent the latter from fully developing their potential.[40] Yet, these inegalitarian effects of the market on democracy have been much more evident in America than in Europe. As we have seen, in terms of distribution of wealth, the regulatory pattern did not prevent America from becoming the most inegalitarian democracy among the established democracies of the Atlantic (as we have seen in chapter 4, the Gini index of income inequality increased from 0.396 in 1971 to 0.466 in 2001 [US Census Bureau, various years]).

If we consider the relation between groups and individuals, then one could argue that the competitive approach has produced a vital pluralism, albeit with an evident conservative bias. In fact, pluralism has tended to preserve the status quo in the structure of public policies because it entails the use of a resource (the organization) that is unequally distributed among interests and individuals. Social groups with greater resources or better opportunities for self-organization can exert greater influence on policy-making than groups with fewer resources or opportunities. Consequently, once a particular trajectory is imposed on public policies (as was the case with the denial of civil rights to African-Americans after the Civil War), the well-organized groups are able to preserve it to the detriment of the less well organized, according to a process that we may call the factionalism of minorities.[41] Although freedom of association is normatively constitutive of any democracy, its use in America has become a factor in the curtailment of democracy, in the sense that public policy has tended to reflect more the interests of insiders than those of outsiders.

The acknowledgement of the inegalitarian effects of the regulatory market and organizational pluralism is especially necessary in Europe, where both constitute the social bases of the EU's compoundness. In particular, in the "disjointed and competitive setting of the EU," as Schmitter noted, "Euro-associations may not be preferred over more specialized ones. They must compete for influence with a wide variety of other units: national states, para-state corporations, sub-national governments, large private firms, and even lobbyists and lawyers intervening on behalf of individual clients."[42] Unfamiliar with pluralism, EU officials seemed to have underestimated its political implications. In order to answer the criticism that the EU policy-making process is not sufficiently democratic, the EU institutions (and the Commission in particular) paradoxically reinforced that criticism looking for the support (and the involvement) of a growing number of interest groups. Again Schmitter observes: "[e]specially since the signing of the Single European Act in 1985, Brussels has been literally invaded by 'Euro-lobbies' . . . While all this pluralism (to use the American expression) is entirely appropriate in modern democracy, its highly skewed nature does raise some questions about whether these channels for the expression of particular interests are freely and fairly available to all citizens of Europe. So far, the evidence suggests a mobilization of bias in favor of business interests."[43]

Also at the *institutional* level, the competitive method has had significant drawbacks. Competition (if not combat) among separated institutions certainly made reciprocal checking possible. However, a political system with diffused and fragmented powers, both horizontally and vertically, has also helped to preserve the inequalities of income, wealth, status, information, and opportunity produced by the market economy and the culture of racial segregation. In fact, power-sharing systems tend to institutionalize veto points. In these systems, a decision can be taken only with the consent of a large number of actors, to the extent that they are endowed with specific institutional resources. In America, this institutional context has constituted a powerful barrier against choices not supported by a wide consensus; a good condition to prevent bad outcomes. But this context has also furnished powerful minorities with the resources to prevent any changes which might challenge their social, economic, or political privileges.

Consequently, while separation of power has prevented the tyranny of (diffused) majorities it has simultaneously facilitated domination by (concentrated) minorities. It has saved American democracy, but it has also contributed to make it less egalitarian than other democracies. In large democracies with a pronounced heterogeneity of territorial, ethnic, racial, social, economic, and ideological interests, it is extremely difficult to construct political coalitions to bring about change (e.g. the abolition of segregation, the promotion of redistributive policies, the introduction of universal social security). By contrast, it is much less difficult to construct negative political coalitions for conservation of existing policies. The American separation of powers has institutionalized a bias in favor of continuity, rather than the opposite. Institutional pluralism has been an effective antidote against hierarchical and hegemonic conceptions of the public good. But it has been less effective in counteracting those conceptions that engender unequal relations among groups and individuals. The historical development of the American compound democracy has led to the formation of a balanced politics and an unfair society.[44] In sum, if "the 'Madisonian' theory of democracy (represents) an effort to bring off a compromise between the power of majorities and the power of minorities, between the political equality of all adult citizens on the one side, and the desire to limit their sovereignty on the other,"[45] then one might say that that effort has not been entirely successful.

The experience of the EU is similar. Decisions emerge from multiple negotiations between multiple actors in multiple arenas. As Scharpf explained some time ago, this system implies a joint decision trap: [46] if a broad consensus is needed to change the policy status quo, then the outcome will be as close as possible to the policy status quo itself. Also in the EU, powerful national or subnational actors can exercise an effective veto power, through their control of one of the many arenas in which the decision-making process takes place. Institutionally nested veto powers have protected various (social or state) minorities from undesired decisions, but they have also prevented the adoption of popular decisions when they conflicted with the interests of powerful (national or economic or social) minorities. This is why the American experience might be useful for understanding the evolution of the EU compound polity. Assuming that it would be very difficult for the EU to return to the era of the sovereignty of its member states, then the American experience of dealing with compoundness might prove to be fruitful for understanding the antinomies that a compound democracy has to face.

Which trade-off does the EU have to find between institutional compoundness and social equality? Bryce wrote at the end of the nineteenth century:

> America has in some respect anticipated European nations. She is walking before them along a path which they may probably follow. She carries behind her, to adopt a famous simile of Dante's, a lamp whose light helps those that come after her more than it always does herself, because some of the dangers she has passed through may not recur at any other point in her path; whereas they, following in her footsteps, may stumble in the same stony places or be entangled in the quagmires into which she slipped.[47]

Certainly, the same Bryce reminded us that "the reader . . . must not expect the problems America has solved, or those which still perplex her, to reappear in Europe in the same forms," however "nothing can be more instructive than American experience if it be *discreetly* used. . . . "[48] (The italics are mine.)

6.6   Conclusion

The American method for resolving antinomies has enjoyed a solid underpinning in the predominant culture of the country. This method has been sustained by an altogether liberal political culture, i.e. a political culture that has formed in the knowledge that the conflicts of a compound democracy are both inevitable and unsolvable. Ever since 1787, the American political culture has been characterized by its realistic awareness that democracy (or the republic as it was then called) necessarily must come to terms with differences of territorial interests and human imperfections. As Madison said in *Federalist* no.51: "But what is government itself, but the greatest of all reflections on human nature? If men were angels, no government would be necessary. If angels were to govern men, neither external nor internal controls on government would be necessary."[49]

This realism has made its mark on the constitutional culture of the country from the beginning, by instituting an operational link between liberty and change.[50] In fact, America is the homeland of modern constitutionalism, because it has known how to preserve its spirit and not just its letter. It has succeeded in doing so precisely by providing for the possibility of amending its Constitution, although this possibility is rigorously regulated. This idea was unprecedented for those times, and it was immediately taken up as the Constitution was amended (with the ten amendments of the Bill of Rights) already the year after it was approved.[51] At least since the Civil War of 1861–5, the Constitution has furnished the normative frame through which conflicts between states, groups, and individuals have been waged. It is for this reason that, as has been observed, the Americans have become so attached to their Constitution, turning it into the "holy book" of their secular religion.[52] The EU, instead, although a constitutionalized regime, is still lacking a formal document able to frame the conflicts between member states, groups, and individuals.[53] America shows that compound democracies are open systems, wherein it is implausible to settle conflicts, given the difference between their constituent units. This is why America can hardly be interpreted as a model to emulate.

Its realistic foundation (i.e. the recognition of the contradictions among states and individuals that stand at the basis of a compound democracy) and liberal inspiration (i.e. the idea that all interests are legitimate) are the reasons why American political culture came to be informed by a pluralistic vision of social and institutional interests. What counts in such a vision is the guarantee of an acceptable competition between the diverse interests rather than an acceptable outcome of that competition. As long as there is competition between the institutions of government, the personalization of the presidency is not a threat. As long as there is competition between the various wielders of public power, the decline of the political parties and of electoral participation is not the expression of a political crisis. As long as there is competition among states and among the federal state and the federated states, the threat of territorial centralization will be neutralized. As long as there is competition in the market, the growth of inequality is not a challenge to its functioning. As long as there is an open decision-making process in foreign policy, the imperial outcome of some decisions does not call into question the democratic nature of the country.

Precisely because of their different historical roots, the dominant political cultures in Europe instead were not content with safeguarding the competition between interests and values, but have sought to establish a hierarchy amongst them. Only with difficulty has pluralism found a way into these societies, as they had formed on the basis of a normative vision of society. It was probably not easy to provide for the recognition of all the "ambitions" in a context of scarce resources for a growing population and in the presence of unjustifiable hereditary privileges. The liberalism of continental European countries has been molded by this context, frequently turning into an ideology (in defense of the dominant classes and strata) rather than a method (which presupposed the recognition of the interests of all groups and of all classes). Thus, in European countries, the outcome was a less personalized and more participatory political system than in America, but also a more paternalistic and hierarchical one. Simultaneously, the outcome has been a more egalitarian society than the American one, but also less dynamic and less inclusive. Collectivist and communitarian European countries have embraced social solidarity as their priority, even to the detriment of individual liberty. This has made European democracies more solidaristic, but also more exposed to the tyranny of the majority; America, by contrast, is much more exposed to the tyranny of minorities.

Yet, European political culture has undergone great transformations in the post-Second World War period. The process of supranational integration has tested the preconditions of social and cultural cohesion on which European societies had rested in the past. Indeed, the EU is as institutionally compound and socially differentiated as any of the countries that have helped to create it. Such transformations have confronted Europeans with novel problems in the market and in politics. Europeans have to learn to manage their institutional and social contrasts without having the possibility of returning to the hierarchical solutions of the nation state. America has dealt with those contrasts through a competitive method that is constitutionally regulated. This being so, it is worth knowing the American method for dealing with similar problems, in order to understand both the virtues it has instilled and the vices it has not managed to avoid. Although it is true that in America competition has been able to produce public goods, it is also true that this has not always occurred. In fact, competition has revealed itself to be a double-edged sword, in the sense that it at times has worsened, rather than mitigated, relevant institutional, social, and political problems. In the end, as a method, competition and the outcomes it produces are not beyond empirical verification. Knowing America better, Europe might perhaps become aware not only of the latter's vices and virtues, but also of the challenges that lie before it.

Notes

Chapter 1   Anti-Americanism in Europe

1   P. Chamorel, *Anti-Europeanism and Euroskepticism in the United States*, Florence, European University Institute, Schuman Centre for Advanced Studies, working paper, 2004; T. Garton Ash, "Anti-Europeanism in America," *New York Review of Books*, 50, 2 (February 13, 2003).
2   T. Judt and D. Lacorne (eds), *With US or Against US: Studies in Global Anti-Americanism* (New York: Palgrave Macmillan, 2005).
3   S. Fabbrini (ed.), *The United States Contested: American Unilateralism and European Discontent* (London: Routledge, 2006).
4   S. Fabbrini, "The Domestic Sources of European Anti-Americanism," *Government and Opposition*, 37, 1 (2002).
5   There is a growing literature on the argument. See the four volumes edited by B. O'Connor, *Anti-Americanism: History, Causes and Themes* (Oxford: Greenwood World Publishing, 2007); P. J. Katznelson and R. O. Keohane (eds), *Anti-Americanism in World Politics* (Ithaca: Cornell University Press, 2007); G. Chiozza, *Love and Hate: Anti-Americanism and the American World Order*, Ph.D. dissertation, Duke University, Department of Political Science, 2004.
6   P. Hollander, *Anti-Americanism: Critique at Home and Abroad* (Oxford: Oxford University Press, 1992).
7   D. W. Ellwood, *Anti-Americanism in Western Europe: A Comparative Perspective*, Johns Hopkins University, Bologna Center, Occasional Paper no. 3, 1999, p. 3.
8   T. Judt, "America and the War," *New York Review of Books*, 48 (November 15, 2001), p. 4.
9   S. Hoffmann, "The US and International Organizations," in R. J. Lieber (ed.), *Eagle Rules?* (Boston: Prentice Hall, 2001).

10 I. Buruma and A. Margalit, *Occidentalism: The West in the Eyes of its Enemies* (New York: Penguin, 2004); P. Scowen, *Rogue Nation: The America the Rest of the World Knows* (Toronto: MandS, 2003).

11 D. W. Ellwood, "Comparative Anti-Americanism in Western Europe," in H. Fehrenbach and U. G. Poiger (eds), *Transactions, Transgressions, Transformations: American Culture in Western Europe and Japan* (New York: Berghahn, 2000).

12 W. Drzdick, "Even Allies Resent US Dominance," *Washington Post*, November 4, 1997.

13 P. Pinzler, "The Row with America," *Die Zeit*, September 3, 2002, p. 3.

14 R. Singh, "Anti-Americanism in the United Kingdom," in O'Connor, *Anti-Americanism*, vol. 3.

15 P. Deer, "The Dogs of War: Myths of British Anti-Americanism," in A. Ross and K. Ross (eds), *Anti-Americanism* (New York: New York University Press, 2004).

16 C. Ross, "The French Declaration of Independence," in A. Ross and K. Ross (ed.), *Anti-Americanism* (New York: New York University Press, 2004).

17 S. Meunier, "The French Exception," *Foreign Affairs*, 79, 4 (2000), p. 106.

18 See F. Viviano, "Bitter Debate in Europe on US Role: Washington's Dominance of Nato Creates Waves of Anti-Americanism," *San Francisco Chronicle*, April 15, 1999, pp. 1, 7.

19 P. Roger, *L'ennemi américain: Généalogie de l'antiaméricanisme français* (Paris: Seuil, 2002).

20 C. Nettelbeck, "Anti-Americanism in France," in O'Connor, *Anti-Americanism*, vol. 3.

21 Cited by Viviano, "Bitter Debate."

22 M. Nolan, "Anti-Americanization in Germany," in Ross and Ross, *Anti-Americanism*.

23 V. Berghahn, *America and the Intellectual Cold Wars in Europe* (Princeton: Princeton University Press, 2001).

24 S. Fabbrini, "Layers of Anti-Americanism: Americanization, American Unilateralism and Anti-Americanism in a European Perspective," *European Journal of American Culture*, 23, 2 (2004).

25 A. Giddens and W. Hutton, "In Conversation," in A. Giddens and W. Hutton (eds), *Global Capitalism* (New York: The New Press, 2000), p. 41.

26 W. Wallace, 2002, "Living with the Hegemon: European Dilemmas," in E. Hershberg and K. W. Moore (eds), *Critical Views of September 11: Analysis From Around the World* (New York: New Press, 2002).

27 P. Isernia and S. Fabbrini, "Bush, the Iraq War and Anti-Americanism," in O'Connor, *Anti-Americanism*, vol. 1; R. Crockatt, *America Embattled: September 11, Anti-Americanism and the Global Order* (London: Routledge, 2003).

28 R. Crockatt, *America and Anti-Americanism* (London: Taylor and Francis, 2002).
29 B. Rubin and J. Colp Rubin, *Hating America: A History* (Oxford: Oxford University Press, 2004).
30 S. M. Lipset and G. Marks, *It Didn't Happen Here: Why Socialism Failed in the United States* (New York: W.W. Norton, 2000).
31 C. Ruzza and E. Bozzini, "Anti-Americanism and the European Peace Movement: The Iraq War," in Fabbrini, *United States Contested*.
32 Giddens and Hutton, "In Conversation," p. 34.
33 Ibid., p. 15.
34 Rubin and Rubin, *Hating America*.
35 G. Wood, *The Radicalism of the American Revolution* (New York: Alfred. A. Knopf, 1992).
36 Indeed, as Alexis de Tocqueville pointed out (*Democracy in America*, New York: Anchor Books, 1969, p. 114), since "(t)he new federal government took up its duties in 1789," one may say that "the American Revolution ended exactly when ours (the French n.d.r.) began."
37 De Tocqueville, *Democracy in America*, p. 241.
38 Robert H. Wiebe, *Self Rule: A Cultural History of American Democracy* (Chicago: University of Chicago Press, 1995), in an amusing chapter entitled "The Barbarians" draws on the travel diaries and letters as well as the literature published in the course of the nineteenth century to provide a detailed survey of the interpretation of *homo americanus* by (aristocratic) Europeans. There is little difference between that literature and a certain type of contemporary journalism. For the Americans are uncouth and ill-mannered. What essential difference is there between the lofty disdain shown by the well-educated English lady Marie Lundie Duncan when she expresses in her *America as I Find It*, 1852 (cited in Wiebe, *Self Rule*, 45) her disdain for a society "[w]here a scavenger was a *gentleman* and a whore was a *lady*" and that of many European journalists or cultural correspondents in America when reporting snobbishly on the habit of Americans to call each other by the first name and eat hot dogs.
39 De Tocqueville, *Democracy in America*, p. 186.
40 M. Nacci, *L'anti-americanismo in Italia negli anni Trenta* (Turin: Bollati Boringhieri, 1989).
41 M. Kazin, *The Populist Persuasion: An American History* (New York: Basic Books, 1995).
42 R. D. Putnam, *Bowling Alone: The Collapse and Revival of American Community* (New York: Simon and Schuster, 2000).
43 S. Verba, K. Schlozman, and H. Brady (eds), *Voice and Equality: Civic Volunteerism in American Politics* (Cambridge: Harvard University Press, 1995).
44 G. Wills, *Papal Sin: Structure of Deceit* (New York: Random House, 2001).

45 M. Walzer, *What It Means To Be an American: Essays on the American Experience* (New York: Marsilio, 1996), p. 108.
46 C. S. Steiker, "Capital Punishment and American Exceptionalism," in M. Ignatieff (ed.), *American Exceptionalism and Human Rights* (Princeton: Princeton University Press, 2005).
47 S. M. Lipset, *American Exceptionalism: A Double-Edged Sword* (New York: Norton, 1996), p. 19.
48 J. Neusner, *World Religions in America: An Introduction* (Louisville, KY: Westminster John Knox Press, 2003).
49 M. Walzer, *On Toleration* (New Haven, CT: Yale University Press, 1997), p. 67.
50 J. T. McGreevy, *Catholicism and American Freedom: A History* (New York: W.W. Norton, 2003).
51 J. D. Dolan, *In Search of an American Catholicism: A History of Religion and Culture in Tension* (Oxford: Oxford University Press, 2003).
52 Lipset, *American Exceptionalism*, pp. 62–3.
53 L. Banning, *The Jeffersonian Persuasion: Evolution of a Party Ideology* (Ithaca, NY: Cornell University Press, 1983).
54 J. Krammick and R. L. Moore, *The Godless Constitution: The Case Against Religious Correctness* (New York: W.W. Norton, 1997); see also J. A. Hall and C. Lindholm, *Is America Breaking Apart?* (Princeton: Princeton University Press, 1999).
55 G. Wills, *Why I Am a Catholic* (New York: Houghton Mifflin, 2002).
56 G. M. Fredrickson, "Mosaics and the Melting Pot," *Dissent* (Summer 1999). See also G. M. Fredrickson, *The Comparative Imagination: On the History of Racism, Nationalism, and Social Movements* (Berkeley: University of California Press, 1997).
57 "I admit that I saw in America more than America; it was the shape of democracy itself which I sought, its inclinations, character, prejudices, and passions," wrote A. de Tocqueville in the introduction to his *Democracy in America*, p. 19. Having accepted uncritically this coincidence between America and democracy, it was inevitable, for many observers after de Tocqueville, to transform the country into an ideology.
58 S. M. Lipset, *The First New Nation: The United States in Historical and Comparative Perspective*, 2nd edn (New York: W.W. Norton, 1979); see also C. Offe, J. Thompson, and G. Schott, *Reflections on America: Tocqueville, Weber and Adorno in the United States* (Cambridge: Polity Press, 2005).
59 On the self-centered outlook of American public culture see S. Fabbrini, "American Democracy from a European Perspective," *Annual Review of Political Science*, 2 (1999).
60 J. W. Ceaser, *Reconstructing America: The Symbols of America in Modern Thought* (New Haven, CT: Yale University Press, 1997), p. 248.

61 The literature on this topic is vast. See H. Spruyt, *The Sovereign State and Its Competitors* (Princeton: Princeton University Press, 1994), and C. Tilly, *Coercion, Capital, and European States, AD 990–1990* (Oxford: Basil Blackwell, 1990).
62 See S. Fabbrini, *Compound Democracies: Why America and Europe Are Becoming Similar* (Oxford: Oxford University Press, 2007); S. Fabbrini, "A Single Western State Model? Differential Development and Constrained Convergence of Public Authority Organization in Europe and America," *Comparative Political Studies*, 36, 6 (2003).

Chapter 2 A Plebiscitary Democracy

1 D. Losurdo, *Democrazia o bonapartismo: Trionfo e decadenza del suffragio universale* (Torino: Bollati Boringhieri, 1993), p. 285. (Translation mine.)
2 Harald Muller, "Das zerrissen Erbe der Aufklärung: Die ideologische Polarisierung zwischen Deutschland und den USA," *Internationale Politik*, 50 (2004), pp. 11–12.
3 Geffrey Gedmin, "Warum Europaer George W. Bush hassen," *Die Welt*, November 15, 2006.
4 I have discussed these issues on several occasions. See, in particular: S. Fabbrini, *Compound Democracies: Why the United States and Europe Are Becoming Similar*; S. Fabbrini, "The American System of Separated Government: An Historical-Institutional Interpretation," *The International Political Science Review*, 20, 1 (1999); S. Fabbrini, *La representacion y el presidencialismo estadunidense*, in A. Hernandez-Chavez (ed.), *Presidencialismo y system politico. México y los Estados Unidos* (El Colegio de Mexico: Fondo de Cultura Economica, 1994).
5 C. Beard (ed.), *The Enduring Federalist* (New York: Frederick Ungar Publishing Co., 1948, original edn 1788), p. 34.
6 G. S. Wood, *The Creation of the American Republic, 1776–1787* (New York: Norton, 1969).
7 G. S. Wood, *American Revolution* (New York: Modern Library, 2002); J. G. A. Pocock, *The Machiavellian Moment: Florentine Political Thought and the Atlantic Republican Tradition* 2 vols (Princeton: Princeton University Press, 1975).
8 D. C. Hendrickson, *Peace Pact: The Lost World of American Founding* (Lawrence: University Press of Kansas, 2003), xii.
9 J. S. Shklar, *Redeeming American Political Thought*, ed. S. Hoffmann and D. F. Thompson (Chicago: University of Chicago Press, 1998); R. Hofstadter, *The American Political Tradition and the Men Who Made It* (New York: Alfred A. Knopf, 1948); M. Forsyth, *Unions of States: The Theory and Practice of Confederation* (New York: Leicester University Press, 1981).
10 Beard, *Enduring Federalist*, p. 225.

11 Wood, *Creation of the Republic.*
12 Beard, *Enduring Federalist,* p. 34.
13 Letter to William Stephens Smith of November 13, 1787, now in A. Koch and W. Peden (eds), *The Life and Selected Writings of Thomas Jefferson* (New York: Random House, 1944), p. 436.
14 Beard, *Enduring Federalist,* p. 234.
15 S. P. Huntington, *Political Order in Changing Societies* (New Haven, CT: Yale University Press, 1968).
16 R. E. Neustadt, *Presidential Power and the Modern Presidents: The Politics of Leadership from Roosevelt to Reagan,* 3rd rev. edn (New York: The Free Press, 1990), p. 29 (italics in the original).
17 M. Forsyth, *Unions of States: The Theory and Practice of Confederation* (New York: Holmes and Meier Publishers, 1981), pp. 64, 65.
18 B. Ackerman, "The New Separation of Powers," Harvard Law Review, 113, 3 (2000).
19 With the exception, in Europe, of Switzerland which has an institutional structure based on multiple separations of power and a functional logic marked by the absence of a government similar to the American ones.
20 *Caucus* generally refers to a party conference. The word is of native-American origin and is said to roughly mean "meeting in front of the tent."
21 W. Wilson, *Congressional Government. A Study in American Politics* (Baltimore: Johns Hopkins University Press, 1981).
22 T. Lowi and B. Ginsberg, *American Government: Freedom and Power* (New York: W.W. Norton, 1990), p. 191.
23 N. W. Polsby, *Congress and the Presidency,* 4th edn (Englewood Cliffs: Prentice Hall, 1986), pp. 116–19.
24 See the, by now, classical analysis of M. L. Mezey, *Congress, the President and Public Policy* (Boulder: Westview Press, 1989), ch. 3.
25 See M.-F. Toinet, (ed.) *L'Etat en Amérique* (Paris: Presses de la fondation nationale de sciences politiques, 1989).
26 See the classic study by M. Einaudi, *The Roosevelt Revolution* (New York: Harcourt, Brace, and World, 1959).
27 C. Tilly, "War Making and State Making as Organized Crime," in P. Evans, D. Rueschemeyer, and T. Skocpol, (eds), *Bringing the State Back In* (Cambridge: Cambridge University Press, 1985).
28 E. S. Corwin, *The President: Office and Powers* (New York: New York University Press, 1957), p. 2.
29 M. Farrand, *The Records of the Federal Convention of 1787* (New Haven, CT: Yale University Press, 1966).
30 See R. A. Dahl, *Democracy in the United States: Promise and Performance,* 3rd edn (Chicago: Rand McNally, 1967), part 2.
31 On the relations between the two, see R. K. Matthews, *If Men Were Angels: Madison and the Heartless Empire of Reason* (Lawrence: University Press of Kansas, 1995), ch. 7.

32 See L. Banning, *The Jeffersonian Persuasion: Evolution of a Party Ideology* (Ithaca, NY: Cornell University Press, 1978).

33 See R. Scigliano, *The Supreme Court and the Presidency* (New York: Free Press, 1971).

34 As argued convincingly by A. Wildavsky, *New Politics of the Budgetary Process*, 2nd edn (Glenview, IL: Scott, Foresman and Company, 1988).

35 On this see R. J. Spitzer, *The Presidential Veto: Touchstone of the American Presidency* (Albany: State University of New York Press, 1988).

36 N. W. Polsby, *How Congress Evolves: Social Bases of Institutional Change* (Oxford: Oxford University Press, 2004).

37 See L. N. Rieselbach, *Congressional Reform* (Washington, DC: C.Q. Press, 1986).

38 M. P. Wattenberg, *The Rise of Candidate-Centered Politics: Presidential Elections of the Eighties* (Cambridge, MA: Harvard University Press, 1991); R. J. Dalton, *Citizen Politics: Public Opinion and Political Parties in Advanced Industrial Democracies* (New York: Chatham House, 2002).

39 S. Kernell, *Going Public: New Strategies of Presidential Leadership*, 4th edn (Washington, DC: C.Q. Press, 2006).

40 See A. Ware, *The American Direct Primary: Party Institutionalization and Transformation in the North* (Cambridge: Cambridge University Press, 2002).

41 V. O. Key Jr, *Southern Politics* (New York: Alfred A. Knopf, 1949).

42 See M. Margolis and J. Green (eds), *Machine Politics, Sound Bites and Nostalgia: On Studying Political Parties* (New York: University Press of America, 1993).

43 See R. S. Katz and R. Kolodny, "Party Organization as an Empty Vessel: Parties in American Politics," in R. S. Katz and P. Mair (eds), *How Parties Organize* (London: Sage, 1994).

44 S. Skowzomek, "Leadership by Definition: First Term Reflections on George W. Bush's Political Stance," *Perspectives on Politics*, 3, n. 4, pp. 817–31.

45 National conventions meet in the summer to formalize the nomination of the presidential candidate that has emerged victoriously from the long trajectory of direct primaries – and, in some cases, the caucuses.

46 N. W. Polsby, *The Consequences of Party Reform* (Oxford: Oxford University Press, 1988).

47 Yet this conflict has also not prevented important bills from being passed when a consensus existed between the legislators, as shown by D. R. Mayhew, *Divided We Govern: Party Control, Lawmaking, and Investigations 1946–2002*, 2nd edn (New Haven, CT: Yale University Press, 2005).

48 Still the most incisive study is B. Ginsberg and M. Shefter, *Politics by Other Means: The Declining Importance of Elections in America* (New

York: Basic Books, 1990). By "other means" they mainly refer to revelations, investigations and persecutions (RIPs). On the characteristics of the RIPs, see, from the same authors, "Ethics Probes as Political Weapons," *The Journal of Law and Politics*, 11, 3 (1995).

49 See *Congressional Weekly Report*, December 14, 2002, p. 3240.
50 E. Schickler, "Congress," in G. Peele et al. (eds), *Developments in American Politics* (New York: Palgrave, 2002), p. 99.
51 R. Dworkin, "The Wounded Constitution," *New York Review of Books*, 46 (March 18, 1999).
52 As has been well documented by L.-E. Nelson, "The Republican's War," *New York Review of Books*, 46 (February 4, 1999).
53 This decision, in fact, had made it possible to initiate legal proceedings against President Clinton for sexual harassment (during his tenure as Governor of Arkansas) of Paula Jones. These proceedings subsequently led to the Lewinsky scandal, when the president, four years on from the start of the proceedings, finally committed a crime by falsely denying to the lawyers of Paula Jones that he had sexual relations with Monica Lewinsky.
54 As was brilliantly argued by T. Lowi, *The Personal President: Power Invested Promise Unfulfilled* (Ithaca, NY: Cornell University Press, 1985).
55 See A. M. Dershowitz, *Supreme Injustice: How the High Court Hijacked Election 2000* (Oxford: Oxford University Press, 2001).

Chapter 3   A Democracy without the People

1 C. Leggewie, "Die neue selbstverstandlichkeit," *Die Zeit* (online), 45, 2000, p. 13.
2 See M. P. Wattenberg, *Where Have All the Voters Gone?* (Cambridge, MA: Harvard University Press, 2002).
3 The term "dynasty" is used by K. Phillips, *American Dynasty: Aristocracy, Fortune, and the Politics of Deceit in the House of Bush* (New York: Penguin, 2004).
4 J. N. Shklar, *American Citizenship: The Quest for Inclusion* (Cambridge, MA: Harvard University Press, 1991); E. Foner, *The Story of American Freedom* (New York: W.W. Norton, 1998).
5 S. M. Lipset, *American Exceptionalism: A Double-Edged Sword* (New York: W. W. Norton, 1996), pp. 43–4.
6 A. Ranney, "Referendums," *Public Opinion*, 11, 1 (1989), p. 15.
7 See V. Ostrom, *The Political Theory of a Compound Republic: Designing the American Experiment*, 2nd edn (Lincoln: University of Nebraska Press, 1987).
8 R. A. Dahl, *A Preface to Democratic Theory: Expanded Edition* (Chicago: University of Chicago Press, 2006, original edn 1956). The fact that the formation of a cross-party majority is hindered by the full institution-

alization of the separation of powers obviously does not imply that such a majority cannot come about anyway, in particular when critical events, such as the Great Depression of 1929 or the terrorist attacks of 2001, erase the differences between the interests represented by the various institutions of government.

9   B. E. Cain and W. T. Jones, *Madison's Theory of Representation*, in B. Grofman and D. Wittman (eds), *The Federalist Papers and the New Institutionalism* (New York: Agathon Press, 1989).

10   L. Epstein, *Political Parties in the American Mold* (Madison: University of Wisconsin Press, 1986).

11   M. F. Toinet, *Le Système politique des États-Unis* (Paris: PUF, 1987), p. 426.

12   Ibid., p. 427.

13   D. Butler and B. Cain, "Reapportionment: A Study in Comparative Government," *Electoral Studies*, 4, 3 (1985).

14   There is a vast literature on the so-called *gerrymandering*, i.e. designing electoral districts in such a way as to give a decisive advantage to a certain party. The term derives from a combination of the name of the governor of Massachusetts, Elbridge Gerry (who, at the beginning of the Republic had an electoral district designed for him in such a way as to assure his re-election) and the shape of the district thus designed, which resembled a salamander.

15   N. W. Polsby and A. Wildavsky, *Presidential Elections: Strategies of American Electoral Politics*, 12th edn (Lanham, MD: Rowman and Littlefield, 2007).

16   In 1876 the Republican Rutherford B. Hayes was elected president by the presidential electors, having received only 48 percent of the popular vote, whereas his rival, the Democratic Samuel J. Tilden, had polled 51 percent. In 1888, the Republican Benjamin Harrison was elected president, with about 0.6 percent fewer popular votes than his rival Grover Cleveland.

17   With the exception of Maine and Nebraska that elect presidential electors for each congressional district on the basis of a first-past-the-post system and then elect two presidential electors for the entire state on the basis of who obtained most votes. As a result, the presidential electors of both Nebraska and Maine (currently 5 and 4 respectively) may support different candidates.

18   Toinet, *Le Système politique des États-Unis*, p. 425.

19   A. Ranney, *Governing: An Introduction to Political Science*, 5th edn (Englewood Cliffs: Prentice Hall, 1990).

20   S. M. Milkis, *The President and the Parties: The Transformation of the American Party System Since the New Deal* (Oxford: Oxford University Press, 1993), p. 5.

21   B. Cain, "The American Electoral System," in G. Peele, C. J. Bailey, and B. Cain (eds), *Developments in American Politics* (London: Macmillan, 1992), p. 39.

22 G. C. Jacobson, *The Electoral Origins of Divided Government: Competition in US House Elections 1946–1988* (New Haven, CT: Yale University Press, 1990).

23 B. Cain, J. Ferejohn, and M. Fiorina, 1987, *The Personal Vote: Constituency Service and Electoral Independence* (Cambridge, MA: Harvard University Press, 1987), pp. 214–8.

24 F. J. Sorauf (ed.), *Inside Campaign Finance: Myth and Realities* (New Haven, CT: Yale University Press, 1992).

25 See B. Ginsberg, *The Consequences of Consent: Elections, Citizens and Popular Acquiescence* (Reading, MA: Addison-Wesley, 1982).

26 N. W. Polsby, *Consequences of Party Reform* (Oxford: Oxford University Press, 1983).

27 H. Heclo, "The Emerging Regime," in R. A. Harris and S. M. Milkis (eds), *Remaking American Politics* (Boulder, CO: Westview Press, 1989).

28 R. A. Dahl, *The New Political (Dis)order* (Berkeley: Institute of Governmental Studies Press, 1994).

29 J. E. Cantor, *Campaign Finance*, CRS Issue Brief for Congress, Congressional Research Service, The Library of Congress, Washington, DC: December 15, 2003, p. 5.

30 See D. Donnelly, J. Fine, and E. S. Miller (eds), *Are Elections For Sale?* (Boston: Beacon Press, 2001). For a colorful journalistic description of the topic, see G. Palast, *The Best Democracy Money Can Buy* (New York: A Plume Books, 2003).

31 A. Grant, "Campaign Finance," in G. Peele et al. (eds), *Developments in American Politics* (New York: Palgrave, 2002).

32 R. Texeira and J. Rogers, *America's Forgotten Majority: Why the White Working Class Still Matters* (New York: Basic Books, 2000); R. Texeira, *The Disappearing American Voter* (Washington, DC: Brookings, 1992); R. Texeira, *Why Americans Don't Vote: Turnout Decline in the United States 1960–1984* (Westport, CT: Greenwood Press, 1987).

33 G. W. Cox, *Making Votes Count* (Cambridge: Cambridge University Press, 1997); J. H. Aldridge, "When Is It Rational to Vote?," in D. C. Mueller (ed.), *Perspectives on Public Choice: A Handbook* (Cambridge: Cambridge University Press, 1997); R. McKelvey and P. Ordeshook, "A General Theory of the Calculus of Voting," in J. F. Herndon and J. L. Bernd (eds), *Mathematical Applications in Political Science* (Charlottesville: University Press of Virginia, 1972); W. Riker and P. C. Ordeshook, "A Theory of the Calculus of Voting," *American Political Science Review*, 62, 1 (1968).

34 As shown by D. R. Mayhew, *Congress: The Electoral Connection* (New Haven, CT: Yale University Press, 1974).

35 See M. D. Martinez, *Turnout Effects on the Composition of the Electorate: A Multinomial Logit Simulation of the 2000 Presidential Election*, presented at the Annual Meeting of the Southwestern Political Science Association, New Orleans, March 27–30, 2002.

36 F. F. Piven and R. Cloward, *Why Americans Still Don't Vote and Why Politicians Want it That Way* (Boston: Beacon Press, 2000); F. F. Piven and R. A. Cloward, *Why Americans Don't Vote* (New York: Pantheon Books, 1988). But see also, by the same authors, *Regulating the Poor: The Functions of Public Welfare* (New York: Vintage, 1971).

37 R. L. McCormick, "Walter Dean Burnham and 'The System of 1896,'" *Social Science History*, 10, 3, 1986.

38 A. J. Reichley, *The Life of the Parties: A History of the American Political Party* (New York: The Free Press, 1992); M. P. Fiorina, *Retrospective Voting in American National Elections*, 3rd edn (New Haven, CT: Yale University Press, 1989); N. W. Polsby, *The Consequences of Party Reform* (Oxford: Oxford University Press, 1988).

39 See W. D. Burnham, "The Turnout Problem," in A. J. Reichley (ed.), *Elections American Style* (Washington, DC: The Brookings Institution, 1987) and W. D. Burnham., "Elections as Democratic Institutions," in K. Lehman Schlozman (ed.), *Elections in America* (London: Allen and Unwin, 1987).

40 A. King, *Running Scared: Why America's Politicians Campaign Too Much and Govern Too Little* (New York: The Free Press, 1997), p. 37.

41 Still worth reading is P. Bonomi, J. Macgregor Burns, and A. Ranney (eds), *The American Constitutional System Under Strong and Weak Parties* (New York: Praeger, 1981).

42 See the argument developed by W. E. Hudson, *American Democracy in Peril: Seven Challenges to America's Future*, 2nd rev. edn (Chatham: Chatham House, 1996), p. 38.

43 See J. H. Aldrich, *Why Parties? The Origin and Transformation of Political Parties in America* (Chicago: University of Chicago Press, 1995).

44 J. L. Sundquist, *Dynamics of the Party System: Alignment and Realignment of Political Parties in the United States*, 2nd edn (Washington, DC: The Brookings Institution, 1983); J. L. Sundquist, *Constitutional Reform and Effective Government*, rev. edn (Washington, DC: The Brookings Institution, 1992).

45 W. D. Burnham, *Critical Elections and the Mainsprings of American Politics* (New York: W.W. Norton, 1970).

46 G. Wills, *A Necessary Evil: A History of American Distrust of Government* (New York: Simon and Schuster, 1999).

47 King, *Running Scared*, p. 52.

48 US Census Bureau, *Statistical Abstracts of the United States* (Washington, DC: 2003); at www.census.gov/.

Chapter 4 A Democracy for the Rich?

1 M. Tarchi, *Contro l'americanismo* (Rome-Bari: Laterza, 2004), p. 9.

2 T. Assheuer, "Schattenboxen im leeren ring," *Die Zeit*, May 28, 2003.

3 J. Rifkin, "Glückliches Europa . . . ," *Die Zeit*, October 14, 2004.

4   A. Gambino, *Perché oggi non possiamo non dirci antiamericani* (Rome: Editori Riuniti, 2003), p. 87.

5   Source, *Public Agenda of the World Bank 1996*, cited in K. Phillips, *Wealth and Democracy* (New York: Broadway Books, 2002), p. 124. See also J. Kopstein and S. Steinmo (eds), *Growing Apart? America and Europe in the Twenty-First Century* (Cambridge: Cambridge University Press, 2008).

6   Congressional Budget Office, *The Economic and Budget Outlook, Fiscal Years 2000–2009* (Washington, DC: 1999).

7   T. M. Smeeding, *Public Policy and Economic Inequality: The United States in Comparative Perspective*, paper prepared for the Campbell Institute Seminar on "Inequality and American Politics," February 20, 2004.

8   See the important study by G. Poggi, *Forms of Power* (Cambridge: Polity Press, 2001).

9   S. M. Lipset, *The First New Nation: The United States in Historical and Comparative Perspective*, 2nd edn (New York: W.W. Norton, 1979).

10 See D. Grimm, "The Modern State: Continental Tradition," in F. X. Kaufman, C. Majone, and V. Ostrom (eds), *Guidance, Control and Evaluation in the Public Sector* (Berlin: De Gruyter, 1985).

11 See C. Tilly, "State and Counterrevolution in France," in F. Fehér (ed.), *The French Revolution and the Birth of Modernity* (Berkeley: University of California Press, 1990).

12 J. P. Nettl, "The State as a Conceptual Variable," *World Politics*, 20, 4 (1968).

13 S. L. Elkin, "Madison and After: The American Model of Political Constitution," *Political Studies*, 44, 3 (1996), p. 597.

14 K. Polanyi, *The Great Transformation* (New York: Beacon Press, 1944).

15 M. Egan, *Constructing a European Market* (Oxford: Oxford University Press, 2001), p. 38.

16 J. T. McDonald, "Building the Impossible State: Toward an Institutional Analysis of State-building in America, 1820–1930," in J. E. Jackson (ed.), *Institutions in American Society: Essays in Market, Political and Social Organizations* (Ann Arbor: University of Michigan Press, 1993), p. 218.

17 J. Bryce, *The American Commonwealth* (London: Macmillan, 1888).

18 M. Mann, "Nation-States in Europe and Other Continents: Diversifying, Developing, Not Dying," *Daedalus*, 122, 3 (1993).

19 Egan, *Constructing a European Market*, p. 35.

20 D. P. Calleo, *Rethinking Europe's Future* (Princeton: Princeton University Press, 2001), p. 48.

21 See S. Fabbrini, "Building a Market Without the State: The EU in an American Perspective," in S. Fabbrini (ed.), *Democracy and Federalism in the European Union and the United States: Exploring Post-National Governance* (London: Routledge, 2005); and S. Fabbrini, "A Single Western State Model? Differential Development and Constrained

Convergence of Public Authority Organization in Europe and America," *Comparative Political Studies*, 36, 6 (2003).

22 A. Stone Sweet, *Governing With Judges: Constitutional Politics in Europe* (Oxford: Oxford University Press, 1999).

23 See L. B. Hartz, *The Liberal Tradition in America* (New York: Harcourt Brace Jovanovich, 1955); C. Tilly (ed.), *The Formation of National States in Western Europe* (Princeton: Princeton University Press, 1975); D. Bell, "The 'Hegelian Secret': Civil Society and American Exceptionalism," in B. E. Shafer (ed.), *Is America Different? A New Look to American Exceptionalism* (Oxford: Clarendon Press, 1991).

24 See, M. Ferrera, *The Boundaries of Welfare: European Integration and the New Spatial Politics of Social Protection* (Oxford: Oxford University Press, 2005).

25 G. V. Rimlinger, *Welfare Policy and Industrialization in Europe, America and Russia* (New York: Wiley and Sons, 1971).

26 G. Esping-Andersen, *Three Worlds of Welfare Capitalism* (Cambridge: Polity Press, 1990).

27 For the European case see A. Pizzorno, "Mutamenti nelle istituzioni rappresentative e svilupo dei partiti politici," in P. Bairoch and E. Hobsbawn (eds), *Storia dell'Europa: L'età contemporanea. Secoli XIX–XX*, vol. V (Turin: Einaudi, 1996).

28 T. Skocpol, "State Formation and Social Policy in the United States," *American Behavioral Scientist* 35, 4/5 (1992).

29 T. Skocpol, *Protecting Soldiers and Mothers: The Political Origins of Social Policy in the United States* (Cambridge: Cambridge University Press, 1992).

30 M. Ferrera, "The Politics of Health Reform: Origins and Performance of the Italian Health Service in Comparative Perspective," in J. Bjorkman and G. Freddi (eds), *Controlling Medical Professionals* (London: Sage, 1989).

31 A. O. Hirschman, *Exit, Voice and Loyalty* (Cambridge, MA: Harvard University Press, 1970).

32 See, J. Micklethwaith and A. Wooldridge, *The Right Nation: Conservative Power in America* (New York: Penguin Press, 2004).

33 K. P. Phillips, *The Emerging Republican Majority* (New Rochelle, NY: Arlington House, 1969).

34 Here, of course, the term liberalism refers to its political and not cultural meaning, i.e. the philosophy that inspired the political program of the Democratic party, as originally developed during the New Deal period (between 1932 and 1940) and subsequently updated with President Johnson's Great Society program (between 1963 and 1968). See, A. Brinkley, *The End of Reform: New Deal Liberalism in Recession and War* (New York: Vintage, 1995).

35 M. J. Crozier, S. P. Huntington, and J. Watanuki, *The Crisis of Democracy: Report on the Governability of Democracies to the Trilateral Commission* (New York: New York University Press, 1975).

36 See, M. Kazin, *The Populist Persuasion* (New York: Basic Books, 1995).

37 T. Lowi, *The End of Liberalism: Ideology, Policy and the Crisis of Public Authority*, 2nd edn (New York: W.W. Norton, 1971).

38 R. D. Dahl, *Democracy in the United States*, 4th edn (Boston: Houghton Mifflin, 1981).

39 R. Hofstadter, *The Age of Reform: From W. Bryan to F. D. Roosevelt* (New York: ACLS History E-Book Project, 1999, original edn 1955).

40 K. P. Phillips, *The Politics of Rich and Poor* (New York: Random House, 1990).

41 N. Elias and J. L. Scotson, *The Established and the Outsider* (London: Sage, 1994).

42 K. P. Phillips, *Post-Conservative America* (New York: Vintage Books, 1983).

43 This dissatisfaction became manifest for the first time in California in 1978 when a referendum approved Proposition 13, which imposed automatic cuts of state taxes. Similar proposals were subsequently adopted by other states.

44 E. J. Dionne Jr, *Why Americans Hate Politics* (New York: Simon and Schuster, 1991).

45 J. Shklar, *American Citizenship: The Quest for Inclusion* (Cambridge, MA: Harvard University Press, 1991).

46 For example, T. Lowi, *The Politics of Disorder* (New York: W.W. Norton, 1971) and E. E. Schattschneider, *The Semisovereign People: A Realist's View of Democracy in America* (Hinsdale, IL: Dryden Press, 1960).

47 L. Goodwin, *The Populist Moment: A Short History of the Agrarian Revolt in America* (Oxford: Oxford University Press, 1980). But see also Hofstadter, *Age of Reform*.

48 E. A. Stettner, *Shaping Modern Liberalism: Herbert Croly and Progressive Thought* (Lawrence: University Press of Kansas, 1993).

49 D. Vogel, *Kindred Strangers: The Uneasy Relationship between Politics and Business in America* (Princeton: Princeton University Press, 1996). More generally, on American anti-statism see J. S. Nye Jr, P. D. Zelikow, and D. C. King (eds), *Why People Don't Trust Government* (Cambridge, MA: Harvard University Press, 1997).

50 See J. Didion, "The Teachings of Speaker Gingrich," *New York Review of Books*, 42 (August 10, 1995) but also N. Gingrich, *To Renew America* (New York: Harper Collins, 1994).

51 This document was turned into a book by E. Gillespie and R. Schellas (eds), *Contract with America: The Bold Plan by Rep. Newt Gingrich, Rep. Dick Armey and the House Republicans to Change the Nation* (Washington, DC: Times Books, 1994). For a critique, see D. Plotke, "Against Government. The Contract With America," *Dissent*, Summer (1995) and L. Fisher, "The 'Contract with America': What It Really Means," *New York Review of Books*, 42 (June 22, 1995).

52 K. Patterson, "The Political Firepower of the National Rifle Association," and J. Judith et al., "Onward Christian Soldiers: Religious Activ-

ists in American Politics," both in A. J. Cigler and B. A. Loomis (eds), *Interest Group Politics*, 5th edn (Washington, DC: C.Q. Press, 1998); and A. J. Reichley, *The Life of the Parties: A History of American Political Parties* (New York: Free Press, 1992).

53 G. Pomper, "The Leninist Republican Party," *Party Line*, Summer (1995).

54 T. Skocpol, *Boomerang: Health Reform and the Turn Against Government* (New York: W.W. Norton, 1997).

55 F. Ross, "Social Policy," in G. Peele et al., *Developments in American Politics* (New York: Palgrave, 2002); B. Rothstein and S. Steinmo (eds), *Restructuring the Welfare State: Political Institutions and Policy Change* (New York: Palgrave, 2002).

56 Adapted from US Social Security Administration, *Social Security Bulletin*, 62, 2 (1999), quoted in US Census Bureau, *Statistical Abstract of the United States* (Washington, DC: 2000).

57 J. Handler, *Welfare Reform: Something Old, Something New* (UCLA, School of Public Policy and Social Research, 2001).

58 US Census Bureau, *Income, Poverty, and Health Insurance Coverage in the United States: 2003*, US Department of Commerce, August 2004, 9–13; and August 2007.

59 Ibid., August 2004, pp. 14–20.

60 G. Benjamin and M. J. Malbin (eds), *Limiting Legislative Terms* (Washington, DC: C.Q. Press, 1992).

61 N. W. Polsby, "The Institutionalization of the US House of Representatives," *American Political Science Review*, 62, 1 (1968).

62 J. S. Nye Jr, P. D. Zelikow, and D. C. King (eds), *Why People Don't Trust Government* (Cambridge, MA: Harvard University Press, 1997).

63 B. Cain, "The United States in Evolution: Majoritarian Reforms in a Madisonian System," in Peele et al., *Developments in American Politics*.

64 Congressional Budget Office, *Historical Effective Federal Tax Rates: 1979 to 2004*, Congress of the United States, December 2006, table 1C.

65 EGTRRA stands for Economic Growth and Tax Relief Reconciliation Act of 2001; JCWAA for Job Creation and Workers Assistance Act of 2002; JGTRRA for Jobs and Growth Tax Relief Reconciliation Act of 2003.

66 Congressional Budget Office, *Effective Federal Tax Rates under Current Laws, 2001–2004*, Congress of the United States, August 2004, p. 5.

67 See C. Swain, *The New White Nationalism in America* (Cambridge: Cambridge University Press, 2002). For a comparative analysis, see Y. Mény and Y. Surel, *Par le peuple, pour le peuple* (Paris: Librairie Arthème Fayard, 2000).

68 The Constitution of 1787 even counted a black person for three fifths of a white person, albeit for the purpose of calculating the size of electoral districts.

69 The theoretical and historical literature on this topic is vast. See e.g. A. Brinkley, *Liberalism and Its Discontents* (Cambridge, MA: Harvard University Press, 1998).

70 See A. Ryan, *John Dewey and the High Tide of American Liberalism* (New York: W.W. Norton, 1995).

71 M. Ferrera, "Il crepuscolo delle opportunità," *Il Sole-24 Ore*, December 29, 2002, p. 28.

72 US Census Bureau, *Statistical Abstract of the United States* (Washington, DC: 2007), p. 8, at www.census.gov/.

73 R. D. Putnam, *Bowling Alone: The Collapse and Revival of American Community* (New York: Simon and Schuster, 2000).

74 T. Skocpol, "Voice and Inequality: The Transformation of American Civic Democracy," *Perspectives on Politics*, 2, 1 (2004); *Encyclopedia of Associations*, Gale Group, Farmington Hills, Annual Report.

75 Bryce, *American Commonwealth*, vol. 2, p. 278.

Chapter 5   An Imperial Democracy

1 M. Tarchi, *Contro l'Americanismo* (Rome-Bari: Laterza, 2004), p. 92.

2 Ibid., p. 162.

3 A. Gambino, *Perché oggi non possiamo non dirci antiamericani* (Rome: Editori Riuniti, 2003), p. 69.

4 Ibid., p. 77.

5 Ibid., p. 8.

6 W. Schaeuble, "Warnung vor welpolitischer dominanz der USA," *German News.De*, March 22, 2003, at www.germnews.de/archive/gn/2003/03/22.html5.

7 Radio interview with Peter Gauweiler, January 5, 2007, at www.dradio.de/dif/sendungen/interview_ dif/57965/.

8 "Wird Amerika wieder dekratish," *Der Spiegel*, March 1, 2004.

9 P. Sloterdijk, "Kohls Erbe wirkt bis heute nach," *Profil*, online, 39 (2002).

10 M. Winter, "Der Riss zwischen den kulturen," *Frankfurter Rundschau*, January 20, 2003, p. 3.

11 M. Brumlik, "Wider die US-Hegemonie," *TAZ*, January 16, 2003, p. 12.

12 T. Sommer, "Die Achse der Betonköpfe," *Die Zeit* (online), 10, 2002, p. 4.

13 Gambino, *Perché oggi non possiamo non dirci antiamericani*, p. 25.

14 F. H. Hartman and R. L. Wendzel, *America's Foreign Policy in a Changing World* (New York: HarperCollins, 1994).

15 G. J. Ikenberry (ed.), *American Foreign Policy: Theoretical Essays* (New York: Longman, 1999), parts 2 and 3.

16 M. L. Mezey, *Congress, the President and Public Policy* (Boulder, CO: Westview Press, 1989).

17 D. M. Snow and D. M. Drew, *From Lexington to Desert Storm: War and Politics in the American Experience* (New York: M. E. Sharpe, 1994).

18 W. R. Mead, *Special Providence: American Foreign Policy and How It Changed the World* (London: Routledge, 2002), pp. 17, 18.

19 W. M. Lunch, *The Nationalization of American Politics* (Berkeley: The University of California Press, 1987).

20 A. Wildavsky, *The Two Presidencies*, in A. Wildavsky (ed.), *Perspectives on the Presidency* (Boston: Little Brown, 1975, original edn 1966).

21 The personal presidency is composed of the president, a restricted group of his personal advisors from the White House Office (such as the head of the National Security Council and the various special assistants), in addition to the secretaries of State, Defense and of the Executive Office. As some of the personal advisors of the president (but not the head of the National Security Council) can be appointed without the "advice and consent" of the Senate, they express the point of view of the president, more so than the secretaries of State and Defense, who instead need to obtain the "advice and consent." In addition to the personal presidency, the departmental presidency and the administrative presidency are of significance. The departmental presidency is composed of the various secretaries, whereas the administrative presidency is composed of the various regulatory agencies. On the concept of the "stratified presidency," see S. Fabbrini, *Il presidenzialismo degli Stati Uniti* (Rome-Bari, Laterza, 1993) and S. Fabbrini, *Compound Democracies: Why the United States and Europe Are Becoming Similar* (Oxford: Oxford University Press, 2007).

22 C. V. Crabb Jr and P. M. Holt, *Invitation to Struggle: Congress, the President, and Foreign Policy*, 4th edn (Washington, DC: C.Q. Press, 1991).

23 D. M. Oldfield and A. Wildavski, "Reconsidering the Two Presidencies," *Society*, 26, 5 (1989).

24 We need to remember that L. B. Johnson, in his role as vice-president, became president for the period November 22, 1963 – December 31, 1964, because of the killing of the incumbent President J. F. Kennedy. In fact, the American Constitution in art. II, sec. 1.6, states that "in case of the removal of the President from office, or of his death, resignation, or inability to discharge the powers and duties of the said office, the same shall devolve on the Vice-President."

25 N. W. Polsby, *The Evolution of an American Establishment: Congress, the President, and the Contemporary Foreign Policy Community*, University of California at Berkeley, Institute of Governmental Studies, mimeo, 1991.

26 B. S. Morris, "Presidential Accountability in Foreign Policy: Some Recurring Problems," *Congress and the Presidency*, 13, 2 (1986).

27 A. Schlesinger Jr, *The Imperial Presidency* (New York: Houghton Mifflin, 1973).

28 G. J. Ikenberry, *After Victory: Institutions, Strategic Restraint, and the Rebuilding of Order After Major Wars* (Princeton: Princeton University

Press, 2001). See also M. Cox (ed.), *Twentieth Century International Relations* (London: Sage, 2006).

29 Subsequently turned into an article, "The Sources of Soviet Conduct," published in *Foreign Affairs* in 1947 and now in J. F. Hoge Jr and F. Zaakaria (eds), *The American Encounter: The United States and the Making of the Modern World* (New York: Basic Books, 1997).

30 Already at Bretton Woods the American economic delegation (led by the economist Harry Dexter White) and the English delegation (led by John Maynard Keynes) were at loggerheads on the issue of liberalizing trade. The agreement eventually reached envisaged a system sufficiently open to promote the American trade interests and sufficiently controlled so as to permit the Europeans to protect the reconstruction of their ravaged economies.

31 In Ikenberry, *After Victory*, p. 166.

32 On the convergence of the views of the Wilsonian (idealist) and Hamiltonian (materialist) elites on the post-Second World War internationalism, see Mead, *Special Providence*, ch. 8.

33 For an effective interpretation of American foreign policy as the expression of a tension between identity and interests, see J. G. Ruggie, "The Past as Prologue? Interests, Identity and American Foreign Policy," *International Security*, 21 (1997).

34 G. J. Ikenberry (ed.), *America Unrivaled: The Future of the Balance of Power* (Ithaca, NY: Cornell University Press, 2002).

35 M. Cox, "The 1980s Revisited or the Cold War as History – Again," in O. Njolstadt (ed.), *The Last Decade of the Cold War: From Conflict Escalation to Conflict Transformation* (London: Frank Cass, 2004).

36 E. R. Wittkopf, "Introduction: Setting Priorities for a Post-Cold War World," in E. R. Wittkopf (ed.), *The Future of American Foreign Policy* (New York: St. Martin's Press, 1994), p. 2.

37 Despite the information sent to Washington, DC by American ambassador April C. Glaspie on her meeting with Saddam Hussein, on August 2, 1990, the day Kuwait was invaded, none of the main political leaders was present in the capital, nor were the American ambassadors to the most important Arab countries on their posts. See House of Representatives, *Joint Hearings of the Committee on Foreign Affairs and the Joint Economic Committee on the Persian Gulf Crisis*, House of Representatives, August 8–December 11, 1990, Washington, DC: US Government Printing Office.

38 A. Lewis, "Presidential Power. Bush Framed the Question for Congress," *New York Times*, January 14, 1991, p. A15.

39 In fact, "again and again Bush practically ignored Capitol Hill as he made his decisions (on the Gulf crisis). While the administration spoke positively of consultation with Congress, it engaged only in notification – and usually after the fact. . . . In the six months of the Gulf crisis, Democratic leaders of the Senate and House of Representatives had less influence upon the Bush White House than Margaret Thatcher,

who resigned as British prime minister in November 1990, or Prince Bansar bin Sultan, the Saudi Ambassador to Washington," as D. Gergen writes in "America's Missed Opportunities," *Foreign Affairs*, 71, 1 (1991/1992): 7.

40 *Weekly Compilation of Presidential Documents*, March 6, 1991, p. 284. See also T. H. Draper, "Presidential Wars," *New York Review of Books*, 38 (November 21, 1991).

41 See, L. Henkin, *Constitutionalism, Democracy, and Foreign Affairs* (New York: Columbia University Press, 1992).

42 T. H. Draper, "The True History of the Gulf War," *New York Review of Books*, 39 (January 30, 1992), p. 45.

43 D. C. Hendrickson, "The Renovation of American Foreign Policy," *Foreign Affairs*, 71, 2 (1992): 59.

44 Between the fall of 1986 and the winter of 1987 details were made public concerning the involvement of the Reagan presidency, and in particular of National Security Council officials, in the illegal sale of arms to Iran, by way of Israel. The proceeds of the sales were subsequently transferred, by means of a complicated series of transactions in private bank accounts, to the Nicaraguan Contras to finance their guerilla war against the Sandinista government. These activities of the presidency were clearly illegal as they violated both an American decision not to maintain diplomatic relations with Iran (issued after the Iranians had taken hostage several Americans at the American embassy in Tehran in the late 1970s) as well as a decision of Congress not to financially support the anti-Sandinista guerrillas and to promote, instead, a diplomatic initiative in the Central America region. See Congressional Joint Committees, *Report of the Congressional Committees Investigating the Iran-Contra Affair*, US Congress, Washington, DC: US Government Printing Office, 1987.

45 L. V. Sigal, "The Last Cold War Election," *Foreign Affairs*, 71, 5 (1992–3): 9.

46 J. S. Nye Jr, "What New World Order?," in Wittkopf, *Future of American Foreign Policy*.

47 D. P. Calleo, *Rethinking Europe's Future* (Princeton: Princeton University Press, 2001), p. 326, n.57.

48 One of the most influential articles certainly was C. Krauthammer, "The Unipolar Moment," *Foreign Affairs*, 70, 1 (1991).

49 D. P. Calleo, "The US Post-Imperial Presidency and Transatlantic Relations," *International Spectator*, 35, 3 (2000), p. 73.

50 W. G. Hyland, "The Case for Pragmatism," *Foreign Affairs*, 71, 1 (1992), pp. 43–4.

51 J. Joffe, "Entangled Forever," in Wittkopf, *Future of American Foreign Policy*, p. 43 (italics in the original).

52 M. Mandelbaum, *The Ideas That Conquered the World: Peace, Democracy, and Free Markets in the Twenty-First Century* (Oxford: Perseus Books, 2002).

53 Hyland, *Case for Pragmatism*, p. 44.
54 W. Lippmann, "The Rise of the United States," *Today and Tomorrow*, September 11, 1945, reproduced in W. Lippmann, *The Essential Lippmann*, ed. E. Rossiter and J. Lare (New York: Random House, 1965).
55 The concept was originally developed by P. Kennedy, *Rise and Fall of the Great Powers: Economic Change and Military Conflict from 1500 to 2000* (New York: Vintage Books, 1989).
56 Two important contributions that laid the basis for this strategy, can be found in J. S. Nye Jr, *Bound to Lead: The Changing Nature of American Power* (New York: Basic Books, 1990) and Z. Brzezinski, *Out of Control: Global Turmoil on the Eve of the 21st Century* (New York: Colliers Book, 1993).
57 Nye, "What New World Order?," in Wittkopf, *Future of American Foreign Policy*, p. 54.
58 Wittkopf, "Introduction: Setting Priorities for a Post-Cold War World," p. 2.
59 A. Tonelson, "Superpower without a Sword," *Foreign Affairs*, 72, 3 (1993).
60 Calleo, "The US Post-Imperial Presidency," p. 73.
61 J. Mc Cormick, "Clinton and Foreign Policy: Some Legacies for a New Century," in S. E. Schier (ed.), *The Postmodern Presidency: Bill Clinton Legacy in US Politics* (Pittsburgh, University of Pittsburgh Press, 2000), p. 61.
62 D. Williams, "Foreign and Security Policy," in G. Peele et al., *Developments in American Politics* (New York: Palgrave, 2002), p. 242.
63 J. S. Nye Jr, *The Paradox of American Power: Why the World's Only Superpower Can't Go Alone* (Oxford: Oxford University Press, 2002), p. 112.
64 R. Jervis, "Mission Impossible: Creating a Grand Strategy," in J. D. Caraley (ed.), *The New American Interventionism: Lessons From Successes and Failures* (New York: Columbia University Press, 1999), p. 217.
65 S. Hoffmann, *Gulliver Unbound: America's Imperial Temptation and the War in Iraq*, interview by F. Bozo (Lanham, MD: Rowman and Littlefield, 2004), p. 12.
66 S. Hoffmann, "On the War," *New York Review of Books*, 48 (November 1, 2001), p. 6.
67 However, it may be interesting to note that the shock of 9/11 did not significantly alter the multilateralist preferences of public opinion, which remains in favor of military solutions supported and legitimized by international institutions, first and foremost the UN. P. Joseph, *Are Americans Becoming More Peaceful?* (Boulder, CO: Paradigm Publishers, 2007), reports that "a comprehensive poll conducted by the Chicago Council on Foreign Relations (*Global Views 2004: American Public Opinion and Foreign Policy*) found strong support among the public for international treaties that have been rejected by the Bush administration" (p. 236). Moreover, Joseph notices, "two thirds of

Americans thought that the United States should be more willing to make decisions within the United Nations even if this means that the United States will sometimes have to go along with a policy that is not its first choice" (p. 237).

68   I. H. Daalder and J. M. Lindsay, *America Unbound: The Bush Revolution in Foreign Policy* (Washington, DC: Brookings Institution Press, 2003).

69   J. Dumbrell, "Unilateralism and 'America First'? President George W. Bush's Foreign Policy," *Political Quarterly*, 73, 3 (2002).

70   Daalder and Lindsay, *America Unbound*.

71   G. W. Bush, *The National Security Strategy of the United States* (Washington, DC, September 20, 2002).

72   Ibid., pp. iv, 29.

73   Bush, *National Security Strategy*, p. 31.

74   B. Emmott, "Present at the Creation. Our Law, Your Law," *The Economist*, June 29–July 5, 2002, p. 20.

75   Bush, *National Security Strategy*, p. 15.

76   Reproduced in G. J. Ikenberry, "America's Imperial Ambition," *Foreign Affairs*, 81, 5 (2002), p. 54.

77   P. Gruber, "Rumsfeld: Gli europei? Non esistono," *La Stampa*, March 24, 2002, p.13.

78   A. Norton, *Leo Strauss and the Politics of American Empire* (New Haven, CT: Yale University Press, 2004).

79   Bush, *National Security Strategy*, p. v.

80   See R. D. Kaplan, *Warrior Politics: Why Leadership Demands a Pagan Ethos* (New York: Random House, 2001).

81   Bush, *National Security Strategy*, p. 6.

82   R. Dworkin, "Terror and the Attack on Civil Liberties," *New York Review of Books*, 50 (November 6, 2003).

83   A. Rudalevige, *The New Imperial Presidency: Renewing Presidential Power After Watergate* (Ann Arbor: University of Michigan Press, 2005).

84   B. Ackerman, "The Emergency Constitution," *Yale Law Journal*, 113, 5 (2001); R. C. Leone and J. G. Anrig (eds), *The War on Our Freedoms: Civil Liberties in an Age of Terrorism* (New York: Public Affairs, 2003); D. Cole and J. X. Dempsey, *Terrorism and the Constitution: Sacrificing Civil Liberties in the Name of National Security* (New York: New Press, 2003); S. J. Schulhofer, *The Enemy Within: Intelligence Gathering, Law Enforcement and Civil Liberties in the Wake of September 11* (New York: Century Foundation, 2003).

85   S. Fabbrini (ed.), *The United States Contested: American Unilateralism and European Discontent* (London: Routledge, 2006).

86   With the support of the German Marshall Fund of the United States and the Compagnia di San Paolo of Italy.

87   R. Kagan and W. Kristol, *Present Dangers: Crisis and Opportunity in American Foreign and Defense Policy* (San Francisco: Encounter Books, 2000).

88 See *The Iraq Study Group Report: The Way Forward, A New Approach*, The United States Institute for Peace, December 6, 2006 (the group was co-chaired by James Baker III and Lee Hamilton).
89 See the debate in A. J. Bacevich (ed.), *The Imperial Tense* (Chicago: Ivan R. Dee Publisher, 2004).
90 As recognized by the repented neoconservative F. Fukuyama, *After the Neo-Cons: America at the Crossroads* (London: Profile Books, 2006). See in particular R. Jervis, *American Foreign Policy in a New Era* (London: Routledge, 2005).
91 C. Campbell, B. A. Rockman, and A. Rudalevige (eds), *The George W. Bush Legacy* (Washington, DC: C.Q. Press, 2008); G. C. Edwards III and D. S. King (eds), *The Polarized Presidency of George W. Bush* (Oxford: Oxford University Press, 2007).
92 M. Cox, T. Dunne, and K. Booth (eds), *Empires, Systems and States: Great Transformations in International Politics* (Cambridge: Cambridge University Press, 2001).
93 M. Walzer, "Is There an American Empire?," *Dissent*, Autumn (2003).
94 Calleo, "The U.S. Post-Imperial Presidency," p. 73.
95 Walzer, "Is There an American Empire?," pp. 28–9.
96 Z. Brzezinski, *The Choice: Global Domination or Global Leadership* (New York: Basic Books, 2004).
97 C. A. Kupchan, *The End of the American Era: US Foreign Policy and the Geopolitics of the Twenty-First Century* (New York: Alfred A. Knopf, 2002).
98 Walzer, "Is There an American Empire?," p. 29.
99 A. Hurrell, *Empire Reborn?*, in A. Hurrell, *On Global Order: Power, Values and the Constitution of International Society* (Oxford: Oxford University Press, 2007), ch. 11.

Chapter 6   America as Method

1 See K. Von Beyme, *America as a Model: The Impact of American Democracy in the World* (Berlin, Gower, 1987).
2 See S. Fabbrini, "American Democracy From a European Perspective," *Annual Review of Political Science*," 2 (1999).
3 This interpretation was revised and updated in S. M. Lipset and G. Marks, *It Didn't Happen Here: Why Socialism Failed in the United States* (New York: W. W. Norton, 2000).
4 S. M Lipset, *The First New Nation: The United States in Historical and Comparative Perspective*, 2nd rev. edn (New York: W.W. Norton, 1979).
5 D. Bell, "The 'Hegelian Secret': Civil Society and American Exceptionalism," in B. Shafer (ed.), *Is America Different? A New Look at American Exceptionalism* (Oxford: Clarendon Press, 1991). But see also L. Cohen-Tanugi, *Le droit sans l'État: Sur la démocratie en France et en Amérique*, pref. S. Hoffmann (Paris: PUF, 1992).

6   An important role, in this respect, was played by the scholars associated with the journal *Studies in American Political Development*.

7   I. Katznelson and M. Shefter (eds), *Shaped by War and Trade: International Influence on American Political Development* (Princeton: Princeton University Press, 2002).

8   G. K. Wilson, *Only in America? The Politics of the United States in Comparative Perspective* (Chatham: Chatham House, 1998), p. 126.

9   P. Pierson, *Dismantling the Welfare State? Reagan, Thatcher and the Politics of Retrenchment* (Cambridge: Cambridge University Press, 1994).

10 R. Rose, *How Exceptional Is American Government?*, University of Strathclyde, Centre for the Study of Public Policy, Working Paper no. 150, 1985.

11 S. Steinmo, "Why Is Government So Small in America?," *Governance*, 8, 2 (1995).

12 As argued by Shafer, *Is America Different?*; E. Glaser and H. Wellenreuther (ed.), *Bridging the Atlantic: The Question of American Exceptionalism in Perspective* (Cambridge: Cambridge University Press, 2002); C. Lockart *The Roots of American Exceptionalism: Institutions, Culture and Policies* (New York: Palgrave, 2004).

13 R. Smith, "Beyond Tocqueville, Myrdal, and Hartz," *American Political Science Review*, 87, 3 (1993).

14 E. B. Haas, *Nationalism, Liberalism, and Progress: The Rise and Decline of Nationalism* (Ithaca, NY: Cornell University Press, 1997).

15 Lipset, *First New Nation*.

16 L. B. Hartz, *The Liberal Tradition in America* (New York: Harcourt Brace Jovanovich, 1955).

17 D. J. Elazar, *The American Constitutional Tradition* (Lincoln: University of Nebraska Press, 1988).

18 R. H. Wiebe, *Self Rule: A Cultural History of American Democracy* (Chicago: University of Chicago Press, 1995).

19 M. F. Toinet, "Introduction, " in M.-F., Toinet (ed.), *Et la Constitution créa l'Amérique* (Nancy: Presses universitaires de Nancy, 1988).

20 R. A. Dahl, *Democracy in the United States: Promise and Performance*, 3rd edn (Chicago: Rand McNally, 1976).

21 D. J. Boorstin, *The Americans: The National Experience* (New York: Vintage Books, 1965).

22 G. M. Friedrickson, *The Comparative Imagination: On the History of Racism, Nationalism, and Social Movements* (Berkeley, University of California Press, 1997).

23 G. Wills, *Explaining America: The Federalist*, 2nd edn (London: The Penguin Group, 2001); G. Wills, *Inventing America: Jefferson Declaration of Independence* (New York: Vintage Books, 1978).

24 Haas, *Nationalism, Liberalism and Progress*.

25 M. Walzer, *What It Means To Be An American: Essays on the American Experience* (New York: Marsilio, 1996).

26 R. A. Dahl, *A Preface to Democratic Theory: Expanded Edition* (Chicago: University of Chicago Press, 2006, original edn 1956).

27 S. P. Huntington, *Political Order in Changing Societies* (New Haven: Yale University Press, 1968).

28 J. A. Morone, *The Democratic Wish: Popular Participation and the Limits of American Government* (New York: Basic Books, 1990).

29 Who wrote, "Extend the sphere, and you take in a greater variety of parties and interests; you make it less probable that a majority of the whole will have a common motive to invade the rights of other citizens; or if such a common motive exists, it will be more difficult for all who feel it to discover their own strength, and to act in unison with each other." Reproduced in C. Beard (ed.), *The Enduring Federalist*, (New York: Frederick Ungar Publishing Co., 1948, original edn 1788), p. 74.

30 S. H Beer, *To Make a Nation: The Rediscovery of American Federalism* (Cambridge, MA: Harvard University Press, 1993).

31 T. J. Lowi, *The End of Liberalism: The Second Republic of the United States*, 2nd edn (New York: W.W. Norton, 1979).

32 G. Lehmbrich and P. C. Schmitter (eds), *Patterns of Corporatist Policy-Making* (London: Sage, 1982).

33 M. Lind, *The Next American Nation: The New Nationalism and the Fourth American Revolution* (New York: Free Press, 1995).

34 T. Lowi, "The State in Political Science: How We Become What We Study," *American Political Science Review*, 86, 1 (1992): 1–6.

35 Of course, an antinomic model is a contradiction in terms, given that models necessarily consist of consistent patterns.

36 S. Fabbrini, *Compound Democracies: Why the United States and Europe Are Becoming Similar* (Oxford: Oxford University Press, 2007).

37 A. Brinkley, *The End of Reform: New Deal Liberalism in Recession and War* (New York: Vintage Books, 1995).

38 S. P. Huntington, *American Politics: The Promise of Disharmony?* (Cambridge, MA: Harvard University Press, 1981).

39 T. R. Dye, *American Federalism: Competition Among Governments* (Lexington: Lexington Books, 1990).

40 R. A. Dahl and C. E. Lindblom, *Politics, Economics, and Welfare: Planning and Politico-Economic Systems Resolved into Basic Social Processes* (Chicago: University of Chicago Press, 1953).

41 I. Katznelson, K. Geiger, and D. Kryder, "Limiting Liberalism: the Southern Veto 1933–1950," *Political Science Quarterly*, 108, 2 (1993).

42 P. Schmitter, *How to Democratize the European Union and . . . Why Bother?* (Lanham, MD: Rowman and Littlefield, 2000), p. 36.

43 Ibid., p. 81.

44 APSA, *American Democracy in a Age of Rising Inequality*, Report of the American Political Science Association Task Force on Inequality and American Democracy, Washington, DC, 2004.

45 Dahl, *Preface to Democratic Theory*, p. 4.

46 F. W. Scharpf, "The Joint-Decision Trap: Lessons from German Federalism and European Integration," *Public Administration*, 66, 3 (1988).

47 Now in J. Bryce, *The American Commonwealth* (London: Macmillan, 1909), p. 608.

48 Ibid., p. 614.

49 Beard, *Enduring Federalist*, p. 225.

50 On Madison's realism, see R. K. Matthews, *If Men Were Angels: The Heartless Empire of Reason* (Lawrence: University Press of Kansas, 1995), who emphasizes that it derives from reason and not from a lack of compassion.

51 S. Levinson (ed.), *Responding to Imperfection: The Theory and Practice of Constitutional Amendment* (Princeton: Princeton University Press, 1995).

52 R. B. Bernstein (with J. Agel), *Amending America: If We Love The Constitution So Much, Why Do We Keep Trying to Change It?* (Lawrence: University Press of Kansas, 1993).

53 I discuss these issues in my *Compound Democracies*. For a discussion of the different constitutional traditions on the two shores of the Atlantic, see R. Bellamy (ed.), *Constitutionalism, Democracy and Sovereignty: American and European Perspectives* (Aldershot: Avebury, 1996).

Index

abuse of power, 26–31, 57–8, 118
Adams, John Quincy, 69
Afghanistan, 135, 160, 162
African Americans
  civil rights, 58, 111, 113, 131, 181
  education, 112
  forced immigrants, 175
  racial integration, 117
  rediscovery of roots, 13
  segregation, 112
  suffrage, 61, 67, 90
  voter turnout, 85
Aid to Families with Dependent
  Children, 113, 116, 122
America first, 161
American democracy
  anti-majoritarian, 21, 29, 63
  assessment, 95–7
  civil society democracy, 109, 134,
    172
  complexity, 16
  compound democracy, 21–2,
    23–6, 62–3, 106, 116, 147, 165,
    176–7
  European Left and, 7–9
  European Right and, 10, 11–12
  frequency of elections, 62
  hyperdemocracy, 96

  manipulated democracy, 9
  model, 170, 180–4
  number of elected positions, 62,
    96
  original state, 90, 95
  permanent electoral campaign,
    96
  plebiscitary democracy, 7, 9, 11,
    16, 20–1
  post-electoral democracy, 61, 95
  preventing abuse of power, 26–31
  see also electoral system; market
    democracy
American Medical Association, 122
anti-Americanism
  Catholic Church, 12–16
  concept, 2–3
  context, 2–5
  Europe, 1–19
  European Left, 5–9, 12
  European Right, 9–12
  misunderstanding, 16–19
  unifying factor, 2
anti-Europeanism, 1, 3
anti-globalization, 5
anti-modernism, 15
anti-statism, 118–19, 171, 174
anti-trust legislation, 8, 19, 106

antinomies, 174–80
arrogance, 3
Ashcroft, John, 164
Assheuer, Thomas, 98
associations, 134
Atlantic Charter (1941), 144, 146
Austria, 18

Belgium, 15, 18, 99, 166
Bell, Daniel, 172
Berlin crisis (1948), 144
Bible Belt, 14
Biological Weapons Convention,
    162
blanket primaries, 49–50
Blue Cross, 111–12
Blue Shield, 112
Boehner, John, 124
Bonapartism, 10, 20
Bosnia, 158
Bretton Woods order, 143
Bryan, William, 118, 134
Bryce, J., 103, 134, 184
Burke, Edmond, 9
Burnham, Walter, 88, 89
Bush, George H., 52, 120, 121, 149,
    149–51, 153, 154
Bush, George W.
    2000 election, 70
    divided government, 52
    growth of poverty, 123–4
    Iraq War, 135–6, 159–65
    neoconservative rule, 1
    social inequalities, 130
business interests, 182

Cain, Bruce, 72
California, 50, 125, 126, 200n43
Calleo, D.P., 107, 152, 154, 157, 167
campaign financing, 74–6
Canada, 99
Cannon, Joseph Gurney, 37
capitalism
    American version, 7
    corporate capitalism, 113

European Left and, 6
    imperial expansion and, 138
Carter, Jimmy, 115, 148
Catholic Church, 4, 12–16
caucuses, 50
Chemical Weapons Convention,
    157
Chile, 166
China, 155
civil liberties, 58, 132, 164, 181
Civil Rights Act (1965), 113
civil rights movement, 86
civil society, 109, 134, 172
Civil War, 110, 178
class, 85, 86, 89, 90, 94, 111, 114–18,
    120, 171
Cleveland, Grover, 52
Clinton, Bill
    constitutional attacks on, 154
    divided government, 52, 121–4
    foreign policy, 153
    health system, 51, 122
    impeachment, 55
    Motor-Voter Act, 86
    multilateralism, 155–9
    post-Gulf War world, 152
closed primaries, 48
Colbert, Jean-Baptiste, 107
Cold War, 6, 10–11, 12, 15, 16, 35,
    43, 65, 136, 167, 179
colonialism, 35, 107, 138, 166
Colorado, 125
commercial society, 84, 101–13,
    146–7
committee government, 32–3
communism, 5–6, 11, 65, 143, 149,
    159, 171
competition, 106, 113, 133
Comprehensive Test-Ban Treaty,
    157
Congress
    adaptation, 41–5
    campaign costs (1994–2006),
        78–9
    committee chairmen, 43

Congress (cont.)
  committee government, 32–3
  decline, 33–7
  defence policy, 139, 151
  divided government, 51–6, 71–7
  electoral system, 64–7
  foreign policy and, 55, 66, 141, 156–9
  Iraq War and, 164–5
  judicial review of legislation, 28, 56, 104–5
  modes of election, 27–8, 36
  original primacy, 31–3
  PAC campaign contributions (1993–2004), 76
  political majorities (1967–2007), 53
  presidential veto, 29, 40–1, 42
  public ignorance of, 20
  renunciation of powers, 39–41
  scapegoat, 128–9
  secondary role, 21
  seniority system, 36–7, 43
  term limits, 29, 125–31
  voter turnout, 59–60, 84
  see also House of Representatives; Senate
conspiracy theories, 5
Constitution
  12th Amendment, 69, 70
  14th Amendment, 67
  15th Amendment, 67
  16th Amendment, 103
  17th Amendment, 66–7
  24th Amendment, 67
  26th Amendment, 67
  1781 Articles of Confederation, 25
  1787 settlement, 22, 23–6, 28, 31, 38, 91–2
  amendment, 185
  Article II, 37–8, 40, 70
  authority, 28
  Commerce Clause, 104
  liberalism, 24, 132, 176
  presidential elections, 68

religion and, 14, 175
  supremacy, 105
constitutional courts, 105
consumerism, 15, 98
contempt, 10
"Contract with America", 120, 125
contractualism, 101–2
Convention on the Rights of the Child, 157
corporate funds, 80, 82
corporate interests, 85–6, 146–7
corporatism, 107
corruption, 82, 117, 165
Corwin, E. S., 37
counter-terrorism
  American strategy, 1
  civil liberties and, 164
  imperialism, 135–7
  unilateralism, 137, 162
crisis of authority, 118
Cuba, 138, 159, 166

Dahl, R. A., 181
Darwinism, 14, 134
Dayton Accords, 158
death penalty, 3, 13, 17
Debray, Regis, 4
decentralization, 18, 21, 74, 101–4, 109, 177
defence policy, 43, 66
Delors, Jacques, 136
Democracy, see American democracy
Democratic Party
  1968 Convention, 47
  low voter turnout and, 84, 87, 89
  particularism, 118, 119
  post-Civil War, 46
  presidencies, 115–16
  selection of presidential candidates, 92
  South, 43
  taxation policy, 117
  weakness of Clinton presidencies, 121–4
Dole, Robert, 120

Draper, T. H., 151
Dulles, John Foster, 136
dynastic regime, 59, 95

economic society, 84, 101–13, 146–7
egalitarianism, 172
Egypt, Suez crisis, 3–4, 144
Eisenhower, Dwight, 114, 140, 141
electoral system
  1828 presidential elections, 69–70
  1896 system, 36, 46, 85, 86, 90
  campaign financing, 74–6
  characteristics, 62–71
  Congressional elections, 64–7
  corruption, 82
  costs, 18, 77–82
  development, 71–82
  direct presidential primaries,
    45–51
  disenfranchisement, 67, 85
  divided votes, 72
  Electoral College, 8, 27, 36, 67–71
  electoral district boundaries, 65
  exclusions, 61
  Florida count (2000), 56, 69
  House of Representatives, 64–5
  incumbency factor, 72–3, 87
  new political disorder, 77
  origins of divided government,
    71–7
  personalized politics, 72–3, 89,
    91, 92–3, 94
  post-electoral democracy, 61, 95
  presidential elections, 27, 36,
    67–71
  property qualifications, 69
  Senate, 65–7
  separation of powers and, 27–8
  types of direct primaries, 47–51
  universal male suffrage, 61, 110,
    177
  voter registration, 83, 87
  voter turnout, *see* voter
    turnoutelites, 1, 2, 3, 4–5, 11,
    17, 96. 115, 118–21, 130, 141,
    143, 146–7, 160, 172

Elkin, S.L., 102
Ellwood, D. W., 2
Engels, Friedrich, 171
Enlightenment, 23, 27
Enron scandal, 82
Euro-lobbies, 182
European Coal and Steel
  Community, 145
European states
  Americanization, 5, 173
  constitutional courts, 105
  corporatism, 107
  health systems, 112
  individualism, 132
  market regulation, 107
  mercantilism, 107, 108
  mixed economies, 108
  nationalizations, 18, 106, 108
  paternalism, 186
  social policies, 109, 110, 111
  social solidarity, 186
  trade unions, 111
  voter turnout, 97
European Union
  constitution, 185
  decision making, 183
  democratic deficit, 182
  European Left and, 7
  integration, 19, 109, 186
  limited power, 153
  origins, 145
  separation of powers, 19, 182
  tyranny of the minorities, 58, 183
Europeanization, 172–3
exceptionalism, 18, 136, 170–4

federalism, 18, 21, 177, 179–80
Fishke, Robert, 55
Florida count (2000), 8, 56, 69
food stamp program, 122
Ford, Gerald, 114, 149, 150
foreign policy
  1990s multilateralist perspective,
    155–9
  1990s schizophrenic power,
    152–9

foreign policy (cont.)
  1990s unilateralist perspective, 152–5
  Cold War, 142–8
  Congress and, 55, 66, 141, 156–9
  consensus, 140–1
  domestic and foreign policy, 137–42
  end of Cold War, 148–52, 155
  European critique, 135–7
  George W. Bush presidency, 159–65
  Gulf War (1991), 149–52, 154–5, 155–6
  hegemonic power, 9, 17
  presidential role, 43
  support for dictatorships, 148–9, 166–7
  see also Iraq War (2003)
founding fathers, 23, 30–1, 36, 38, 43, 69–70, 95, 139, 175
France
  anti-Americanism, 4
  Catholic Church, 15
  colonialism, 137
  communism, 6
  cooperation with Germany, 145
  Enlightenment, 27
  exit from NATO command, 146
  Iraq War and, 166
  mercantilism, 107
  political and economic freedom, 102
  post-war outlook, 144
  Revolution, 9
  social inequalities, 99
  Suez crisis, 4, 144
Fredrickson, G.M., 15
free enterprise, 102, 107, 174
freedom of association, 181–2
freedom of conscience, 175
freedom of expression, 74

Gates, Bill, 99
GATT, 143–4
Gaullism, 10

Gauweiler, Peter, 136
Geneva Conventions, 162, 164
Germany, 4, 7, 10, 15, 18, 99, 102, 145, 166
Giddens, Anthony, 5, 7, 8
Gingrich, Newt, 54, 93, 119–21, 153
Ginsberg, B., 33
global governance, 8
Glorious Revolution (1688), 174
gold standard, 113, 148
Gore, Albert, 70
Great Depression, 34, 37, 107, 108, 172
Great Society program, 116, 117
Greece, 6, 10, 11, 167
Grenada, 166
Grotius, Hugo, 23–4
groups, 178–9
Guantanamo, 162, 164
Gulf War (1991), 149–52, 154–5, 155–6

Hamilton, Alexander, 23, 25–6, 38, 118, 146
Hayes, Rutherford, 52
Head Start, 122
health insurance interests, 122
health system, 51, 98, 111–12, 122, 124
Hendrickson, D. C., 24, 151
Hirschmann, A. O., 112
Hoffmann, Stanley, 3, 160
Homeland Security, 163
homosexuality, 14
House of Representatives
  campaign costs (1994–2006), 78
  competences, 64
  electoral district boundaries, 65
  electoral system, 64–5
  membership, 64
  see also Congress
Humphrey, Hubert, 47
Huntington, Samuel, 27, 115
hyperdemocracy, 96
hyperpower, ix, 152

Idaho, 126
Ikenberry, G. J., 142, 147
immigrants, 13, 17, 133
imperialism
    1990s schizophrenic power,
        152–9
    Cold War, 142–8
    democratic imperialism, 161
    George W. Bush presidency,
        159–65
    Gulf War (1991), 149–52
    imperial democracy, 166–9
    meaning, 166
    mercantilism and, 107
    military imperialism, 15
    post-9/11, 135–7
incumbency factor, 72–3, 87
independent voters, 95
individualism, 11, 98, 132, 172, 174,
    178
institutions
    competition, 180–2, 185, 186
    confidence in, 129
    conflicts, 95
    international institutions, 143–4
interest groups, 34, 75–7, 80–2, 159,
    182
International Criminal Court, 162
International Monetary Fund,
    143
Iran, 3, 166
Iran-Contra Affair, 152
Iraq
    Cold War ally, 149
    neoconservative view, 153–4
Iraq Liberation Act, 157
Iraq War (2003)
    electoral impact, 54
    European reaction, 1–2, 3, 5,
        135–6
    imperialism, 166
    neoconservative agenda, 154,
        164–5
    unilateralism, 168
Islam, 3, 13
Ismay, Lord, 145

isolationism, 17, 136, 137–8, 141,
    151
Israel, 3, 136
Italy, 6, 10, 11, 15, 145

Jackson, Andrew, 9–10, 66, 69, 118,
    149, 154
Jacobins, 28
Japan, 4, 99, 142, 143, 145, 147, 153
Jefferson, Thomas, 23, 38, 91–2, 94,
    95, 118, 175, 178
Jervis, R., 159
Johnson, Lyndon, 11, 44, 113,
    115–16, 141
Jones, Paula, 194n53
Joxe, Alain, 4
Judaism, 13–14
judicial review, legislation, 28, 56,
    104–5
Judt, Tony, 2–3
jungle, 98, 106
Juppé, Alain, 4

Kennan, George, 142, 144–5
Kennedy, John F., 47, 141
Key, V. O., 46
Keynesianism, 110
King, Anthony, 96
Korean war, 39, 140, 142
Kosovo intervention, 4
Kuwait, 149–51
Kyoto Protocol, 162

League of Nations, 138
Left, anti-Americanism, 5–9, 12
Leggewie, Claus, 59
Lenin, Vladimir, 6, 171
Leninism, 121
Lewinsky, Monica, 194n53
liberalism
    Catholic Church and, 14–15
    Constitution, 24, 132, 176–7
    contradictions, 17
    individualism, 178
    interest group liberalism, 115–16,
        124

liberalism (cont.)
  political philosophy, 23
  post-war order, 147
  separation of powers, 21
  social implications of American
    liberalism, 131–4
Libya, 159
Lindblom, C. E., 181
Lippmann, W., 156
Lipset, Seymour Martin, 13, 14, 17,
  62, 172
Locke, John, 23, 174, 176
Lowi, T., 32–3

McCain-Feingold Act, 82
McCarthyism, 164
McDonald, J.T., 103
Machiavelli, Niccolò, 23, 176
Madison, James, 23, 24–5, 26–7, 28,
  38, 66, 72, 91, 92, 94, 95, 116,
  175, 177, 183
marginalized groups, 84, 85, 86, 90,
  116–17
market democracy
  antinomies, 174
  competition regulation, 106, 113,
    133
  decentralized formation,
    101–4
  development, 101–13
  European Union, 19
  institutionalization, 103
  judicial role, 104–9, 111
  meaning, 99–101
  neoconservative revolution,
    114–21
  public agencies, 106, 108, 119
  social inequalities, 131–3, 181
  social responsibility of state,
    109–13, 178
  US choice, 16
Marshall, Chief Justice John, 56
Marshall Plan, 145
Marx, Karl, 171
Massachusetts, 126
materialism, 10

media, 51
Medicaid, 113, 122, 124
Medicare, 113
melting pot, 179
mercantilism, 107, 108
Meunier, Sophie, 4
middle classes, populism, 114–18,
  120
militarism, 3, 8, 15, 16, 35, 135–6,
  139, 147
Milkis, S. M., 71
minimum wage, 122
Mitterand, François, 4
mobility, 97, 133
monopolies, 106, 178
Monroe, James, 69
Monroe doctrine, 138
Montesquieu, Charles de, 27, 176
moralism, 172
Motor-Voter Act (1993), 84, 86, 87,
  91

NAFTA, 157
narcissism, 98
National Rifle Association, 120
nationalizations, 18, 106, 108
Native Americans, 136, 138
NATO, 145, 146, 158, 166
Nebraska, 66
neoconservatives
  anti-Europeanism, 1
  ascendency, 94
  Clinton presidencies and, 121–4
  "Contract with America", 120,
    125
  coup d'état, 55
  Democrats' weakness, 121–4
  George W. Bush presidency,
    159–65
  Gulf War (1991) and, 150
  populism of middle classes,
    114–18
  Reagan presidency, 149, 153
  resources, 93
  revolution, 100–1, 114–21
  September 11 and, 94

successes, 16, 54, 133, 153
term limits and recall, 125–31
unilateralism, 153–5
updated elitism, 118–21
Neustadt, R. E., 27
New Deal, 43, 86, 87, 93–4, 108, 113, 114, 115, 116, 143, 178
new political disorder, 77
New York, 64–5
9/11, 1–2, 54, 94, 160
Nixon, Richard, 11, 44, 71, 113, 114, 118, 148, 149, 150
North Dakota, 126
North Korea, 3, 151
Nuclear Non-Proliferation Treaty, 157
nuclear weapons, 143
Nye, Joseph, 156, 158

oil, 154
Oklahoma, 125
Oldfield, D. M., 141
oligarchy, 18, 43, 59
oligopolies, 106, 180
open primaries, 49
open society, 16
Oregon, 126

papacy, 165
parliamentary supremacy, 28, 105
particularism, 75–7, 118, 119
paternalism, 11
Patriot Act, 164
Perot, Ross, 121
Philadelphia (1787), 22, 23–6
Philippines, 35, 138, 166
Pintzler, Petra, 3
Polanyi, Karl, 103
political action committees, 75–7, 80–2, 87, 120, 156–7
political parties
  abuses, 36
  constitutionalization, 95
  corrupt machines, 117
  decline, 36, 63, 73, 75, 77, 85, 90–5, 179

financing, 74–5, 80, 82
low turnout interpretation, 88–90
market targeting, 86, 87
origin of party system, 52
party affiliation, 51
power, 36
re-alignment, 93–4
registration with, 47, 49
role, 71–2
Polsby, Nelson, 33, 51
populism
  American model, 172
  cyclical movements, 130
  middle classes, 114–18, 120
  neoconservatives and, 124
Portugal, 6, 10, 167
poverty, 98, 123–4
poverty programs, 113, 116, 122
presidents
  1828 elections, 69–70
  civil prosecution, 55
  direct primaries, 45–51
  divided government, 51–6, 71–7
  electoral system, 27, 36, 67–71
  impeachment, 29, 44, 54–5
  imperial drift, 44, 181
  legislative vetoes, 29, 40–1, 42
  original weakness, 31–3
  personalized presidency, 22, 45, 55, 140, 185
  plebiscitary democracy, 11, 20–1
  post-1970 transformation, 22
  powers, 8, 9, 38–41
  presidential wars, 151
  rhetorical presidency, 55
  rise of presidential government, 34–5, 37–41
  Roosevelt revolution, 34–5, 37, 52
  Senate advice to, 66
  term limits, 29
  two-presidency model, 140–1
  voter turnout, 59–60
protestantism, 12–13
public agencies, 106, 108, 119

Racine, Bruno, 4
racism, 17, 111
Reagan, Ronald, 52, 114, 117, 120,
    121, 149, 152, 153, 160
redistribution, 110, 183
Reformation, 12
registration of voters, 83, 87, 90
religion
    freedom of conscience, 175
    fundamentalism, 14, 120
    pluralism, 13–14, 175
    revival, 117, 120
    separation between state and
        church, 14, 175
religious wars, 12
Republican Party
    neoconservative revolution,
        114–21
    religious and populous wing,
        113
    rise of conservative wing, 85, 90
    see also neoconservatives
republicanism, 176
Revolution, 9
Rifkin, Jeremy, 98
Right, anti-Americanism, 9–12
rogue states, 136, 153, 154, 161, 162
Roosevelt, Franklin
    Atlantic Charter (1941), 144
    New Deal, 143
    populism, 117
    powers, 39
    presidential veto, 41
    social policies, 115–16
    turning point, 34–5, 37, 52, 71
Roosevelt, Theodore, 38–9
Rose, Richard, 173
Rumsfeld, Donald, 163

Saddam Hussein, 150, 153
Schaeuble, Wolfgang, 136
Scharpf, F. W., 183
Schmitter, P., 182
sects, 13
segregation, 112, 183
semi-closed primaries, 48–9

Senate
    campaign costs (1994–2006), 79
    classes of Senators, 65–6
    competences, 66
    Comprehensive Test-Ban Treaty
        and, 157
    electoral system, 65–7
    membership, 65–6
    see also Congress
separation of powers
    decision-making and, 8
    effect, 57–8, 110–11, 183–4
    European Union, 19
    post-9/11, 181
    US origins, 23–31
September 11 attacks, 1–2, 54, 94,
    160
Sherman Act, 8, 106
Skocpol, Theda, 110
slavery, 17
Sloterdijk, Peter, 136
social Darwinism, 134
social egoism, 98, 132
social inequalities
    American liberalism, 131–4
    causes, 16
    commercial republic, 101–13
    growth, 99
    international comparisons, 99
    market democracy, 99–101, 181
    statistics, 99–100
social movements, 11, 119
social policies, 109–13, 122–4, 134,
    173, 183
Social Security, 113
social solidarity, 186
socialism, 6, 171
soft money, 75, 80
Sombart, Werner, 6, 171
South, 14, 43, 46, 54, 58, 94, 111,
    113, 114, 117, 120, 174
South Carolina, 46
sovereignty, 26
Soviet Union, 4–5, 140, 148, 150,
    167
    see also Cold War

Spain, 6, 10, 11, 15, 35, 137, 138, 167
special interest groups, 34, 75–7, 80–2, 159, 182
Stalin, Joseph, 165
Starr, Kenneth, 55
state
  American contractualism, 101–2
  anti-statism, 118–19, 171, 174
  European role, 101–2
  expansion, 118
  social responsibility, 109–13, 178
State Children's Health Insurance Program, 124
Suez crisis, 3–4, 144
Supreme Court
  appointments, 29
  Baker v. Carr, 65
  Buckley v. Valeo, 74
  California Democratic Party v. Jones, 50
  Curtiss-Wright case, 39
  Florida count (2000), 8, 56
  judicial review of legislation, 28, 56, 104–5
  Marbury v. Madison, 56
  market economy and, 104–9
  Pink case, 39
  powers, 21, 28
  Re Neagle, 39
  Steel Seizure case, 39
  Term Limits Inc. v. Thornston, 125–6
Switzerland, 18

Tarchi, Marco, 98
taxation, 103–4, 117, 130
Taylor, Zachary, 52
term limits, 125–31
terrorism, *see* counter-terrorism
Thatcher, Margaret, 114
Tocqueville, Alexis de, ix, 9–10, 16, 134
tolerance, 17
Tories, 10
torture, 164
totalitarian factory, 98

trade unions, 51, 80, 98, 110, 111
Trotsky, Leon, 163, 171
Truman, Harry, 39, 41, 140, 141
Tudor England, 27, 176
tyranny of the minorities, 31, 43, 58, 122, 183, 186

unilateralism, 136, 137, 138, 152–5, 159–65, 168
United Kingdom
  anti-Americanism, 3–4
  anti-Europeanism, 3
  colonialism, 137, 144, 147
  naval protection, 139
  social inequalities, 99
  social policy, 110
  special relationship with US, 3–4
  Suez crisis, 3–4, 144
  Thatcherism, 114
United Nations
  affiliated institutions, 144
  creation, 147
  international order, 143, 148
  Iraq resolutions, 150
  Iraq War and, 165
  North Korea resolution, 151
  Westphalian principles, 162
Utah, 126

Védrine, Hubert, ix
Vietnam War, 44, 47, 73, 113, 135, 140, 141, 148, 149, 152
Virginia Company, 25
virtue, 23
voluntarism, 134, 172
voter turnout
  1932–2006 statistics, 60
  1980–2004 statistics, 61
  assessment of theories, 90–1
  cost-benefit analysis, 83
  effects, 96–7
  electoral hurdles, 83, 87
  European states, 97
  instrumentalist theory, 82
  low turnout, 8, 9, 11, 16, 17–18, 59–61

voter turnout (cont.)
  marginalized groups, 84, 85, 86, 87–8, 90
  Motor-Voter Act (1993), 84, 86, 87, 91
  party school interpretation, 88–90, 94
  passive support, 84, 85
  penalizing left, 89–90
  personalized politics, 89, 91
  political market, 85–6
  radical interpretation, 84–8
  rational choice theory, 82
  rational interpretation, 82–4
  reasons for low turnout, 82–91
  registration of voters, 83, 87, 90
  social correlation, 89
  strategy of electoral demobilization, 87–8
  system of 1896, 85–6, 90

Wallace, George, 114
Walzer, M., 13, 166
War Powers Act, 151
Washington state, 126
Watergate Affair, 44
wealth statistics, 99–100, 130–1
Wells, H.G., 171
Westphalian principles, 162
Wildavsky, A., 140, 141
Wilson, Woodrow, 6, 32, 39, 138, 142, 146, 157
Wisconsin, 46, 123
Wittkopf, E.R., 149
women, 61, 90, 131
workfare, 122, 123
World Bank, 99, 143, 144
World War I, 138, 139
World War II, 138, 139–40, 142, 172
WTO, 8, 144